CAMBRIDGE
UNIVERSITY PRESS

G000124125

CAMBRIDGE
Global English

for Cambridge Primary English as a Second Language

Teacher's Resource 4

Nicola Mabbott with Helen Tiliouine

Series Editor: Kathryn Harper

CAMBRIDGE
UNIVERSITY PRESS

University Printing House, Cambridge CB2 8BS, United Kingdom

One Liberty Plaza, 20th Floor, New York, NY 10006, USA

477 Williamstown Road, Port Melbourne, VIC 3207, Australia

314–321, 3rd Floor, Plot 3, Splendor Forum, Jasola District Centre, New Delhi – 110025, India

103 Penang Road, #05-06/07, Visioncrest Commercial, Singapore 238467

Cambridge University Press is part of the University of Cambridge.
It furthers the University's mission by disseminating knowledge in the pursuit of education,
learning and research at the highest international levels of excellence.

www.cambridge.org
Information on this title: www.cambridge.org/9781108934015

© Cambridge University Press 2021

First edition published 2014
Second edition 2021

20 19 18 17 16 15 14 13 12 11 10 9 8 7 6 5 4

Printed in Great Britain by CPI Group (UK) Ltd, Croydon CR0 4YY

A catalogue record for this publication is available from the British Library

ISBN 978-1-108-93401-5 Paperback with Digital Access

Additional resources for this publication at www.cambridge.org/9781108934015

....

....

› Contents

Digital resources

The following items are available on Cambridge GO. For more information on how to access and use your digital resource, please see inside front cover.

Active learning

Assessment for Learning

Developing learner language skills

Differentiation

Improving learning through questioning

Language awareness

Metacognition

Skills for Life

Letter for parents

Lesson plan template

Curriculum framework correlation

Scheme of work

Audio files and audioscripts

Progress tests 1–3 and answers

Progress report

Learner's Book answers

Workbook answers

Wordlist

You can download the following resources for each unit:

Differentiated worksheets and answers

Photocopiables

Sample answers

End-of-unit tests and answers

⟩ Introduction

Welcome to the new edition of our Cambridge Global English series.

Since its launch, the series has been used by teachers and learners in over 100 countries for teaching the Cambridge Primary English as a Second Language curriculum framework.

This exciting new edition has been designed by talking to Global English teachers all over the world. We have worked hard to understand your needs and challenges, and then carefully designed and tested the best ways of meeting them.

As a result of this research, we've made some important changes to the series, whilst retaining the international and cross-curricular elements which you told us you valued. This Teacher's Resource has been carefully redesigned to make it easier for you to plan and teach the course. It is available in print for all Stages.

The series still has extensive digital and online support, including Digital Classroom which lets you share books with your class and play videos and audio. This Teacher's Resource also offers additional materials, including tests, available to download from Cambridge GO. (For more information on how to access and use your digital resource, please see inside front cover.)

The series uses successful teaching approaches like active learning and metacognition and takes a 21st-century skills approach, with a focus on developing critical thinking skills. This Teacher's Resource gives you full guidance on how to integrate them into your classroom.

Formative assessment opportunities help you to get to know your learners better, with clear learning intentions and success criteria as well as an array of assessment techniques, including advice on self and peer assessment. This Teacher's Resource also includes example responses to writing tasks, together with comments from the authors to help you and your learners understand what 'good' looks like.

Clear, consistent differentiation ensures that all learners are able to progress in the course with tiered activities, differentiated worksheets, open-ended project tasks and advice about supporting learners' different needs.

All our resources are written for teachers and learners who use English as a second or additional language. In this edition of Global English we focus on four aspects of language:

- there is more grammar presentation and practice in the Workbook and on the Digital Classroom
- we have introduced scaffolded writing lessons with models of a range of text types
- we have included a range of literature
- and we have worked to ease the transition between stages, especially between primary and secondary.

We hope you enjoy using this course.

Eddie Rippeth

Head of Primary and Lower Secondary Publishing, Cambridge University Press

> About the authors

Jane Boylan

Jane Boylan is a freelance author, consultant, and creator of ESL materials for print and digital resources. She has worked for a range of publishers and educational organisations, creating and developing language learning materials for young learners and teachers of English. She has taken a leading role in educational resource projects for specific cultural contexts in East Asia, the United Arab Emirates, Pakistan, West Africa and Kazakhstan, consulting on content development and classroom application. Formerly, Jane worked on British Council teacher development projects primarily in East Asia, managing, writing and delivering a diverse range of training courses to state sector primary and secondary teachers of English. Earlier in her career, she worked as an English language teacher in Spain, Portugal, Thailand and Vietnam.

Claire Medwell

Passionate about quality English teaching, **Claire Medwell** is a teacher, teacher trainer and independent materials writer. She has 26 years of experience in ELT and ESL specialising in infant and primary learners.

Her publications include Cambridge Global English Stages 4–6 and the New Fun Skills 1 and 2.

Nicola Mabbott

Nicola Mabbott is a linguist who began her teaching career in Nottingham, England in 1998, teaching English as a Foreign Language to young adults. Since then, she has taught learners of all abilities and ages (from preschool age to retired adults) in Italy. She also regularly works as a tutor in English for Academic Purposes.

Nicola has been writing for a variety publishers in the UK and Italy – mostly resources for teachers of EFL to young learners and adolescents – for over 10 years. These resources include games, quizzes, communicative activities, worksheets, self-study resources, short stories and reading and listening activities for school coursebooks.

Nicola has a passion for language and languages and also works as a translator and examiner.

Kathryn Harper

Kathryn Harper is a freelance writer, publisher and consultant. Early on in her career, she worked as an English Language teacher in France and Canada. As an international publisher at Macmillan and Oxford University Press, she published teaching materials for Europe, the Middle East, Africa, Pakistan and Latin America. Her freelance work includes publishing reading schemes, writing electronic materials, language courses and stories for markets around the world. Her primary French whiteboard course for Nelson Thornes, *Rigolo*, won the 2008 BETT award. She also volunteers as an English teacher for child refugees and a mentor for young African writers.

Helen Tiliouine

Helen Tiliouine is an experienced teacher and writer of test materials. She has been involved in writing a range of ESL and ELT test materials, including *Cambridge Global English Teacher's Resource tests, Cambridge English Prepare! Test generator,* and *Complete First for Schools.* She is an experienced examiner.

Alison Sharpe

Alison Sharpe is a freelance teacher, writer and publisher. She started her career teaching English in Japan, Taiwan and the UK. She then worked for many years at Cambridge University Press and Oxford University Press publishing learning, teaching, exams and assessment materials for teachers and students all around the world. As a freelancer, she has been involved in a wide range of projects, including developing online teacher training materials, the assessment of children's writing and editing language learning materials for young learners and adults. She is also currently a part time tutor of academic literacy at Oxford University's Department of Continuing Education.

> How to use this series

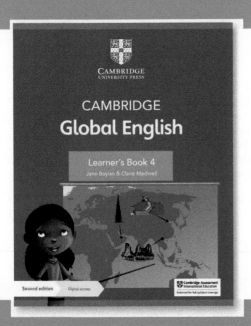

The Learner's Book is designed for learners to use in class with guidance from the teacher. It offers full coverage of the curriculum framework. The cross-curricular content supports success across the curriculum, with an international outlook. There is a focus on critical thinking, reading and writing skills with a literature section in every unit and a scaffolded approach to the development of written skills, with model texts. End-of-unit projects provide opportunities for formative assessment and differentiation so that you can support each individual learners' needs.

Digital Access with all the material from the book in digital form, is available via Cambridge GO.

The write-in Workbook offers opportunities to help learners consolidate what they have learned in the Learner's Book and is ideal for use in class or as homework. It provides plenty of differentiated grammar practice at three tiers so that learners have choice and can support or extend their learning, as required. Activities based on Cambridge Learner Corpus data give unique insight into common errors made by learners.

Digital Access with all the material from the book in digital form, is available via Cambridge GO.

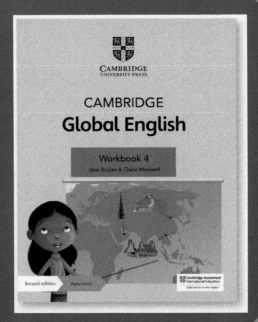

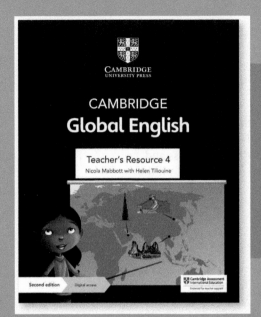

In the print Teacher's Resource you'll find everything you need to deliver the course, including teaching ideas, answers and differentiation and formative assessment support. Each Teacher's Resource includes:

- a print book with detailed teaching notes for each topic.
- a digital edition with all the material from the book plus editable unit and progress tests, differentiated worksheets and communicative games.

The Digital Classroom is for teachers to use at the front of the class. It includes digital versions of the Learner's Book and Workbook, complete with pop-up answers, helping you give instructions easily and check answers. Zoom in, highlight and annotate text, and support better learning with videos, grammar slideshows and interactive activities.

 A letter to parents, explaining the course, is available to download from Cambridge GO (as part of this Teacher's Resource).

> How to use this Teacher's Resource

This Teacher's Resource contains both general guidance and teaching notes that help you to deliver the content in our Cambridge Global English resources. Some of the material is provided as downloadable files, available on **Cambridge GO**. (For more information about how to access and use your digital resource, please see inside front cover.) See the Contents page for details of all the material available to you, both in this book and through Cambridge GO.

Teaching notes

This book provides **teaching notes** for each unit of the Learner's Book and Workbook. Each set of teaching notes contains the following features to help you deliver the unit.

The **Unit plan** summarises the lessons covered in the unit, including the number of learning hours recommended for the lesson, an outline of the learning content and the Cambridge resources that can be used to deliver the lesson.

Lesson	Approximate number of learning hours	Outline of learning content	Learning objectives	Resources
1 Why are all families special?	1–1.5	Talk about why families are special	4Ld.02 4Ld.04	Learner's Book Lesson 1.1 Workbook Lesson 1.1 **Digital Classroom:** Family activities Family vocabulary fun

The **Background knowledge** feature provides information which helps the teacher to familiarise themselves with the cross-curricular and international content in the unit.

Learners' prior knowledge can be informally assessed through the **Getting started** feature in the Learner's Book.

The **Teaching skills focus** feature covers a teaching skill and suggests how to implement it in the unit.

BACKGROUND KNOWLEDGE

It is useful to have a good understanding of a range different literary genres (historical fiction, traditional folk and fairy tales and myths, science fiction, mystery stories, fantasy fiction, adventure stories, etc.).

TEACHING SKILLS FOCUS

The challenge with active learning is to stop yourself telling learners things that they could discover for themselves.

Reflecting the Learner's Book, each unit consists of multiple lessons.

At the start of each lesson, the **Learning plan** table includes the learning objectives, learning intentions and success criteria that are covered in the lesson.

It can be helpful to share learning intentions and success criteria with your learners at the start of a lesson so that they can begin to take responsibility for their own learning.

LEARNING PLAN

Learning objective	Learning intentions	Success criteria
4Rm.01	• **Reading:** Understand the main points of a short text about a sports star's life.	• Learners can answer questions on a short text about a sports star's life.
4Us.06	• **Use of English:** Use an increasing range of verbs followed by infinitive and gerund forms.	

There are often **common misconceptions** associated with particular grammar points. These are listed, along with suggestions for identifying evidence of the misconceptions in your class and suggestions for how to overcome them. At Cambridge University Press, we have unique access to the Cambridge Learner Corpus to help us identify common errors for key language groups.

Misconception	How to identify	How to overcome
Learners often, incorrectly, leave out *to* with *hope* and *want*. Learners often use *to* and *-ing* in the same sentence.	Elicit correct examples of sentences with *hope and want* + infinitive; *love and enjoy* + *verb + ing*, e.g. *I hope to be a doctor.* *I want to have rice for lunch.*	Practise, for example, using **Photocopiable 1:** While using the activity, circulate and correct learners when they make these errors.

For each lesson, there is a selection of **starter ideas, main teaching ideas** and **plenary ideas**. You can pick out individual ideas and mix and match them depending on the needs of your class. The activities include suggestions for how they can be differentiated or used for assessment. **Homework ideas** are also provided, with home-school link suggestions to enable learners to continue their learning at home.

Starter ideas

Talk about athletes with disabilities (10 minutes)

- Ask learners if they know any athletes with disabilities (blindness, artificial limbs, etc.).

- Gain interest in the subject of inspirational athletes who have overcome disabilities. Show video clips of athletes with a variety of disabilities competing in different events. Elicit what disabilities the athletes have. You can easily find clips by searching the internet for events like the 2020 Paralympic 100m final. Make sure you include a clip of an athlete with an artificial leg.

Main teaching ideas

1 Match the words to the pictures (5–10 minutes)

- Look at the pictures on page 14 in the Learner's Book. First, check that learners understand the vocabulary and know that for football, rugby and basketball they should use *play;* for long jump and karate, *do;* and for the sports ending in *–ing, go*.

- Elicit sentences like: *I play both football and rugby. I go surfing, but I don't go snowboarding.*

The **Language background** feature contains information to help you present the grammar in the unit.

LANGUAGE BACKGROUND

Use of *infinitive* and *ing* after *like, love, enjoy, hope, want* and *learn*

The use of the infinitive and *-ing* form after verbs is the focus of the Language detective in this lesson.

In the text, the writer uses the six verbs to talk about what Ezra *likes, enjoys, loves doing* and activities he *hopes, wants* and *learns* to do.

The **Cross-curricular links** feature provides suggestions for linking to other subject areas.

CROSS-CURRICULAR LINKS

PE: After reading about Ezra, brainstorm vocabulary and have a discussion about the movements and training learners do for competitive sports.

> **Differentiation ideas:** This feature provides suggestions for how activities can be differentiated to suit the needs of your class.

> **Critical thinking opportunity:** This feature provides suggestions for embedding critical thinking and other 21st-century skills into your teaching and learning.

> **Assessment ideas:** This feature highlights opportunities for formative assessment during your teaching.

> **Digital Classroom:** If you have access to Digital Classroom, these links will suggest when to use the various multimedia enhancements and interactive activities.

Answers: Answers to Learner's Book exercises can be found integrated within the lesson plans and Learner's Book and Workbook answer keys are also available to download.

Note: Some texts used in the Learner's Book and Workbook have been abridged, so please be aware that learners may not be presented with the full version of the text.

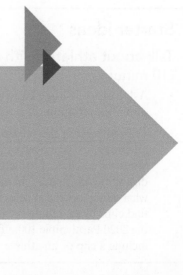

Digital resources to download

This Teacher's Resource includes a range of digital materials that you can download from Cambridge GO. (For more information about how to access and use your digital resource, please see inside front cover.) This icon 📥 indicates material that is available from Cambridge GO.

Helpful documents for planning include:

- **Letter for parents:** a template letter for parents, introducing the Cambridge Global English resources.
- **Lesson plan template:** a Word document that you can use for planning your lessons. Examples of completed lesson plans are also provided.
- **Curriculum framework correlation:** a table showing how the Cambridge Global English resources map to the Cambridge Primary English as a Second Language curriculum framework.
- **Scheme of work:** a suggested scheme of work that you can use to plan teaching throughout the year.

Each unit includes:

- **Differentiated worksheets:** these worksheets cater for different abilities. Worksheet A is designed to support learners who don't feel confident about the topic. Worksheet B is designed for learners who have a general understanding of the topic. Worksheet C is aimed at learners who want a challenge. Answer sheets are provided.
- **Photocopiable resources:** these include communicative language game, templates and any other materials that support the learning objectives of the unit.
- **Sample answers:** these contain teacher comments, which allow learners and teachers to assess what 'good' looks like in order to inform their writing.
- **End-of-unit tests:** these provide quick checks of the learner's understanding of the concepts covered in the unit. Answers are provided. Advice on using these tests formatively is given in the Assessment for Learning section of this Teacher's Resource.
- **Project checklists:** checklists for learners to use to evaluate their writing and project work.

Additionally, the Teacher's Resource includes:

- **Progress test 1:** a test to use at the beginning of the year to discover the level that learners are working at. The results of this test can inform your planning. Answers are provided.
- **Progress test 2:** a test to use after learners have studied Units 1–5 in the Learner's Book. You can use this test to check whether there are areas that you need to go over again. Answers are provided.
- **Progress test 3:** a test to use after learners have studied all units in the Learner's Book. You can use this test to check whether there are areas that you need to go over again, and to help inform your planning for the rest of the year. Answers are provided.
- **Progress report:** a document to help you formatively assess your classes' progress against the learning objectives.
- **Audioscripts:** available as downloadable files.
- **Answers to Learner's Book questions**
- **Answers to Workbook questions**
- **Wordlist:** an editable list of key vocabulary for each unit.

In addition, you can find more detailed information about teaching approaches.

🎧 **Audio** is available for download from Cambridge GO (as part of this Teacher's Resource and as part of the digital resources for the Learner's Book and Workbook).

🎥 **Video** is available through the Digital Classroom.

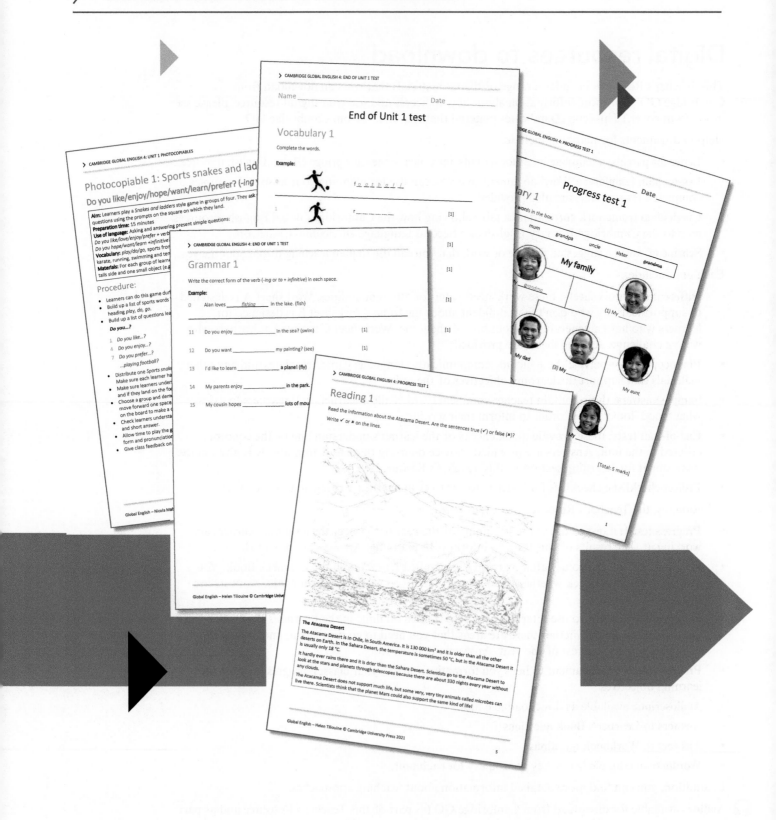

⟩ CAMBRIDGE GLOBAL ENGLISH 4: UNIT 1 PHOTOCOPIABLES

Photocopiable 1: Sports snakes and ladders
Do you like/enjoy/hope/want/learn/prefer? (-ing ...

Aim: Learners play a *Snakes and ladders* style game in groups of four. They ask ...
questions using the prompts on the square on which they land.

Preparation time: 15 minutes

Use of language: Asking and answering present simple questions:
Do you like/love/enjoy/prefer + verb ...
Do you hope/want/learn +infinitive ...
Vocabulary: play/do/go, sports fron ...
karate, running, swimming and ten ...
Materials: For each group of learne ...
tails side and one small object (e.g ...

Procedure:

- Learners can do this game dur ...
- Build up a list of sports words ...
  heading play, do, go.
- Build up a list of questions lea ...

  Do you...?
  1 *Do you like...?*
  4 *Do you enjoy...?*
  7 *Do you prefer...?*
      ...playing football?

- Distribute one *Sports snake* ...
  Make sure each learner ha ...
- Make sure learners under ...
  and if they land on the foo ...
- Choose a group and dem ...
  move forward one space ...
  on the board to make a ...
- Check learners understa ...
  and short answer.
- Allow time to play the g ...
  form and pronunciation ...
- Give class feedback on ...

Global English – Nicola Mab...

⟩ CAMBRIDGE GLOBAL ENGLISH 4: END OF UNIT 1 TEST

Name _____   Date _____

End of Unit 1 test

Vocabulary 1

Complete the words.

Example:

0   [icon]   f o o t b a l l

1   [icon]   r _ _ _ _ _ _ _   [1]

                                           [1]

                                           [1]

                                           [1]

                                           [1]

⟩ CAMBRIDGE GLOBAL ENGLISH 4: END OF UNIT 1 TEST

Grammar 1

Write the correct form of the verb (*-ing* or *to + infinitive*) in each space.

Example:

0   Alan loves ____*fishing*____ in the lake. (fish)

_____

11   Do you enjoy _____ in the sea? (swim)   [1]   [1]

12   Do you want _____ my painting? (see)   [1]

13   I'd like to learn _____ a plane! (fly)

14   My parents enjoy _____ in the park.

15   My cousin hopes _____ lots of mou...

⟩ CAMBRIDGE GLOBAL ENGLISH 4: PROGRESS TEST 1

Reading 1

Read the information about the Atacama Desert. Are the sentences true (✓) or false (✗)?
Write ✓ or ✗ on the lines.

[illustration of desert landscape]

The Atacama Desert

The Atacama Desert is in Chile, in South America. It is 130 000 km² and it is older than all the other deserts on Earth. In the Sahara Desert, the temperature is sometimes 50 °C, but in the Atacama Desert it is usually only 18 °C.

It hardly ever rains there and it is drier than the Sahara Desert. Scientists go to the Atacama Desert to look at the stars and planets through telescopes because there are about 330 nights every year without any clouds.

The Atacama Desert does not support much life, but some very, very tiny animals called microbes can live there. Scientists think that the planet Mars could also support the same kind of life!

Global English – Helen Tiliouine © Cambridge University Press 2021

                                                                    5

...DGE GLOBAL ENGLISH 4: PROGRESS TEST 1

...ary 1   **Progress test 1**   Date _____

...words in the box.

        mum   grandpa   uncle   sister
... grandma ...   ~~grandma~~

My family

... grandma   (1) My _____

                        My dad   (3) My _____

                                                        My aunt

...My _____

                                              [Total: 5 marks]

                                                           1

> About the curriculum framework

*This series supports the Cambridge Primary English as a Second Language curriculum framework from 2020. You should always refer to the appropriate curriculum framework document to confirm the details of the framework and for more information. Visit **www.cambridgeinternational.orglprimary** to find out more.*

The Cambridge Primary English as a Second Language curriculum framework is designed to enable young learners from an ESL background (who speak little or no English at home) to communicate effectively and with confidence in English. Cambridge Global English is designed to deliver this curriculum. It does this by developing the skills to access and understand a wide range of information, media and texts. It achieves this by focussing on active learning, developing critical thinking skills and intellectual engagement with a range of topics.

Our scheme is designed to fully support teachers to deliver the framework by providing an integrated approach to planning and teaching to develop effective communication skills in English. The five strands, and their respective learning objectives, work together to support the development of knowledge, skills and understanding in:

- Reading
- Writing
- Use of English
- Listening
- Speaking.

The new curriculum framework includes some important changes. For example, there is a new sub-strand of learning objectives within the Speaking strand, with new learning objectives concerning fluency and accuracy of pronunciation.

> About the assessment

Information concerning the assessment of the Cambridge Primary English as a Second Language curriculum framework is available on the Cambridge Assessment International Education website: **www.cambridgeinternational.org**.

The resources provide support for the Cambridge Primary English as a Second Language curriculum framework from 2020.

⟩ Approaches to learning and teaching

The following are the teaching approaches underpinning our course content and how we understand and define them.

Active learning

Active learning is a teaching approach that places student learning at its centre. It focuses on how students learn, not just on what they learn. We, as teachers, need to encourage learners to 'think hard', rather than passively receive information. Active learning encourages learners to take responsibility for their learning and supports them in becoming independent and confident learners in school and beyond.

Assessment for Learning

Assessment for Learning (AfL) is a teaching approach that generates feedback which can be used to improve learners' performance. Learners become more involved in the learning process and, from this, gain confidence in what they are expected to learn and to what standard. We, as teachers, gain insights into a learner's level of understanding of a particular concept or topic, which helps to inform how we support their progression.

Differentiation

Differentiation is usually presented as a teaching approach where teachers think of learners as individuals and learning as a personalised process. While precise definitions can vary, typically the core aim of differentiation is viewed as ensuring that all learners, no matter their ability, interest or context, make progress towards their learning intentions. It is about using different approaches and appreciating the differences in learners to help them make progress. Teachers therefore need to be responsive, and willing and able to adapt their teaching to meet the needs of their learners.

Language awareness

For many learners, English is an additional language. It might be their second or perhaps their third language. Depending on the school context, students might be learning all or just some of their subjects through English.

For all learners, regardless of whether they are learning through their first language or an additional language, language is a vehicle for learning. It is through language that students access the learning intentions of the lesson and communicate their ideas. It is our responsibility, as teachers, to ensure that language doesn't present a barrier to learning.

Metacognition

Metacognition describes the processes involved when learners plan, monitor, evaluate and make changes to their own learning behaviours. These processes help learners to think about their own learning more explicitly and ensure that they are able to meet a learning goal that they have identified themselves or that we, as teachers, have set.

Skills for Life

How do we prepare learners to succeed in a fast-changing world? To collaborate with people from around the globe? To create innovation as technology increasingly takes over routine work? To use advanced thinking skills in the face of more complex challenges? To show resilience in the face of constant change? At Cambridge, we are responding to educators who have asked for a way to understand how all these different approaches to life skills and competencies relate to their teaching. We have grouped these skills into six main Areas of Competency that can be incorporated into teaching, and have examined the different stages of the learning journey and how these competencies vary across each stage.

These six key areas are:

- Creativity – finding new ways of doing things, and solutions to problems
- Collaboration – the ability to work well with others
- Communication – speaking and presenting confidently and participating effectively in meetings
- Critical thinking – evaluating what is heard or read, and linking ideas constructively
- Learning to learn – developing the skills to learn more effectively
- Social responsibilities – contributing to social groups, and being able to talk to and work with people from other cultures.

Cambridge learner and teacher attributes

This course helps develop the following Cambridge learner and teacher attributes.

Cambridge learners	Cambridge teachers
Confident in working with information and ideas – their own and those of others.	**Confident** in teaching their subject and engaging each student in learning.
Responsible for themselves, responsive to and respectful of others.	**Responsible** for themselves, responsive to and respectful of others.
Reflective as learners, developing their ability to learn.	**Reflective** as learners themselves, developing their practice.
Innovative and equipped for new and future challenges.	**Innovative** and equipped for new and future challenges.
Engaged intellectually and socially, ready to make a difference.	**Engaged** intellectually, professionally and socially, ready to make a difference.

Adapted from Approaches to learning and teaching series, courtesy of Cambridge University Press and Cambridge Assessment International Education: cambridge.org/approachestolearning

More information about these approaches to learning and teaching is available to download from Cambridge GO (as part of this Teacher's Resource).

> Setting up for success

Our aim is to support better learning in the classroom with resources that allow for increased learner autonomy while supporting teachers to facilitate student learning. Through an active learning approach of enquiry-led tasks, open-ended questions and opportunities to externalise thinking in a variety of ways, learners will develop analysis, evaluation and problem-solving skills.

Some ideas to consider to encourage an active learning environment are as follows:

- Set up seating to make group work easy.

- Create classroom routines to help learners to transition between different types of activity efficiently, e.g. move from pair work to listening to the teacher to independent work.

- Source mini-whiteboards, which allow you to get feedback from all learners rapidly.

- Start a portfolio for each learner, keeping key pieces of work to show progress at parent–teacher days.

- Have a display area with learner work and vocab flashcards.

Planning for active learning

We recommend the following approach to planning. A blank lesson plan template is available to download to help with this approach.

1 **Plan learning intentions and success criteria:** these are the most important feature of the lesson. Teachers and learners need to know where they are going in order to plan a route to get there.

2 **Plan language support:** think about strategies to help learners overcome the language demands of the lesson so that language doesn't present a barrier to learning.

3 **Plan starter activities:** include a 'hook' or starter to engage learners using imaginative strategies. This should be an activity where all learners are active from the start of the lesson.

4 **Plan main activities:** during the lesson, try to: give clear instructions, with modelling and written support; coordinate logical and orderly transitions between activities; make sure that learning is active and all learners are engaged; create opportunities for discussion around key concepts.

5 **Plan assessment for learning and differentiation:** use a wide range of Assessment for Learning techniques and adapt activities to a wide range of abilities. Address misconceptions at appropriate points and give meaningful oral and written feedback which learners can act on.

6 **Plan reflection and plenary:** at the end of each activity and at the end of each lesson, try to: ask learners to reflect on what they have learned compared to the beginning of the lesson; build on and extend this learning.

7 **Plan homework:** if setting homework, it can be used to consolidate learning from the previous lesson or to prepare for the next lesson.

To help planning using this approach, a blank lesson plan template is available to download from Cambridge GO (as part of this Teacher's Resource).

For more guidance on setting up for success and planning, please explore the Professional Development pages of our website **www.cambridge.org/education/PD**

› 1 Our community

Unit plan

Lesson	Approximate number of learning hours	Outline of learning content	Learning objectives	Resources
1 Why are all families special?	1–1.5	Talk about why families are special	4Ld.02 4Ld.04	Learner's Book Lesson 1.1 Workbook Lesson 1.1 **Digital Classroom:** Family activities Family vocabulary fun
2 An inspirational sports player	1–1.5	Use different verb patterns to talk about what we like Read about an inspirational sports player	4Rm.01 4Us.06	Learner's Book Lesson 1.2 Workbook Lesson 1.2 ⬇ Photocopiable 1 **Digital Classroom:** Revising verb patterns An inspirational sports player
3 Our school community	1–1.5	Interview people who make our school a great place to learn!	4Sc.03 4Ug.03 4Uv.03	Learner's Book Lesson 1.3 Workbook Lesson 1.3 ⬇ Photocopiable 2 ⬇ Differentiated worksheet 1 **Digital Classroom:** Where do you work?
4 Organise a community event	1–1.5	Write a leaflet about an event in our community	4Wor.03	Learner's Book Lesson 1.4 Workbook Lesson 1.4 ⬇ Photocopiable 3 **Digital Classroom:** Make a leaflet ⬇ Sample answer for Unit 1
5 *The Treasure*	1–1.5	Enjoy a story about special people in 'The Treasure'	4Rm.02	Learner's Book Lesson 1.5 Workbook Lesson 1.5 **Digital Classroom:** *The Treasure*
6 Project challenge	1–1.5	Project A: A day in the life of a school helper Project B: Write about an inspirational person you know in your community	4Wc.02/4Wca.04 4Wc.02/4Wc.03	Learner's Book Lesson 1.6 Workbook Lesson 1.6 ⬇ Unit 1 project checklists

Cross-unit resources
⬇ Unit 1 Audioscripts
⬇ End of Unit 1 test
⬇ Progress test 1
⬇ Unit 1 Progress report
⬇ Unit 1 Wordlist

BACKGROUND KNOWLEDGE

Before starting this unit, you may want to use Progress test 1. This diagnostic test can help you to identify gaps in learners' knowledge or understanding, which you can help them address before beginning this unit.

Unit 1 focuses on different kinds of communities or groups of people who have something in common, or a common identity. Although communities are important all over the world, the types of community and their importance vary in different countries and cultures. As an introduction to the topic, you may find it useful to watch a child-friendly video about communities. For instance, search for the Kids Academy YouTube video about social communities.

Learners are encouraged to explore why members belong to a community. Different-sized communities are considered. Lesson 1 focuses on a very small community, the family. A medium-sized community, the school community, is the subject of Lesson 3. Learners are encouraged to think about different-sized communities, from their block or neighbourhood, to their city, to very large communities like countries or continents.

Learners are encouraged to appreciate the role of school helpers in Lesson 3 and other community helpers (the ice-cream seller, the librarian, police officer and vet) in Lesson 5. Community helpers are people who play an important role in the community. Learners also read about different community events, like a fun run, a spelling bee and a fun day. A spelling bee is a competition where children compete to see who can spell the most words correctly.

In Lesson 2, learners read about an inspirational sportsman who has overcome disabilities to achieve success. In Lesson 6, learners either write about an inspirational person in their community or a school helper.

TEACHING SKILLS FOCUS

Differentiation

What is differentiation?

General information on differentiation is on page 14 of this resource and more information can be found at the Cambridge Assessment International Education PDF called *The Differentiation Game.*

How and when can I differentiate in my class?

This resource gives suggestions on how to tailor activities for your classes to stimulate and involve learners with differing abilities, interests and motivation. Look for the differentiation ideas. There are also plenty of strategies you can devise yourself.

Consider the following questions:

1 Think about the content of the lesson. Are your learners already familiar with the general theme of the unit? If not, think of ways to support them. For example, you could show them a child-friendly video.

2 Think about the process of learning and the product of the lesson. What are the learners' strengths and weaknesses? How can you use their strengths? Do your learners comprehend information more efficiently by listening or reading, or by actively participating in communicative methods? If the latter, you could incorporate activities such as *Photocopiable 1: Sports snakes and ladders game.* Do your learners perform well when giving oral presentations, writing reports or designing posters? Do tests and competitions stimulate them? Experiment with different types of activities to help you find the best ways to encourage your learners. Assess whether they perform better in written homework or group projects.

3 The learning environment. Do you have a mixed-ability class? Think about ways to maximise learning potential by changing the classroom layout for collaborative activities. Mix more confident and less confident learners. Put tables together for group work.

> CONTINUED
>
> **Your challenge**
>
> At the end of the unit, think about how successful you have been at supporting and challenging learners. Build a class profile of strengths and weaknesses. Review this list after Unit 3. How could you improve further?

1.1 Think about it: Why are all families special?

LEARNING PLAN

Learning objective	Learning intentions	Success criteria
4Ld.02 4Ld.04	• **Listening:** Understand questions which ask for information about our families. • **Listening:** Understand, with little support, what is special about families. • **Vocabulary:** *They are into…, They are keen on…, my neighbourhood, my block, my sports club, my country, my continent.*	• Learners can, with support, answer an increasing range of questions which ask for information about their families. • Learners can, with little or no support, talk about what is special about families.

21st-century skills

Social responsibilities: Identify a variety of groups learners belong to.

Critical thinking: Think critically by asking *Wh-* questions and comparing two sets of information.

Materials: Learner's Book pages 11–13; Workbook pages 8–9; Video about what a community is, e.g. about communities we belong to at, for instance, search for the Kids Academy YouTube video about social communities

Starter ideas

Thirty-second families game (5 minutes)

- Start by revising words for family members. Nominate learners and give them 30 seconds to talk about their family. Write words that learners find difficult on the whiteboard.

- Allow learners 30 seconds to tell a partner about their families.

Getting started (10 minutes)

- Focus on the big question *What is a community?* Elicit names of different types of communities.

> **Social responsibilities:** Tell learners to identify a variety of groups they belong to. Write 'Communities I belong to' on the board and build up a list of communities.

- Match the words to a picture. If necessary, show a simple video to reinforce these ideas, like the one in Materials. Then complete the sentences as a class.

- Familiarise learners with words for communities by asking them to put communities in size order. Give each group of 3–4, nine small paper squares with the following communities to sort: *my family, my block/street, my neighborhood, my sports team, my band, my school, my village/city, my country/state, my continent.*

> **Critical thinking opportunity:** When ordering the communities, encourage critical thinking by asking how many people there are in each community. Ask learners why they have chosen a particular word to describe each community.

Answers

a   Top right: neighbourhood; middle right: sports team; bottom left: family; bottom centre: school; bottom right: community helpers

b   Learner's own answers.

> **Digital Classroom:** Use the video 'Family activities' to give examples of activities that families do together. The i button will explain how to use the video.

Main teaching ideas

1   Name the family members in each photo (5 minutes)

*   Point at the family members in each photo and ask: *Who is this?*

*   Encourage critical thinking and elicit differences and similarities between the photos and learners' families. Ask questions, e.g. *How many people are there?* Be sensitive to difficult family situations.

*   Revise family member vocabulary and write *Wh-* question prompts on the board.

*   Elicit why families are special.

Answers
Learner's own answers.

2   Complete the family word chart (5 minutes)

*   Learners complete the family word chart with the male and female words for their family members.

*   Learners use the words to help describe their families.

Answers
Female: mum, granddaughter, aunt, sister, grandma, daughter, cousin
Male: brother, dad, grandson, grandpa, uncle, son, cousin

3   Listen and number the photos (10 minutes)

*   Tell learners they only need to understand the main idea of each speaker. Encourage them to make predictions about what they will hear by looking at the pictures of the families.

*   Listen to the first speaker. Elicit which picture the girl is talking about. Ask learners which words helped them to make this choice.

*   Listen to the other speakers and match each of them with a photo.

*   Pre-teach the expressions in Activity 4, which learners will hear on the audio. For extra support, pause the audio and give feedback after every speaker.

Audioscript: Track 01

See Learner's Book page 13.

Girl A: It can be quite noisy when my family are together because **we are really into music**. In fact, we are all musicians. I play the violin and my brother plays the clarinet. We usually practise every day because we are <u>both</u> in the school band. My grandparents play instruments <u>too</u>. My grandpa plays the piano and my grandma plays the guitar.

Boy B: We are a very active family. We're always outside or in a sports centre practising some sport or another. **My sister and I are keen on tennis,** <u>but</u> we also like to play table tennis with the rest of the family. My dad and grandpa are really good players. My grandpa was even a local champion when he was younger.

Girl C: I got a mobile phone for my birthday and I love it! In fact **I really like any kind of new technology**. I use the internet a lot to learn and find out new things and I like playing online games <u>too</u>. My grandma really wants to learn about how to use my phone to take selfies!

Boy D: I live on a farm with my family, so I don't just have pets like cats, <u>but</u> we've also got cows, sheep and horses <u>too</u>. **We love animals** and caring for them is my parents' job. I help at the weekends feeding and cleaning the animals <u>too</u>.

Answers
a4 b1 c3 d2

4 What's special about each family? (5 minutes)

Learners complete the examples. If necessary, replay the audio.

Answers
a animals b music c new technology
d sports

Language focus (5 minutes)

- The Language focus looks at *both*, *too* and *but*. Learners will have heard the speakers using these in the listening activity, so a good starting point is for learners to underline examples in the audio script.

- Play Audio Track 1 again. Focus on the sentences containing *both*, *too* and *but*, and pause after each.

- Elicit that *too* and *both* are used to emphasise that two people do the same thing or have the same characteristic. To check that learners understand, ask concept check questions, e.g. for Speaker A: *Who is in the school band? Who plays musical instruments?*

- Focus on the word order and elicit the position of *both* and *too*. Look again at Speaker B. Find places where *too* or *both* could be added.

5 Interview your partner about their family (5 minutes)

> **Critical thinking opportunity:** Use activities 5–7 to encourage learners to think critically. Learners ask the *Wh-* questions to gain information about their partners' families. Learners will compare their own family with their partner's in Activity 6.

- In pairs, learners ask and answer questions about their families. They need to take notes on their partner's answers for Activities 6 and 7.

> **Differentiation ideas:** If learners need support with this task, provide a prompt sheet with the expressions from Activity 4 and useful prompts such as: *There are ... people in my family; I have ... brothers and ... sisters; My family lives ...;*

6 Complete the diagram (5 minutes)

- Learners use the information from the previous activity to complete the Venn diagram.

7 Talk about similarities and differences (10 minutes)

- Using the Venn diagram as support, learners talk to their partners about the similarities and differences between their families. Encourage learners to use *both*, *too* and *but* when they are talking.

- Before learners start the activity, identify different ways to express differences using *but*. For example: *There are four people in A's family, but in B's family there are eight. C has one sister, but D has four. E's family lives in Church Street, but F's lives in Main Street. G has a cat, but H hasn't. I's family likes doing sports, but my family does not.*

> **Digital Classroom:** Use the activity 'Family vocabulary fun' to revise family vocabulary. The i button will explain how to use the activity.

Plenary ideas

Consolidation (15 minutes)

- Invite two learners to the 'hot seat' at the front of the class. Divide the rest of the class into teams of four. Team members ask the learners in the 'hot seat' questions from Activity 5. They memorise the answers, without writing them down.

- Make true and false statements based on the answers to the questions, e.g. *Mahmoud has a dog, but Salma does not. They both have two brothers.* The teams decide whether the sentences are true and false. Award 1 point for each correct answer. The winning team has the most points at the end of the game.

Homework ideas

> **Workbook**
>
> Questions 1–5 on pages 8–9.

- Learners write a paragraph comparing their family with their partner's family. They should use *but*, *too* and *both* in their writing.

> **Assessment ideas:** As a class, write a short checklist so that learners can self-assess their work before handing it in. For example: *Have I used the new vocabulary from the lesson? Have I made comparisons? Have I used* but, too *and* both?

1.2 P.E.: An inspirational sports player

LEARNING PLAN

Learning objective	Learning intentions	Success criteria
4Rm.01 4Us.06	• **Reading:** Understand the main points of a short text about a sports star's life. • **Use of English:** Use an increasing range of verbs followed by infinitive and gerund forms. • **Vocabulary:** *long jump, football, skateboarding, rugby, basketball, snowboarding, karate, running, surfing, hope, love, enjoy, want, learn.*	• Learners can answer questions on a short text about a sports star's life. • Learners can use an increasing range of verbs followed by infinitive and gerund forms to talk about themselves and their families.

21st-century skills

Collaboration: Collaborate with others when making choices.

Learning to learn: Use practical skills for learning independently when completing a task.

Materials: Learner's Book pages 14–15; Workbook pages 10–11; **Photocopiable 1**; Pictures or video clips of inspirational sports players with disabilities

LANGUAGE BACKGROUND

Use of *infinitive* and *ing* after *like, love, enjoy, hope, want* and *learn*

The use of the infinitive and *-ing* form after verbs is the focus of the Language detective in this lesson.

In the text, the writer uses the six verbs to talk about what Ezra *likes, enjoys, loves doing* and activities he *hopes, wants* and *learns* to do.

- *Like* or *love* can be used with the *-ing* form or the infinitive: *I like/love playing tennis; I like/love to play tennis.* In US English, the infinitive is more common. In British English, choosing

the *-ing* form implies that the speaker enjoys the action, whereas the infinitive emphasises the consequences of the action, or the fact that it is a habit.

- In both UK and US English, *enjoy* is followed by the *-ing* form and not the infinitive: *I enjoy playing tennis; I enjoy ~~to play~~ tennis.*

- *Hope, want* and *learn* are followed by the infinitive.

- None of the verbs can be followed by the base form of the verb. For example: *I hope ~~learn~~ English.*

Common misconceptions

Misconception	How to identify	How to overcome
Learners often, incorrectly, leave out *to* with *hope* and *want*. Learners often use *to* and *-ing* in the same sentence.	Elicit correct examples of sentences with *hope and want + infinitive; love and enjoy + verb + ing*, e.g. I <u>hope</u> to be a doctor. I <u>want</u> to have rice for lunch. I <u>love</u> playing football. I <u>enjoy</u> watching films. Elicit that with *hope* and *want*, *to* cannot be left out, and *to* and *-ing* cannot be used in the same sentence.	Practise, for example, using Photocopiable 1: Sports snakes and ladders game. While using the activity, circulate and correct learners when they make these errors.

Starter ideas

Talk about athletes with disabilities (10 minutes)

- Ask learners if they know any athletes with disabilities (blindness, artificial limbs, etc.).

- Gain interest in the subject of inspirational athletes who have overcome disabilities. Show video clips of athletes with a variety of disabilities competing in different events. Elicit what disabilities the athletes have. You can easily find clips by searching the internet for events like the 2020 Paralympic 100m final. Make sure you include a clip of an athlete with an artificial leg.

Main teaching ideas

1 Match the words to the pictures (5–10 minutes)

- Look at the pictures on page 14 in the Learner's Book. First, check that learners understand the vocabulary and know that for football, rugby and basketball they should use *play;* for long jump and karate, *do;* and for the sports ending in *–ing, go.*

- Elicit sentences like: *I play both football and rugby. I go surfing, but I don't go snowboarding.*

- Ask learners the questions. Then ask them to match the sports to the pictures.

Answers

a long jump   b football   c skateboarding
d rugby   e basketball

---

2 Read about Ezra Frech (10 minutes)

- Tell learners that they are going to read about an athlete with an artificial leg. Check that they understand what an artificial leg is.

- Before you start reading, ask learners to predict which sports would be the most challenging for Ezra, and why.

- The length of the text, and new words and expressions, could cause problems for learners. Developing reading strategies should help. Explain that learners should first scan the text, looking only for the names of the sports. See who can find the sports first, to ensure learners are not distracted by the difficult words.

> **Learning to learn:** Learners use the Vocabulary box on page 15 to help them understand the text.

CROSS-CURRICULAR LINKS

P.E.: After reading about Ezra, brainstorm vocabulary and have a discussion about the movements and training learners do for competitive sports.

- Once learners have familiarised themselves with the text, ask them which of the sports in Activity 1 Ezra doesn't play.

> **Differentiation ideas:** If learners need support with this task, turn it into a matching activity. Underline in the text the sports that Ezra does play and ask learners to match these with the sports in Activity 1. Then ask learners to name the sports he doesn't play.

Answers
Rugby and karate.

Audioscript: Track 02
See Learner's Book page 14.

 3 Match the headings with the paragraphs (5 minutes)

- Learners work in pairs or small groups to decide which heading goes with each paragraph. Encourage them to focus on key words in each paragraph, to give them clues about the correct headings.

- Give feedback about correct answers after re-listening.

Answers
a3 b4 c2 d1 e2

4 Play a game (5–10 minutes)

- Start by miming a couple of verbs and asking learners to guess them. Learners should then practise in pairs.

- If learners are particularly interested in sports, encourage them to mime different activities about the sports they do. Tell them the new expressions to describe the actions.

5 Language detective and write sentences (10 minutes)

- The focus of the Language detective is the use of the infinitive and -ing form after verbs. Read the sentences in the box. There are more examples of these structures in the text. Ask learners to underline them or point them out.

- Write two headings on the whiteboard: *Verb + to* and *Verb + ing*. Elicit when we use the -ing form and when we use the infinitive. Build up a list under the headings (*like, enjoy* and *love* under the *verb + ing* heading, and *hope, want* and *learn* under the *verb + to* heading).

- To check learners have understood the use of the *verb + ing* and *verb + infinitive*, ask

questions like: *Which sports do you like playing/doing? (I like playing/doing/going…) What does your brother/sister want to be? (He/She wants to be…)*

- Now ask learners to complete Activity 5.

> **Differentiation ideas:** If learners don't feel confident about the task, ask them to focus on writing three sentences. Extend the activity by asking more confident writers to complete six sentences.

- For communicative practice, please see **Photocopiable 1**.

6 Do you play or like a sport? (10 minutes)

- Check that learners understand the verb *train* in this context.

- Build up a bank of useful expressions on the board for learners to use.

- Learners then ask and answer the questions in pairs.

> **Digital Classroom:** Use the grammar presentation 'Revising verb patterns' to revise verb + *ing* and verb *to* infinitive. The i button will explain how to use the grammar presentation.

Workbook

For further practice, learners look at the Language detective and do Questions 1–3 on pages 10–11.

7 Identify three difficulties Ezra faces (10 minutes)

- First, as a class, talk about some of the difficulties that athletes with disabilities might face.

- Put some useful vocabulary on the whiteboard.

- Then look back at the reading text from this lesson. Focus on Ezra and the types of difficulties he might face.

> **Digital Classroom:** Use the activity 'An inspirational sports player' to reinforce reading comprehension of the text about Ezra Frech. The i button will explain how to use the activity.

Plenary ideas

Consolidation (10 minutes)

Ask learners to write a paragraph about an inspirational sports player they admire. Encourage learners to use vocabulary from the lesson and the structures from the Language detective on Learner's Book page 14.

Homework ideas

| **Workbook** |
| Questions 1–3 on pages 10–11. |

- Learners write a paragraph about the sports and activities they like doing, using the structures from the Language detective (*like* + *ing* and *hope* + *infinitive*).

> **Learning to learn:** To encourage learners to take control of their own learning, the paragraph could be peer-assessed by a partner. They could look for errors with the form of *like* + *ing* and *hope* + *infinitive*, and provide constructive feedback on what went well and what could be improved further.

1.3 Talk about it: Our school community

LEARNING PLAN		
Learning objective	**Learning intentions**	**Success criteria**
4Sc.03	• **Speaking:** Ask questions to find out general information about a school worker's day and responsibilities.	• Learners can ask questions to find out general information about a school worker's day and responsibilities, and respond accordingly.
4Ug.03	• **Use of English:** Use imperative forms [positive and negative] of an increasing range of verbs to give a short sequence of commands and instructions.	• Learners can use imperative forms to encourage people to do things.
4Uv.03	• **Use of English:** Use adverbs of indefinite time, e.g. ever, always. • **Vocabulary:** *cook, headmistress, class teacher, caretaker, school nurse, librarian, P.E. teacher.*	• Learners can use adverbs of indefinite time to talk about what school workers do for them.
21st-century skills		
Learning to learn: Join in learning activities with other children; Show awareness of own progress in learning a subject. **Critical thinking:** Before listening, predict the words that might give clues about the school helpers' jobs.		

Materials: Learner's book pages 16–17; Workbook pages 12–13; **Photocopiable 2**; **Differentiated worksheet 1**

Common misconceptions

Misconception	How to identify	How to overcome
The adverbs of frequency *sometimes*, *often* and *usually* can go in different positions, e.g. *Sometimes I arrive early.* *I sometimes arrive early.* *I arrive early sometimes.* The adverbs *never*, *always* and *hardly ever* usually go between the subject and the main verb (except with *be* and auxiliary verbs).	Write some incorrect sentences on the board and elicit the correct sentences, e.g. *I go to school <u>never</u> late.* → *I <u>never</u> go to school late.* *My house door is open for you <u>always</u>.* → *My house door is <u>always</u> open for you.*	Ask learners to practise making sentences about themselves containing adverbs of frequency. Make sure they are using the correct word order.

Starter ideas

My school community (5 minutes)

- Write the title 'People who make up my school community' on the board. Allow groups of 3–4 learners a few minutes to think of as many people from their school community as they can. Support learners by helping with vocabulary they don't know in English.

- Build up a list of people on the board.

Main teaching ideas

1 Look at the map of the school (10 minutes)

- Create a mind map of the places at school and corresponding activities. Start by eliciting and writing the places. Leave space to write around each place. Elicit and write words connected to the activities that people do in each place, e.g. *classroom – learn (English, etc.), study, listen to the teacher, read.*

- Learners answer the question in the Learner's Book.

  > **Learning to learn:** This is a good opportunity for learners to join in learning activities with other children.

Answers
Learner's own answers.

2 Match the jobs to the people (5 minutes)

- Point at each person in the pictures. Ask learners if they know the name of each job.

- Match the jobs to the people together. Write the names of the jobs on the board and practise the pronunciation.

- Pre-teach difficult vocabulary in a fun way. For instance, write c_r_t_k_r; learners guess the missing letters (*caretaker*).

Answers
a class teacher   b caretaker   c school nurse
d librarian   e cook   f headteacher
g P.E. teacher

3 Match the sentences (5 minutes)

- Focus on the first job (teacher). Ask learners for suggestions about how their teachers help them.

- Demonstrate the activity by asking learners to look for the most suitable answer to 1 (f).

- Learners work in pairs. For each job they should talk about the ways in which each person helps and then find the most appropriate answers.

Answers
a 2   b 4   c 5   d 3   e 6   f 1

4 Listen to the three school helpers (5 minutes)

- **Listening strategies:** The length of the text may cause difficulties for learners of this age and level. Make clear that it isn't necessary to understand every word. Learners should only focus on understanding what the job of each speaker is.

> **Critical thinking opportunity:** Before listening, encourage learners to predict the words that might give them clues about the school helpers' jobs. Look back at Activities 2 and 3.

- Learners listen to Audio Track 3 and guess the jobs. Ask which words helped them to guess the correct answer.

- If necessary, pause the audio for feedback after the first speaker. After listening, you could highlight words in the audio script that help to identify the job.

Audioscript: Track 03

See Learner's Book page 17.

1   I always get up very early in the morning to open the school gates. Then I check that the classrooms are clean and tidy before the children and teachers arrive to start class. During the day, I usually have to fix things that don't work and I change things like light bulbs. When the children go home I stay at the school with the cleaners. I take out the rubbish and then I lock the school gates before I go home. I love my job because I meet lots of great children and teachers every day.

2   I always get up at 7 o'clock in the morning. I live near the school, so it usually only takes me 10 minutes to ride my bike to school. I arrive at 8.45 and classes start at 9 in the morning. I teach the children how to play all kinds of different sports and show them how important it is to look after their health and fitness. My working day finishes at 4.30p.m., but I sometimes work on Saturday mornings as I train the school sports teams, who often play against other schools at the weekend. I love my job, because I enjoy working with children and I love playing sport!

---

3   I work from 9a.m. to 4p.m. in the local school. You'll always find me in the kitchen, cutting vegetables, cooking pasta and rice and preparing desserts in time for lunch in the school dining room. The worst part of my job is washing up all the pans and dishes, but the best part is when the children and teachers say how nice their lunch was.

Answers

1 caretaker   2 P.E. teacher   3 cook

---

5 Listen again (10 minutes)

- Focus on Speaker 1. Replay Audio Track 3 and give learners time to write down what's special about each speaker's job. Learners compare what they have written in groups of 3–4.

- Nominate a group spokesperson to tell the class what the group has written.

- Repeat the procedure for speakers 2 and 3 with a different group spokesperson.

Answers

1   He/she meets lots of great children and teachers every day.

2   He/she enjoys working with children and playing sports.

3   He/she is happy when the children and teachers say how nice their lunch was.

Language detective (5 minutes)

- Write the heading 'Adverbs of frequency' on the board. Brainstorm *always, sometimes, usually* from the audio. Project the audio script on the whiteboard and tell learners to point them out.

- Focus on the adverbs of frequency in the Language detective. Elicit the difference in meaning between the adverbs.

- Encourage learners to make observations on the position of adverbs of frequency in the sentences. This should help prepare them for Activity 6.

> **Workbook**
>
> For further practice, learners look at the Language detective and do Questions 1–4 on pages 12–13.

> **Differentiation ideas:** Learners could also try **Differentiated worksheet 1** at this point, to consolidate their understanding.

6 Talk about school workers (5 minutes)

- Ask learners to think back to the text they have listened to. Put them in groups of 3–4 and give them a few minutes to answer the questions.

- Share feedback at the end of the activity. Nominate groups to answer each question.

Answers
Answers will vary.

7 Write questions (10 minutes)

- Focus on the questions.

- Ask each group of 3–4 learners to decide which school worker to interview.

- Use Audio script 3 as a starting point to brainstorm questions. For example:
  *I always get up very early in the morning to open the school gates… **What** time do you get up? **Why** do you get up early?*

  *I teach the children how to play all kinds of different sports... **What** do you teach the children?*

  *I sometimes work on Saturday mornings as I train the school sports teams… **Why** do you work on Saturday mornings?*

- Circulate and support learners while they write 5–10 questions to ask their chosen school worker.

> **Digital Classroom:** Use the activity 'Where do you work?' to focus on the pronunciation of 'do you' in connected speech. The i button will explain how to use the activity.

8 Listen and repeat the sentences and Speaking tip (5 minutes)

- Ask learners to look at the Speaking Tip box.

- Listen to the questions and then ask learners to practise the pronunciation of the questions.

Audioscript: Track 04
See Learner's Book page 17.

9 Arrange a time to interview the school worker (10 minutes)

- Learners interview the school worker using the questions they have prepared.

- If interviewing a school worker in English is not practical, choose a learner to assume the role of each school worker.

> **Assessment ideas:** Listen to the interview recordings and check for the use of language and pronunciation. Make notes on areas where learners might benefit from further support.

Plenary ideas

Consolidation (15 minutes)

- Follow the instructions at the Puzzlemaker website to create a word search puzzle with different school-related jobs.

- Learners could do **Photocopiable 2**.

Homework ideas

> **Workbook**
>
> Questions 1–4 on pages 12–13.

- Learners use the answer notes from their interview to write up their questions and answers.

1.4 Write about it: Organise a community event

LEARNING PLAN

Learning objective	Learning intentions	Success criteria
4Wor.03	• **Writing:** Use, with support, an appropriate layout for a leaflet. • **Vocabulary:** *leaflet, event, raising money, craft activities, charity slogan*.	• Learners can create, with support, an appropriate layout for a leaflet to advertise an event.

21st-century skills

Creative thinking: Develop a new leaflet, based on a model.

Critical thinking: Compare different information and say which they like best and why.

Collaboration: Participate in a group project.

Learning to learn: Present a leaflet before displaying it in the classroom or putting it in a learner portfolio.

Materials: Learner's Book pages 18–19; Workbook pages 14–15; **Photocopiable 3**; Examples of simple leaflets similar to those in the Learner's Book, if possible created by other learners

Starter ideas

Community events (5 minutes)
• Build up a list of different events that take place in learners' communities.

CROSS-CURRICULAR LINKS

PE: Encourage learners to compare different information about sporting events and say which they like best and why/why not. Nominate learners and ask if they like these types of events. Elicit simple reasons why they do or don't like them, e.g. *I don't like fun runs because I don't like running! I like fun runs because I like to keep fit!*

Main teaching ideas

1   Look at these leaflets (5–10 minutes)
   • Look at the leaflets and ask learners what they can see. Elicit the meaning of *Spelling Bee, Family Fun Day* and *Fun Run*. Build up a list of useful words on the board. Include adjectives like *boring, fun*, etc.

• Encourage learners to participate by asking them if they like the activities and to give a reason why/why not.

• Learners work in pairs and tell their partner which activity they like best and why.

• Nominate learners to report on what they have learned about their partners.

2   Read the leaflets (5–10 minutes)
   • Read the leaflets as a class. Learners will be producing their own leaflets later, so encourage them to think about the kind of information the leaflets contain. Ask Wh- questions like *Who is the…for? When? What time? What is it? Why?*, etc.

   • Demonstrate the activity by asking learners where they could find the information for the first question. Ask the class to vote on whether they think the answer is true or false.

   • Learners read the other statements and decide if they are true or false.

   • Share feedback, pointing out where learners can find the relevant information.

Answers

a True
b False – there are six
c False – it takes place at the community centre
d True
e False – it is for all the family
f True

3 Which event is for you if...? (5 minutes)

- Pre-teach *raising money* by giving examples from the learners' country/countries.

- Introduce the activity by asking learners if they are interested in sports, reading, raising money and craft activities.

- Demonstrate the activity by focusing on the first question and eliciting the correct answer (*Fun Run*).

- Learners answer the other questions in pairs.

- Share feedback, indicating the relevant information on the leaflets, if necessary.

Answers

a Fun Run
b Spelling Bee
c Fun Run
d Family Fun Day
e Family Fun Day

4 Match the slogans and Language focus (10 minutes)

- Explain the concept of a slogan. Encourage learners to think of slogans from their country. Look at the Language focus and explain that slogans often include imperatives. Build up a list of other imperatives that learners are familiar with, e.g. **Read** the text. **Sit** down.

- Ask concept check questions to test learners have understood the purpose of slogans, e.g. *Do they want people to buy something? (What?) Do they want people to go somewhere or to do something? (Where? What?)*

- Focus on the slogan: 'Buy your activity pass today!' Encourage learners to speculate what an activity pass might be used for.

- Match the first slogan to an event in Activity 1.

- Repeat for the other slogans.

Answers

Join us at the local community centre – Spelling Bee
Run for Royal Children's Hospital! – Fun Run
Come and try sculpture painting! – Family Fun Day
Buy your activity pass today! – Family Fun Day

› **Digital Classroom:** Use the activity 'Make a leaflet' to prepare learners for writing, editing and proofreading a leaflet. The i button will explain how to use the activity.

5 Write and design a leaflet (20 minutes)

› **Creative thinking:** Learners follow the instructions, exploring their ideas to create a new leaflet, based on a model.

- Focus on Step 1: Research (Collaboration) and brainstorm ideas about local charities and places which need a 'Big Clean Up'. As part of this step, show learners examples of similar leaflets, if possible created by other learners.

- Encourage learners to be creative and produce artwork for the leaflet.

- Learners follow Step 2: Planning and Step 3: Writing in groups. Circulate and offer support. Encourage learners to use expressions from the Learner's Book. Give feedback after each step.

- Before completing Step 4: Read and check, encourage learners to read the checklist and add any information they have forgotten.

- Once the leaflet has been written, focus on the writing checklist on **Photocopiable 3**.

› **Assessment ideas:** Print out the sample answer. Ask learners to assess it against **Photocopiable 3** before they finalise their own leaflets.

6 Present, display or publish work (5 minutes per group of learners)

- Learners could present their leaflet to the class before displaying in the classroom or putting in a learner portfolio.

› **Assessment ideas:** While learners are presenting, check their use of vocabulary and pronunciation. Make notes on areas where learners might need further support.

Plenary ideas

Consolidation (5 minutes)

Learners ask and answer questions orally about other learners' leaflets.

Homework ideas

Workbook

Questions 1–6 on pages 14–15.

- Learners write a paragraph about one of the events described in another group's leaflet.

1.5 Read and respond: *The Treasure*

LEARNING PLAN		
Learning objective	**Learning intentions**	**Success criteria**
4Rm.02	• **Reading:** Read, with support, a short story, with confidence and enjoyment. • **Vocabulary:** *slide, swings, sandpit, treasure, treasure hunt, neighbourhood, surgery, hidden, follow.*	• Learners can read, and answer questions about, a short simple text.

21st-century skills

Communication: Encourage learners to describe the stories they know.

Collaboration: Explain reasons for own suggestions in a simple way; Take part in a group discussion.

Social responsibilities: Understand personal responsibilities as part of a group and in society.

Materials: Learner's Book pages 20–23; Workbook pages 16–17

Starter ideas

Treasure tales (10 minutes)

- Tell learners that you are going to read a story about finding treasure in the community. Pre-teach the expression *Treasure Hunt* and the words *hidden* and *follow*.

- Ask learners if they know any stories about finding treasure. Ask questions about *Who* found the treasure, *Where* they found it and *What* kinds of treasure were found.

- If learners don't know any treasure stories, get them to ask you questions about a treasure story.

  > **Communication:** Encourage learners to describe the stories they know.

Main teaching ideas

1 Look at the pictures (5–10 minutes)

- The length of the story may make it challenging for learners of this level. To overcome this, encourage learners to look at the pictures and make predictions about the treasure that the children might find.

- Build up a list of useful words on the board and see the differentiation ideas for Activity 2.

2 Read and listen (10 minutes)

- Learners read and listen to the whole story and see if their ideas were right.

- Make sure learners understand that all they need to do is check their ideas. Tell them not to look at the questions now, as there will be time to look at these and the story details later.

- Check that learners know the key words before reading. For example, in the third section (playground): *slide*, *swings* and *sandpit*. If learners find it hard to concentrate on texts of this length, pause after each section and ask the questions in activities 3, 4 and 5, to check learners have understood what they have read, before continuing. If you have time, add some personalised questions. For instance: *How do you feel on Fridays? Do you get homework over the weekend? Do you think this is interesting homework?*

- Learners work together in groups of 3–4. After reading, ask them to write down all the 'treasure' words from the story that they remember.

> **Differentiation ideas:** If learners want an extra challenge, ask them to note down or tell a group member why they think each is a 'treasure', e.g. '*Omer's mum says Omer is a treasure because he is special to her.*'

- Choose a learner from each group to report back to the class.

Audioscript: Track 05
See Learner's Book pages 20–23.

3 Answer the questions (5–10 minutes)

- Before answering the questions in Activity 3, allow learners a minute to re-read the first paragraph. To encourage learners to focus on the task and avoid being distracted by difficult words, be strict on the time limit.

- Learners should then read the next part of the story.

Answers
a To find treasure in their neighbourhood.
b Because they don't usually get homework over the weekend.
c Because the final bell rang and it was Friday.

4 True or false? (5 minutes)

- Tell learners to read the sentences.

- Allow a few minutes for learners to re-read the rest of the text and find the information.

- Read the relevant information in the text for each statement and nominate learners to interpret whether the questions are true or false.

Answers
a True
b False – he wanted to do the treasure hunt
c True

5 Trace Omer's and Azra's route (5 minutes)

- Focus on the map. Introduce the activity by asking learners to point to where the first X is.

- Allow learners 2–3 minutes to find the other places and trace the route on the map.

- Nominate learners to show the route on the board.

Answers
The route is: Azra's house → the park and ice cream van → library → road crossing → community centre → vet's → Azra's house

6 Read the story again. Find these words (10 minutes)

- Demonstrate part a by reading the first sentence of the text and eliciting that the first community helper is the teacher.

- Ask learners to work individually to find the remaining words. Then come together as a class and share the answers.

> **Differentiation ideas:** If learners don't feel confident about this task, ask them to focus on finding the names of three helpers, one thing you can find in a park and one type of food.

Answers
a ice-cream man, librarian, police officer, gardener, vet, class teacher
b slide, swings, sandpit
c kitten
d ice-cream, cakes

〉**Digital Classroom:** Use the activity 'The Treasure' to reinforce reading comprehension of the story. The i button will explain how to use the activity.

7 Values: Helping people in our community (10–15 minutes)

〉**Social responsibilities:** This activity encourages learners to think about social responsibilities, including their own, as part of a group and in society. It also tests learners' understanding about the 'treasures' in the story.

〉**Collaboration:** Allow learners 5–10 minutes to discuss these questions in groups of 3–4.

〉**Differentiation ideas:** If learners need support with this task, provide them with a prompt sheet, with phrases such as *I think… What do you think? Do you agree?*

Answers

a   Suggested answer: Because when we think of treasure, we think of gold or jewels. We don't think about things like our home, the library and people who help us, which are really important to us (but perhaps we should!).

b–d   Learner's own answers.

Plenary ideas

Consolidation (10 minutes)

- Ask learners to revise the ideas from the lesson in small groups. Following the discussion, ask each group of learners to choose one of the people from the story and explain to the class how the person helps in the community.

- Learners write a paragraph about how they could help their class or the community, or about the communities they belong to.

Homework ideas

> **Workbook**
>
> Questions 1–5 on pages 16–17.

- Learners write a short story about a treasure hunt.

〉**Assessment ideas:** As a class, write a short checklist for learners to use to self-assess their story. For example: *Have I used the past simple in my story? Have I used past simple verbs? Have I used the vocabulary from the lesson?*

1.6 Project challenge

LEARNING PLAN

Learning objective	Learning intentions	Success criteria
4Wc.02/4Wca.04	• **Writing:** Write an article which describes a day in the life of a school worker using a short sequence of simple sentences.	• Learners can write, with support, a short sequence of simple sentences.
4Wc.02/4Wc.03	• **Writing:** Write a description about an inspirational person you know using a short sequence of simple sentences. • **Writing:** Express, with support, opinions and feelings.	• Learners can use some simple grammatical structures and sentence patterns correctly in their article or description, allowing for some mistakes. • Learners can express, with support, their opinions and feelings in the article or description.

21st-century skills

Learning to learn: Portfolio opportunity – dating and filing the projects, photos or scans of learners' work; Participate in shared writing activities.

Communication: Share thoughts with others to solve problems and use polite forms to make and respond to suggestions.

Materials: Learner's Book pages 24–25; Workbook page 18; **Unit 1 project checklists**; Examples of articles/descriptions about the day in the life of a school helper/inspirational people, ideally written by other learners

Starter ideas

Raise interest in the projects (10–15 minutes)

- If possible, raise interest in the projects by showing articles about a day in the life of a school helper and descriptions about inspirational people written by other learners.

- Build up a list of school helpers on one half of the white board and people that learners consider to be inspirational on the other half.

- Elicit information about what is special about the school helpers and the inspirational people. Make sure you include information on different special people.

Main teaching ideas

Introduce projects (60 minutes)

- Encourage learners to choose one of the projects and then follow the steps for their chosen project.

- Learners work in groups, managing and sharing the tasks in the project.

Project A: A day in the life of a school helper

- Focus on Step 1. Learners work in groups of 3–4. Circulate and offer groups advice while they design the map of their school.

- For Step 2, re-read/re-play the interview the learners did with a school helper. Support learners by building up a mind map on the board of different parts/times in the school helper's day. Encourage learners to draw their own mind maps about a school helper.

- When learners are writing their article, circulate and give each group help and advice. Encourage them to use suggestions from the Starter activity, their mind-map and their notes from their interview of a school helper.

⟩ **Assessment ideas:** Learners use the **project checklist** to assess how well they carried out the task and make suggestions for improvement.

Project B: Write about an inspirational person you know

- Learners work in groups of 3–4.

- First, look back at the list of people who learners consider to be inspirational (from the Starter).

- For Steps 2–3, allow learners time to read the description to find out who the person is. Then read the questions and allow groups time to find the answers.

- Check that all learners have chosen an inspirational person. Before they start step 4, ask them to read through the 'Remember to' points. More support may be needed for this project than for Project A, so brainstorm suggestions for each point. When learners are writing their description, circulate and offer support where necessary, encouraging them to use these suggestions, as well as those from the Starter activity and the sample answer.

⟩ **Assessment ideas:** Learners use the **project checklist** to assess how well they carried out the task and make suggestions for improvement.

Answers
a her dad
b kind, caring, does nice things
c He helps her with her homework / playing sport (running).
d He coaches them (running).

Plenary ideas

Consolidation (10–15 minutes)

- Have a class discussion about what learners enjoyed most about the projects and what they would like to work on for next time.

Homework ideas

Workbook
Questions 1–11 on page 18.

- Photocopy the projects (with language mistakes corrected) of the other learners, and learners can read them at home.

1.7 What do you know now?

What is a community?

⟩ **Learning to learn:** Learners have the opportunity to reflect and evaluate their own learning success.

- Reintroduce the question from the start of the unit: *What is a community?* Discuss learners' responses to the question now and compare them with their comments at the beginning of the unit. How much has changed?

- Ask learners to work on the questions in pairs.

- Focus on the first task and elicit examples. Allow learners time to work together and build up their lists before giving class feedback.

- Do the same for questions 2–3. Elicit example sentences for each task, e.g. *Parents look after their children.* Allow time for learners to write sentences together and then give class feedback.

- If learners find questions 4 and 5 difficult, encourage them to look back at the events in Lesson 1.4 and the 'treasures' in Lesson 1.5.

Answers

1   Learner's own answers.

2   Suggested answers: Parents look after their children. A caretaker fixes things in a school. A firefighter fights fires. A street cleaner clears away rubbish in public places. A vet looks after animals. A football coach trains a football team.

3   Learner's own answers.

4   Learner's own answers.

5   ice-cream man, librarian, police officer, gardener, vet, class teacher

6   Learner's own answers.

Look what I can do!

• There are six 'can do' statements. Learners read through the statements and tick the things they can do. Encourage them to reflect on how well they can do these things. Also invite them to think of ways they can improve further, e.g. what strategies they can use or learn to use.

• If learners find it challenging to read the statements, look through the unit with them and support them to find the relevant information.

• Finally, ask learners to work through the questions on page 19 of the Workbook. Encourage them to talk about what they enjoyed and also about any further support they might need.

> 2 Earth and beyond

Unit plan

Lesson	Approximate number of learning hours	Outline of learning content	Learning objectives	Resources
1 Planet Earth	1–1.5	Compare Earth's natural landscapes	4Ld.04 4Ug.11 4Sc.03	Learner's Book Lesson 2.1 Workbook Lesson 2.1 **Digital Classroom:** The Earth from space Comparatives: Our planet
2 Planets and orbits	1–1.5	Explore our solar system	4Rd.01 4Sc.03/4Ug.11	Learner's Book Lesson 2.2 Workbook Lesson 2.2 ⬇ Photocopiable 4 **Digital Classroom:** Guess the planet! Superlative adjectives
3 Natural miracles	1–1.5	Describe natural events	4Sc.02 4Ld.04	Learner's Book Lesson 2.3 Workbook Lesson 2.3 ⬇ Differentiated worksheet 2 **Digital Classroom:** Present continuous The Northern Lights
4 Finding out about space technology	1–1.5	Write a fact file about a spacecraft	4Rm.01 4Wor.03	Learner's Book Lesson 2.4 Workbook Lesson 2.4 ⬇ Photocopiable 5 and 6 **Digital Classroom:** The Mars Rovers ⬇ Sample answer for Unit 2
5 *Not a Planet Anymore*	1–1.5	Read a poem about Pluto	4Rm.02	Learner's Book Lesson 2.5 Workbook Lesson 2.5 **Digital Classroom:** Poem: find the rhyming pairs
6 Project challenge	1–1.5	Project A: Create your own adjective poem Project B: Design your own space shuttle	4Wc.03 4Wor.03 4Wc.02	Learner's Book Lesson 2.6 Workbook Lesson 2.6 ⬇ Unit 2 project checklists
Cross-unit resources ⬇ Unit 2 Audioscripts ⬇ End of Unit 2 test ⬇ Unit 2 Progress report ⬇ Unit 2 Wordlist				

BACKGROUND KNOWLEDGE

Unit 2 encourages learners to think about the different landscapes on Earth, to explore planets that orbit our solar system and to think about natural miracles like rainbows, constellations and lightning. The content is linked to science lessons, as learners are encouraged to discover the world around them and beyond, as well as classifying and looking more closely at natural phenomena, describing characteristics, and gathering and analysing data.

Learners will discover space technologies like spaceships, satellites and rovers, which have been designed to explore the mysteries of our solar system. They will investigate people's fascination with Mars (also known as the Red Planet) and Pluto, the subject of the poem in Lesson 5. Pluto was considered the ninth planet of the solar system until it was reclassified as a dwarf planet in 2006. Mars rovers, which are the subject of the fact file in Lesson 4, are motorised vehicles that travel across the surface of the planet and are used to examine its territory.

TEACHING SKILLS FOCUS

Assessment for learning

What is assessment for learning (AfL)?

AfL is a teaching approach. You integrate feedback into your classroom teaching. This feedback can be from you, self-assessment or peer assessment. There are examples of all three types of assessment throughout this resource. For example: through you providing specific written or oral feedback, learners self-assessing by comparing their work with a checklist or sample answer, and peer assessment by exchanging work with another learner and providing feedback on specific points.

Your challenge

Try to incorporate the following ideas in your teaching. You may have already made a start.

1   At the beginning of each lesson, tell the learners the learning intentions.

2   Tell learners the *success criteria* (at the start of the teacher notes for each lesson).

3   Encourage learners to assess their own learning by referring to *can do* statements (in the Learner's Book at the end of each unit).

4   Offer learners oral or written feedback about errors related to the learning goals of a task (see Common misconception feature boxes in lessons that include grammar intentions).

5   Encourage learners to assess their own performance, particularly in Lesson 6, including asking what they did well and where they think they need to improve. Encourage peer feedback.

6   Use open questions to check learners have understood a task.

At the end of Unit 2, write down a list of what you have found out about your learners and improvements in their learning compared to the previous unit.

2.1: Think about it: Planet Earth

LEARNING PLAN

Learning objective	Learning intentions	Success criteria
4Ld.04	• **Listening:** Understand, with little or no support, most specific details comparing natural landscapes.	• Learners can answer questions on a short talk comparing natural landscapes.
4Ug.11	• **Use of English:** Use an increasing range of adjectives and comparative and superlative adjectives [regular and irregular].	• Learners can use an increasing range of comparative adjectives to write a quiz about landscapes.
4Sc.03	• **Speaking:** Ask and answer quiz questions about landscapes.	• Learners can ask questions to find out about a range of global landscapes and respond accordingly.
	• **Vocabulary:** *freezing, icy, dry, huge, wide, wet, beautiful, humid, cool, warm.*	

21st-century skills

Learning to learn: Practical skills/strategies for listening – learners listen only for the information they need.

Critical thinking: Being aware of diversity of landscapes worldwide.

Creative thinking: Generate ideas around the topic to write a quiz.

Materials: Learner's Book pages 27–29; Workbook pages 20–21 and 22–23; Pictures of famous spectacular landscapes in your country; if necessary, a world map

LANGUAGE BACKGROUND

Comparative and superlative adjectives

Comparative adjectives are used to compare two different nouns. Superlative adjectives are used to make comparisons between three or more nouns.

This includes comparing one object or place with the rest of a group, e.g. *The biggest shop in London.*

One-syllable comparative and superlative adjectives are formed as follows:

Comparative	Superlative
add –**er** e.g. *wide* → *wid**er** (than)*	add –**est** e.g. *wid**est***

For adjectives with **two syllables** that end in **–ly**:

Comparative	Superlative
delete the **y** and add –**er** e.g. → *friendly* → *friend**lier** (than)*	delete the y and add –**est** e.g. the *friend**liest***

CONTINUED

For other adjectives with **two syllables or more**:

Comparative	Superlative
add **more** e.g. *dangerous* → **more** *dangerous (than)*	add **most** e.g. *the* **most** *dangerous*

A few adjectives are irregular. The most common irregular forms are:

good	→ *better (than)*	*the best*
bad	→ *worse (than)*	the worst
far	→ *farther/further (than)*	the farthest/furthest

Common misconceptions

Misconception	How to identify	How to overcome
Learners may wrongly think that they can add 'more' to all adjectives (including short adjectives) to make comparatives, as in some other languages.	Ask questions, e.g. • *How do you form the comparative of short adjectives / adjectives with two syllables or more?* • *Why do some comparatives have 'more' and others don't?* • *What's the comparative of 'hot'/ 'wide'/'dangerous'?*	Practise using the comparative form of the short adjectives. Write the base form of short adjectives on the board. Learners make comparative sentences.
Replacing *than* with *that* in pronunciation or forgetting to add *than* after the comparative adjective when making a full sentence comparing two nouns.	If necessary, focus on examples in the audio script.	Practise. Make fun 'half sentence' cards – see Differentiation idea for Activity 5. If learners forget to add, or mispronounce *than*, ask them to memorise sentences and recall in a memory game.

Starter ideas

Opposites game (5 minutes)

- Pre-teach the comparative adjectives that will be used in Lesson 1, by playing a game.
- Write the adjectives on the board in random order: *higher, lower, hotter, colder, huge, tiny, warmer, cooler, drier, wetter / more humid, wider, narrower, longer, shorter, freezing, icy, more beautiful, uglier.*
- Elicit the pairs of opposites, e.g. *higher, lower.* Although *high, low, short, tiny, ugly* and *narrow* are not used in the listening activities, they

may come in useful for the quiz writing activity (Activity 6).

Getting started (5 minutes)

- Learners explore the photo of Planet Earth on page 27 and answer the questions.
- Discuss: *Where are the lights coming from?* Encourage learners to spot geographical features such as ocean clouds, land mass and mountain ranges.

> **Digital Classroom:** Use the video 'The Earth from space' to introduce the subject of the unit topic. The i button will explain how to use the video.

Main teaching ideas

1 Look at the pictures (5 minutes)

- Generate interest by showing pictures of spectacular landscapes in your country.
- Focus on the pictures on page 28 and ask the question: *Which landscapes can you find in your country?*
- If you have time, show learners where the places are on a world map.

Answers
Learner's own answers.

2 Choose the adjectives (5 minutes)

- The aim of this activity is to check learners are familiar with the vocabulary they will hear in Activity 3.
- Ask learners to choose which picture is the desert, which is the tropical rainforest, the Arctic and the mountains.
- Ask learners if they know what the other landscapes are (the Amazon River and the Great Barrier Reef).
- Learners work in pairs to complete the activity.

> **Differentiation ideas:** Learners could work in mixed-ability pairs. More confident readers and writers could provide language support if necessary.

Answers
The desert: dry, hot, huge, wide, beautiful, warm
The tropical rainforest: long, hot, huge, wide, wet, beautiful, humid, warm
The Arctic: freezing, icy, huge, wide, beautiful
The mountains: high, freezing, icy, huge, wide, beautiful, cool

3 Listen and check (5 minutes)

- Explain that although there is a lot of information, learners just need to listen for specific words and expressions to identify the place being described. Focus on the questions and elicit examples of such words before listening and identifying the places.
- If helpful, pause the audio after the first paragraph and elicit which place the speaker is referring to (the tropical rainforest), before moving on to the following two paragraphs.

Audioscript: Track 06

See Learner's Book page 28.

1 The River Nile is the longest river in the world, but the Amazon is the widest. The Amazon is 11 km wide in some places and it's 6400 km long. Only the River Nile is longer than the Amazon River but the Amazon is wider than the Nile. The Amazon flows through many countries. It forms part of a larger area called the Amazon Rainforest, which is home to 33 per cent of the Earth's plants and animals.

The Amazon is also home to many interesting mammals and fish, such as pink dolphins and piranhas (man-eating fish). There are 950 species of bats, too, and the Amazon is home to the only real vampire bat. Be careful at night if you are in the Amazon rainforest!

2 There are three deserts in Africa: the Sahara Desert, the Namib Desert and the Kalahari Desert. The Sahara is very big; in fact it covers approximately 9 million square kilometres. The Sahara is hotter and drier than the Namib and Kalahari deserts, which have an average temperature of 30 degrees. Sometimes the temperature is more than 50 degrees centigrade in the hottest months. The Namib Desert is older than the others. It's at least 80 million years old!

3 Hawaii is beautiful but is it more dangerous than you think? The Kilauea volcano in Hawaii is always erupting. It is more active than its neighbour volcano, the Mauna Loa (Long Mountain). This volcano has erupted 33 times since 1843. Mauna Loa, however, is much bigger than Kilauea. It is 100 kilometres long and 50 kilometres wide – that's half of the island of Hawaii! At night you can see the beautiful colours of the erupting volcano; the bright orange and yellow of the burning lava and the blues and purples of the gases.

Answers
1 tropical rainforest (the River Nile and the Amazon)
2 the desert (the three deserts in Africa: the Sahara, the Namib and the Kalahari)
3 the volcano (Kilauea in Hawaii).

4 Listen again and choose the correct answer (5 minutes)

- Look at the questions together as a class. Remind learners to listen carefully for the key vocabulary. Then listen to the audioscript again.

- If necessary, replay audio track 6 and pause after the relevant information is given.

> **Critical thinking opportunity:** If learners find it difficult to choose the correct answer, encourage them to evaluate all the options and discard the incorrect ones, stating why these options are wrong.

Answers
1b   2b   3a

Language detective (10 minutes)

- Before focusing on Activity 5, read the sentences in the Language detective. Your learners may know some comparative adjectives already. A good way to elicit forms they already know is to ask them if they can remember the forms they have just heard after listening to Activities 3 and 4.

- To reinforce comparatives, you could download the audioscript for learners and tell them to highlight the comparative forms.

- Check learners know irregular comparatives: *good → better, bad → worse, far → farther/further, many/ a lot → more.*

5 Describe the pictures (10 minutes)

- Learners work on the activity in pairs, taking it in turns to say a sentence.

> **Differentiation ideas:** If learners need support with this activity, ask them to match sentence halves, e.g. *The North Pole is colder than… the Sahara Desert. The Mauna Loa volcano is more dangerous than… the Great Barrier Reef.*

- At the end of the activity, give feedback on common errors with the form of comparative adjectives.

Answers
Learner's own answers.

> **Workbook**
>
> For further practice of comparative adjectives, learners can look at the Language detective and complete Questions 1–4 on pages 22–23.

6 Write a true/false quiz (20 minutes)

- Ask learners to do some research about specific places in their country (e.g. deserts, mountains, beaches, etc.). They can work on their own or in pairs/small groups. If necessary, research can be set for homework or (if you have access to a computer room) during the class.

- Elicit examples of quiz statements, e.g. *Mount Everest is taller than…*

- Monitor and correct mistakes with the form of the comparative adjectives and make sure learners have six sentences – some true and some false.

> **Differentiation ideas:** If learners want a challenge, ask them to write 10 sentences.

7 Do the quiz (10 minutes)

- Ask groups to exchange their quizzes.

- Circulate and monitor while learners are doing the quiz.

- Once the groups have completed the quiz, check the answers. Go through any misunderstandings.

> **Digital Classroom:** Use the activity 'Comparatives: Our planet' to revise comparative adjectives. The i button will explain how to use the activity.

Plenary ideas

Consolidation (10 minutes)

- To reinforce what has been learnt, play a class quiz game. Collate 10 interesting questions from different learners' quizzes to create a new quiz for revision. Nominate learners to say whether the statements are true or false.

- Learners work in groups. Write the adjectives from the Starter activity on the board. Ask learners to write sentences including the adjectives and places from the lesson.

> Assessment ideas: When learners have finished writing their sentences, ask them to exchange them with another group. They give each other feedback on the use of comparative adjectives and punctuation.

Homework ideas

Workbook

Questions 1–5 on pages 20–21.

- Learners write a paragraph about one of the pictures in Activity 1 using comparative adjectives and descriptive vocabulary.

2.2 Science: Planets and orbits

LEARNING PLAN

Learning objective	Learning intentions	Success criteria
4Rd.01	• **Reading:** Understand, with little or no support, most specific information and detail in a short, simple text about the solar system.	• Learners can ask and answer questions on specific information and detail in a text about the solar system.
4Sc.03/4Ug.11	• **Use of English:** Use superlative adjectives to ask and answer questions about the solar system. • **Vocabulary:** *explore, orbit, support, discover, poisonous, the planets: Mercury, Venus, Earth, Mars, Jupiter, Saturn, Uranus, Neptune.*	• Learners can ask questions to find out general information about the solar system and respond accordingly. • Learners can use superlative adjectives to ask and answer questions about the solar system.

21st-century skills

Learning to learn: Practical skills/strategies for reading – learners look only for the information they need.

Critical thinking: Decide which information is essential when note taking.

Materials: Learner's Book pages 30–31; Workbook pages 22–23; Fascinating pictures or simple songs about planets – easily searchable on the internet (please see suggestion in the Starter activity); **Photocopiable 4**

Common misconceptions

Misconception	How to identify	How to overcome
Learners may wrongly think that they can add 'the most' to all adjectives (including short adjectives) to make superlatives.	Brainstorm the superlatives from the quiz and Language detective. Elicit that the reason some superlative adjectives contain *the most* and others don't is that it depends on the length of the adjective.	Write the base form of the adjectives on the board and ask learners to practise writing sentences using them.

Misconception	How to identify	How to overcome
Learners sometimes forget to double the final consonant when it is required, e.g. *big* → *the bigest* rather than *the biggest*.	Remind learners that (only) in the case of a final consonant–vowel–consonant combination, the final consonant is doubled, e.g. *hot* → *the hottest*.	Write the base form of short adjectives, which require doubling on the board. Ask learners to practise writing sentences using these.

Starter ideas

Planet pictures (5 minutes)

- To interest learners in the topic of the reading texts, show fascinating pictures or play simple songs about planets.

- You may need to pre-teach some planet facts and vocabulary, for example the names of the planets and *orbit*.

Planet cards (5 minutes)

- Write the name of each planet in large letters on a piece of card. Give each card to a learner and ask the learners with cards to stand at the front.

- The other learners re-order the 'planets', starting with the nearest to the Sun.

- Ask the class for suggestions. Then write the correct order on the board so learners with the cards can stand in the correct order.

Main teaching ideas

1   Test yourself (5 minutes)

- Learners do the quiz in small groups. Make it clear that this is a fun activity, not a test.

- Give class feedback on the answers.

Answers

1   a

2   Mercury, Venus, Earth, Mars, Jupiter, Saturn, Uranus and Neptune

3   No, it is a 'dwarf' planet (because it is so small)

4   c

5   b

6   b

2   Read and listen (5 minutes)

- Learners read and listen to the introduction text and check their answers.

- You may need to indicate the parts of the texts where the answers are found.

⟩ **Learning to learn:** Encourage learners to use the vocabulary from the quiz to help them understand the text. Discuss how they do not need to understand the meaning of all the new words. (Scientific words are dealt with later in the lesson.)

Audioscript: Track 07

See Learner's Book page 31.

3   Read and listen (10 minutes)

- Learners read and listen to the rest of the text. They should make notes on each planet using the example as a model.

⟩ **Critical thinking opportunity:** When taking notes, learners often have trouble deciding which information is essential. Start by focusing on the example. Encourage learners to cross out the words in the text that aren't used in the notes.

⟩ **Assessment ideas:** When learners have finished writing their planet notes, ask them to exchange them with a partner. They give each other feedback on whether the information they have included is accurate and essential.

Audioscript: Track 08

See Learner's Book page 31.

⟩ **Digital Classroom:** Use the slideshow 'Guess the planet!' to consolidate what learners have discovered about planets. The i button will explain how to use the slideshow.

Key words: science (5 minutes)

- Read the words and their definitions.

- It is often easier to remember new words when we use them or see them in context. Tell learners to underline the related sentences in the text and take turns to read them to a partner.

> **Differentiation ideas:** If learners want a challenge, ask them to write a different sentence using each word.

Language detective (10 minutes)

- Before focusing on Activity 4, read the sentences in the Language detective.

- To check learners understand the concept, write prompts in the board, e.g. *the tallest → the smallest, the quietest,* etc. Ask the learners questions about the class, e.g. *Who is the tallest?*

- Use learners' knowledge as a basis to predict the rules for forming the superlative of one-syllable adjectives, e.g. *the tallest*, and adjectives with two syllables or more, e.g. *the friendliest* and *the most beautiful.*

- To check learners know how to form the superlative form of adjectives, ask questions like: *How do you form the superlative of short adjectives? What about for adjectives with two syllables or more? What about two-syllable adjectives ending in 'y'? Which adjectives are irregular?*

- Ask learners other questions, e.g. *What's the superlative form of 'hot'/'wide'/'dry'/'dangerous'?*

- Check learners know the irregular superlatives: *good → the best, bad → the worst, far → the farthest/ furthest.*

4 Ask and answer five questions (10 minutes)

- Focus on Activity 4. First, look for and underline the superlative adjectives in the text.

> **Differentiation ideas:** If learners need support with this task, provide them with a prompt sheet to help them ask and answer the questions. For example: *'Which... near... Sun?'* (*'Which planet is nearest (to) the Sun?'*)

> **Digital Classroom:** Use the grammar presentation 'Superlative adjectives' to revise the form and functions of regular superlative adjectives. The i button will explain how to use the grammar presentation.

> **Workbook**
>
> For further practice, learners can look at the Language detective and do Activities 1–4 on pages 24–25.

Plenary ideas

Consolidation (15–20 minutes)

- To reinforce what has been learnt, play a guessing game. Think of a planet and make statements about it. Learners have to guess which planet you are referring to. For example: *It's the nearest planet to the Sun.* (*Mercury*)

- Play a definition matching game. Make flashcards with new words from the unit (e.g. *explore*; *orbit*) and a corresponding card with its definition (e.g. *look for and find out something new; travel around something in space*). Cut up and distribute one set of flashcards to each pair, for learners to match the word with its definition.

CROSS-CURRICULAR LINKS

Science: Learners of this age are often fascinated by planets. As a homework activity, each learner could choose their favourite planet(s)/dwarf planet(s) and find out information about them, e.g. the distance from the Sun, length of orbit, their characteristics.

- Learners could do **Photocopiable 4.**

Homework ideas

> **Workbook**
>
> Questions 1–4 on pages 22–23.

- Learners find more information about one of the planets and write a paragraph about it using superlative adjectives.

2.3 Talk about it: Natural miracles

LEARNING PLAN

Learning objective	Learning intentions	Success criteria
4Sc.02 4Ld.04	• **Speaking:** Describe an experience using a short sequence of sentences. • **Listening:** Understand, with little or no support, specific details of a short commentary describing an experience. • **Vocabulary:** *natural event, lightning, sunset, northern lights, constellation, rainbow.*	• Learners can describe a natural event using a short sequence of sentences. • Learners can answer questions on specific information and detail from commentary describing a natural event.

21st-century skills

Critical thinking: Evaluate what constitutes phenomena; Discuss which words the speaker might use for each picture before listening.

Creative thinking: Imagine they experience one of the natural events.

Materials: Learner's Book pages 32–33; Workbook pages 24–25; **Differentiated worksheet 2**; For the first Starter activity, interesting pictures of the natural events – use a search engine to find images of each event; Access to the Puzzlemaker website

Common misconceptions

Misconception	How to identify	How to overcome

In some languages the present continuous doesn't exist. As a result, learners often wrongly use the present simple when the present continuous is required.	Re-write sentences from the audio (Track 9) in the present simple.
	
	Elicit differences in meaning by asking questions, e.g. *Which form tells us that:*
	
	   ...the lights are only flashing now?
	
	   ...they always flash?
	
	   ...it is a special occasion?
		Discuss whether the present continuous is used in learners' language in the same way as English.
		
		As usual, the best way to overcome this is practice, e.g. Differentiated worksheet 2.

Learners may spell verbs that end in 'e' incorrectly, e.g. *dance* and *shake*.	Remind learners that verbs that end in 'e', e.g. *dance* and *shake*, lose their 'e' in the present participle.	Build up a list of such verbs and display on the classroom wall with example sentences.

Starter ideas

Superlative sentences (5 minutes)

- Revise the superlatives from the previous lesson.

- Write seven superlative adjectives on the board and see which group of 3–4 learners can make the most sentences in a minute.

Natural events (5 minutes)

- In classes that have not studied natural events in science, it may be more challenging to gain interest. Introduce the relevant vocabulary and pictures of natural events.

Main teaching ideas

1 Match the words to the photos (10 minutes)

- Write 'natural event' on the board and elicit/ pre-teach the meaning. If you have shown the pictures in the Starter activity, this shouldn't present difficulties.

- Match the words in the box to the photos.

- Then write *Have you seen lightning?* on the board and elicit answers like *Yes, I have/No, never./No, I haven't.*

- Learners use this model to ask and answer questions about the other events.

Answers

a	lightning	b	sunset
c	northern lights	d	rainbow
e	constellation		

2 Do you know how these events happen? (5 minutes)

- Tell learners they are going to complete the sentences about how certain events happen. Elicit from the learners *How a rainbow happens* (a) by asking questions with *When?/Why?* There is a simple rainbow diagram on the edrawsoft website: search for edrawsoft rainbow template in a search engine.

- Then ask the learners to work in pairs and complete b–e.

- Test your memory! Learners memorise the reasons why the events occur. Then cover up the sentences and write on the board: *Why do rainbows happen?* Elicit the reply. Learners ask their partners what they remember about the other natural events.

Answers

a	rainbows	b	lightning
c	sunsets	d	northern lights
e	constellations		

3 Listen (10 minutes)

- Make it clear that learners do not have to understand every word in the text. Tell them that they only need to understand which place is being described. They will listen again later.

> **Critical thinking opportunity:** Before listening, elicit/discuss which words the speaker might use for each picture.

- After listening, if learners need more support, highlight the words in the audioscript to help identify the picture.

Answers
Photo c: northern lights

Audioscript: Track 09

See Learner's Book page 32.

Zak: Here we are in Iceland, just outside Reykjavik, the capital city. It is very late, nearly midnight, and we're driving in the countryside to see something very special. I'm with my family. This is my little brother, Ben. Say hi, Ben! (Hi!!) We're stopping now and everyone is getting out. Now we're all standing looking at the sky. It's so cold and dark, but I can see lights appearing in the sky. There they are! Oh, they're amazing! I can see bright green lights rising in the sky; the lights are moving and shaking! They look like they're dancing! Wow! Now I can see blue and purple lights and bits of red and pink! The lights are like ribbons across the sky, waving and dancing. Everyone is so excited! Ben's jumping up and down! This is the most amazing thing I've ever seen!

We are very lucky to see these lights because they only happen in places that are very far north.

4 Listen again (5–10 minutes)

- Pause the audio after the first sentence to demonstrate the example.

- Play the rest of the audio without pausing. If you think learners may find it hard to order the sentences, pause the audio after each sentence to allow thinking time.

Answers
Correct order: a4 b1 c6 d3 e5 f2

5 Underline the examples and Language focus (10 minutes)

- This lesson's Language focus concentrates on the present continuous, which is often called the present progressive.

- If learners are unfamiliar with the present continuous, a starting point could be the audioscript from Activity 3. Write the heading *Present continuous* and an example from the audio on the board, e.g. *We're driving in the countryside* to elicit the form (Subject + verb be + verb+ing).

- Show the audioscript and tell learners to look for other examples. Write the examples on the board, e.g. *Ben's jumping up and down!*

- Ask learners to mime the actions and ask the other learners questions to check they understand the concept, e.g. *Is Ben jumping? Does he usually jump in class? Is he sitting?*

- Learners underline the examples of the present continuous in the sentences in Activity 4.

Answers
Now <u>we're standing</u> looking at the sky.

<u>The lights are moving and shaking!</u>

<u>We're driving</u> in the countryside to see something very special.

6 Listen and repeat (5 minutes)

- When learners repeat the sentences, address over-pronunciation or the 'r' sound in the contractions, which is a common problem. This can be done by showing learners how the sound is made with the mouth and repeating.

Audioscript: Track 10

See Learner's Book page 33.

I'm with my family.

We're stopping now …

Oh, they're amazing!

Ben's jumping up and down!

This is the most amazing thing I've ever seen!

Answers
I'm = I am; We're = we are; they're = they are; Ben's = Ben is; I've = I have

> **Digital Classroom:** Use the activity 'Present continuous' to revise the present continuous. The i button will explain how to use the activity.

7 Work in pairs (5 minutes)

- Check learners know the correct pronunciation of the words.

- Elicit one example of an adjective and one of a verb before learners divide the words, and match the adjectives to the photos. If necessary, act out one of the verbs, e.g. *jump*.

Answers
Adjectives: *purple, special, dark, green, amazing, bright, pink, blue, red*

Verbs: *dance, rise, shake, wave, jump*

Suggested answers for matching to photos:

a   lightning: *amazing, bright*

b   sunset: *purple, special, pink, blue, red*

c   northern lights: *purple, special, green, dance, amazing, bright, rise, pink, shake, blue, wave*

d   rainbow: *purple, special, green, amazing, pink, blue, red*

e   constellation: *special, dark, amazing, bright*

> **Digital Classroom:** Use the single image 'The Northern Lights' to give learners a visual representation of the northern lights. The i button will explain how to use the single image.

8 Imagine and create a commentary (10 minutes)

> **Critical thinking opportunity:** Focus on one of the pictures of natural events in Activity 1. Brainstorm possible answers to the four points, offering support if necessary by asking extra questions. For instance, for *Where you are*, ask *Which country? In a car? In a building?*

- Allow learners time to plan their answers using the suggestions and the audio as a model.

Answers
Learner's own answers.

9 Act out your commentary (10 minutes)

- Demonstrate how to act out the commentary by re-playing the audio about the northern lights, to give learners ideas.

Plenary ideas:

Consolidation (10 minutes)

- Create a puzzle for your learners. The Puzzlemaker website is a useful tool: the easy-to-follow instructions allow you to generate tailor-made puzzles (crosswords, word searches, etc.) for your learners. For instance, you could put the adjectives in a word search grid. Depending on how popular puzzles are with your class, you can decide how many words to use.

> **Differentiation ideas:** Learners could do **Differentiated worksheet 2**, to help practise the present continuous.

Homework ideas

> **Workbook**
>
> Questions 1–4 on pages 24–25.

- Learners research another natural event. They write a paragraph about it, answering the points from Activity 8 as prompts.

2.4 Write about it: Finding out about space technology

LEARNING PLAN

Learning objective	Learning intentions	Success criteria
4Rm.01	• **Reading:** Understand, with support, some of the main points of a short fact file about a space shuttle.	• Learners can answer questions on a short fact file about a spacecraft.
4Wor.03	• **Writing:** Use, with support, appropriate layout for a fact file. • **Vocabulary:** *satellite, telescope, space shuttle, rover.*	• Learners can use the headings and appropriate layout for a fact file about a spacecraft.

21st-century skills

Critical thinking: Evaluate predictions about a text; synthesise ideas and information.

Collaboration: Work together towards a task.

Materials: Learner's Book pages 34–35; Workbook pages 26–27; **Photocopiables 5 and 6**; Pictures of the space technologies used in Lesson 4: a high spec spaceship, an orbiting satellite, Mars rovers and space shuttle – two useful websites are the planets.org website (click on Mars under the Planets tab) and the spaceplace Nasa website (search for spaceplace Nasa and then Mars Rover within the website); in the case of country-specific internet restrictions, a simple search should bring up lots of fascinating pictures

Starter ideas

Space technology pictures (5 minutes)

- Generate interest in the topic by showing interesting pictures of the four space technologies and re-showing the video from Lesson 1.

Main teaching ideas

1 Look at the photos (5 minutes)

- Stimulate a general discussion about space technology. Ask learners what they already know.

- If learners have seen the pictures at the start of the lesson, they shouldn't have any problems with the matching activity.

- After matching, ask concept check questions to make sure learners have understood what the sentences mean.

- If necessary, give extra support by building up a model dialogue on the board, e.g. *What's this?* (Point at the first picture.) *It's an orbiting satellite. What can it do? It can orbit planets and (it can) collect information.*

Answers
a2   b1   c4   d3

---

2 Read the fact file (5–10 minutes)

- Revise or pre-teach some space words, e.g. *rocket, into space, discover, huge, reach a speed of* and *amazing.*

> **Critical thinking opportunity:** It is often useful to make predictions before reading a text. However, the predictions that we make are not always correct. Ask learners to make predictions about the space shuttle from the headings. Evaluate their suggestions. For instance, if learners predict the size as 100 metres long, is that practical? How long is an aeroplane? Could they be similar?

- Make sure that learners focus on matching the headings to the sentences, as they will have the opportunity to re-read the text later.

Answers

1	What is it?	2	What does it do?
3	Size	4	Amazing fact

---

3 Circle the information and discuss (5 minutes)

- When learners have circled the facts they didn't know, ask them to tell a partner which fact they thought was the most interesting. Tell them to begin like this: *I think the most interesting fact is that…*

Writing tip (5 minutes)

- Elicit the rules in the Writing tip about the present simple.

- Tell learners to look for examples of the present simple in the fact file.

4 What do you know about Mars? (10 minutes)

- Write some useful question prompts about Mars on the board. For instance, *Where? How big? What…like? Has anyone landed…? What…amazing fact(s)?*

- Guide learners by suggesting they answer these questions. *What is a Mars rover? What do Mars rovers look like? How much do they weigh/cost? What do Mars rovers look for? What other ways have been used to explore Mars? What advantages are there of using a Mars rover? How many Mars Rover missions have there been? Give some details about one of the missions.*

- Give extra support to learners that have not covered this subject in science. Useful, child-friendly information about Mars, Mars rovers and other aspects of space exploration can be found in the websites listed at the start of the lesson.

> **Digital Classroom:** Use the activity 'The Mars Rovers' to consolidate the research and writing learners have done on the different Mars rovers. The i button will explain how to use the activity.

5 Write a fact file (20 minutes)

> **Critical thinking opportunity:** Learners synthesise ideas and information to create the fact file. Suggest the websites (or other similar sites in the case of country-specific internet restrictions) for researching the fact file. If you cannot access the internet during class, print the information for learners to use. Alternatively, learners could look for resources in their local libraries.

> **Collaboration:** Learners could complete the task in small groups, with each learner taking responsibility for answering one or two of the above questions.

- As a class, compare what you've found out. Share any interesting information and discuss any differences in the information.

- Once learners have put the fact file together, focus on the writing checklist on **Photocopiable 5**.

> **Assessment ideas:** Print out the sample answer. Ask learners to assess it against **Photocopiable 5** before they finalise their fact files.

6 Present, display or publish your work (5 minutes per group to present)

- Learners could present their fact file to the class before displaying in the classroom or putting in a portfolio.

> **Assessment ideas:** While learners are presenting, check their vocabulary, pronunciation and the use of connecting devices *and, but* and *because*. Encourage learners to ask follow-up questions to check understanding/find out more.

Plenary ideas

Consolidation (10 minutes)

- To reinforce what has been learnt, make a true/false quiz. Here are some ideas for questions.

  1) *A space shuttle is extremely powerful and very fast.*

  2) *A space shuttle takes astronauts, scientists and other machines into space.*

  3) *A Mars rover is a space shuttle.*

  4) *A space shuttle is about 15 metres long. That's the same as a school bus.*

  5) *A space shuttle can reach a speed of more than 72 000 kilometres per hour!*

- Alternatively, ask learners to do **Photocopiable 6**, which reviews the present simple.

Answers

1   True

2   True

3   False – A Mars rover is a type of motor vehicle used on Mars.

4   False – A space shuttle is about 56 metres long, the same as five school buses.

5   False – A space *shuttle can reach a speed of more than 27 000 kilometres per hour*.

Homework ideas

> **Workbook**
>
> Questions 1–4 on pages 26–27.

- Learners research alternatives to rovers for investigating planets. They write sentences comparing these to rovers, e.g. *Rovers are better than stationary landers because they can move around.*

2.5 Read and respond: *Not a Planet Anymore*

<table>
<tr><td colspan="3">LEARNING PLAN</td></tr>
<tr><td>Learning objective</td><td>Learning intentions</td><td>Success criteria</td></tr>
<tr><td>4Rm.02</td><td>• Read: Read, with support a poem, with confidence and enjoyment.

• Vocabulary: tiny, bold, wondrous, azure.</td><td>• Learners can answer questions and talk about the poem 'Not a Planet Anymore'.</td></tr>
<tr><td colspan="3">21st-century skills</td></tr>
<tr><td colspan="3">Collaboration: Collaborate with others when making choices; Make sure everyone is joining in.

Critical thinking: Talk about why you like or dislike something.</td></tr>
</table>

Materials: Learner's Book pages 36–39; Workbook pages 28–29; Pictures and useful facts from the space-facts website (click on Pluto under the Planets tab) and the planets.org website (click on Pluto under the Planets tab), or similar sites in the case of country-specific internet restrictions; Simple songs about planets – easily searchable on the internet; Optional: Learners bring in a poem that they like in English (for the Plenary activity)

Starter ideas

Just a minute! (5–10 minutes)

• Make a fun quiz about Pluto. Call it something like *Five fun facts about Pluto.* Use the information from the websites suggested in Materials.

Main teaching ideas

1 What do you know about Pluto? (5 minutes)

• Have a class discussion about why the poem is called *Not a Planet Anymore.*

 2 Read and listen (10 minutes)

• Tell learners that they are going to read a poem about Pluto. Explain that they do not have to understand every word to answer the questions.

• Encourage learners to look at the pictures and predict whether Pluto is a happy planet (and the reasons they think this) before reading the text to confirm their expectations.

Answers
Pluto isn't a happy planet because it is small and far away compared to the other planets.

> **Audioscript:** Track 11
> See Learner's Book pages 36–37.

3 Read and listen again (5 minutes)

• Focus on the first of the blue words in the text: *left out.* Encourage learners to read the words around it to help them understand the context of the words.

• Read the possible meanings and encourage learners to try and deduce the correct meaning.

• Repeat for the other blue words.

Answers
a gems   b doubt   c left out
d speck   e longed

4 Work in pairs (5 minutes)

• Find the first word, *tiny,* in the text. Encourage learners to guess the meaning by reading the words around it.

• Then, in pairs, think of synonyms for each word. If possible, learners can check meaning in their dictionaries.

• Repeat for the other words.

> **Differentiation ideas:** For learners who need more support with this activity, turn this into a matching task. Provide (mixed-up) synonyms in a worksheet and ask learners to match them to the adjectives from the poem.

Answers
Suggested answers:

tiny: very small, little

bold: strong, confident

wondrous: amazing, beautiful, wonderful, fantastic, fabulous

azure: blue

5 Read (10 minutes)

* Learners may benefit from re-reading the poem.

> **Collaboration:** Encourage learners to work together in pairs to decide on the correct answers.

Answers
a   Pluto is a long way from the Sun: *'A tiny speck so far away'*.

b   The other planets in the solar system.

c   The 'bigger kids' make Pluto feel left out because they are bigger and have more interesting and beautiful features such as moons, rings and seas.

d   Words to describe Pluto: *left out, speck, far away, tiny, blue, cold, small*.

  Words to describe the other planets: *big, brave, bold, wondrous, shiny gems, lovely rings, azure seas*.

  The words to describe the other planets are more positive and give more attractive images than the words to describe Pluto.

e   Pluto wants to shout and be noticed.

6 Look at the underlined words (5 minutes)

* Focus on verse 1. Read the poem aloud and elicit which words rhyme.

* If learners find it hard to match rhyming words in the rest of the poem with different word patterns, e.g. *out/doubt*, replay the audio.

Answers
Rhyming words: Verse 1: out/doubt; away/play.

Verse 2: them/gems; bold/cold

Verse 3: me/seas; things/rings

Verse 4: out/shout; small/call

> **Digital Classroom:** Use the activity 'Poem: find the rhyming pairs' to revise rhyming words that appear in 'Not a Planet Anymore'. The i button will explain how to use the activity.

7 Did you like this poem? (5 minutes)

> **Critical thinking opportunity:** Encourage learners to talk about why they like their favourite poem.

* Start by asking learners whether they like or dislike the poem before eliciting a possible reason for this. If learners find it hard to say why/why not, suggest they think about the following – the words, the fact that it rhymes, the fact that loneliness is a negative feeling, whether they can relate to Pluto's feelings (if they have ever felt similar to Pluto).

8 Which is your favourite planet? (5 minutes)

* If learners find this activity challenging, use the suggested websites for more information. Learners could also listen to simple songs about planets, which you can find easily on the Internet. Alternatively, give them ideas or suggest prompt words to help them with a voice/personality for their planet, or use a class brainstorming activity to come up with words that could describe various planets. Build up a word bank that learners can draw on.

CROSS-CURRICULAR LINKS

Art and design: Learners draw, colour and label their favourite planet.

9 Values (5 minutes)

⟩ **Collaboration:** Encourage learners to discuss these questions in small groups before giving group feedback to the class.

Answers
Learner's own answers.

Plenary ideas

Consolidation (20 minutes)

- Develop the idea of rhyming words by brainstorming more words that rhyme with the words in the poem.

- Learners bring in a poem that they like in English. They read a verse of the poem to the class and say why they like it. Poems can include books like *The Gruffalo*, which are stories written in a poetic style.

Homework ideas

> **Workbook**
>
> Questions 1–6 on pages 28–29.

- Ask learners to write their own simple poems using the rhyming words they brainstormed in the Plenary.

⟩ **Assessment ideas:** Choose a couple of the learners' poems and read them to the class. Give positive verbal feedback on the use of language and rhyming words in the poem.

2.6 Project challenge

LEARNING PLAN

Learning objective	Learning intentions	Success criteria
4Wc.03	• **Writing:** Express, with support, opinions and feelings about a chosen topic.	• Learners can write their own adjective poem or design their own space shuttle.
4Wor.03	• **Writing:** Use, with support, appropriate layout for a poem or space shuttle project.	• Learners can follow instructions for the layout of their poem or space shuttle project.
4Wc.02	• **Writing:** Write, with support, a short sequence of simple sentences in an adjective poem or commentary.	• Learners can write an adjective poem or complete a commentary.

21st-century skills

Collaboration: Manage and share project tasks.

Learning to learn: File the information away for future use.

Critical thinking: Cause and effect – explain why a space shuttle should be designed in a certain way.

Materials: Learner's Book pages 40–41; Workbook page 30; **Unit 2 project checklists**; Examples of basic poems written in different shapes: if you don't have any examples from previous learners, search the internet for 'shape poems'; A picture of an astronaut taking pictures in space and an astronaut walking on the Moon; Optional: old magazines with pictures for the poem

Starter ideas

Raise interest in the projects (10–15 minutes)

- Raise interest in the projects by showing pictures of astronauts, space shuttles and/or examples of poems in different shapes. If possible, show examples of a learner's work on a similar topic.

Main teaching ideas

Introduce projects (60 minutes)

- Encourage learners to choose one of the projects and then follow the steps for their chosen project.
- Learners work in groups, managing and sharing the tasks in the project.

Project A: Create your own adjective poem

- After completing the first step in the Learner's Book, explain that adjectives can give extra information about a noun; provide examples to demonstrate. Build up a list of adjectives on the board.
- Focus on Step 2. Elicit which adjectives could be used for each of the subjects.
- Focus on Step 3 and elicit examples. If possible, show examples of learners' work from other classes.
- Learners use these suggestions to write their own poems. Circulate and give help or advice.
- In Step 4, if you have any old magazines, learners can cut out pictures from these or draw their own pictures
- As learners present their work to the class, build up a bank of adjectives and ideas from the poems.

⟩ **Assessment ideas:** Learners use the **project checklist** to assess how well they carried out the task and make suggestions for improvement.

Project B: Design your own space shuttle

- Learners work in pairs or small groups to discuss the answers to the questions in Steps 1–3. Build up a bank of ideas on the board for learners to use. Interesting examples of children's creativity can be easily located by typing *spaceships made by kids* into a search engine and selecting *images*.
- Allow learners time to follow Step 4 and label the special parts of their space shuttle. Circulate and offer support.

- Before proceeding with Step 5, ask questions to brainstorm the kind of things that could be included in the commentary, e.g. *What's the spaceship's name? Where is it taking off? What they can see? How many astronauts are there? Who are they? What are they wearing/taking? Where are they going?*

⟩ **Critical thinking opportunity:** Encourage learners to explain why a space shuttle should be designed in a certain way by considering how the design is influenced by the necessary equipment, food, clothing, the number of astronauts, the length of the mission, etc.

- To help give learners ideas, you could also show them a short video, for example a YouTube video on how to build your own space rocket, more pictures taken from space, or pictures of space shuttles that other children have drawn.
- Ask learners to present their work to the class.

⟩ **Assessment ideas:** While learners are presenting, check their use of new words from the unit and speaking fluency.

⟩ **Assessment ideas:** Learners use the **project checklist** to assess how well they carried out the task and make suggestions for improvement.

Plenary ideas

Consolidation (10–15 minutes)

- After learners present their projects to the class, ask the class questions about the other learners' projects.
- Have a class discussion about what learners enjoyed about their project and what they would improve on for next time.

Homework ideas

> **Workbook**
>
> Questions 1–2 on page 30 of the Workbook.

- Photocopy the projects (with language mistakes corrected) of the other learners and learners can read them at home.

2.7 What do you know now?

What can we discover on planet Earth and in our solar system?

⟩ **Learning to learn:** Learners have the opportunity to reflect and evaluate their own learning success.

- Reintroduce the question from the start of the unit: *What can we discover on planet Earth and in our solar system?* Discuss learners' responses to the question now and compare them with their comments at the beginning of the unit. How much has changed?

- Ask learners to work through the questions in pairs.

- Encourage learners to look back at the unit opening page and Lesson 5 to help them answer questions 6 and 7.

Answers

1   Suggested answers: desert, rainforest, the Arctic/Antarctic, forest, jungle, coral reef, volcano, mountains, rivers, lakes, seas, oceans.

2   Learner's own answers.

3   Mercury, Venus, Earth, Mars, Jupiter, Saturn, Uranus and Neptune.

4   Smallest and nearest planet: Mercury. Most beautiful and why: learner's own answers.

5   Learner's own answers.

6   The photo was taken by satellite.

7   Pluto was sad because it felt left out of the group of planets. It felt different to the other planets because they are big and beautiful and it is small, cold and far away.

Look what I can do!

- There are seven 'can do' statements. Learners read through the statements and tick the things they can do. Encourage them to reflect on how well they can do these things. Also invite them to think of ways they can improve further, e.g. what strategies they can use or learn to use.

- If learners find it challenging to read the statements, look through the unit with them and support them to find the relevant information.

- Finally, ask learners to work through the questions on page 31 of the Workbook. Encourage them to talk about what they enjoyed and also about any further support they might need.

> 3 Homes

Unit plan

Lesson	Approximate number of learning hours	Outline of learning content	Learning objectives	Resources
1 How can we describe where we live?	1–1.5	Talk about homes around the world	4Lo.01	Learner's Book Lesson 3.1 Workbook Lesson 3.1 **Digital Classroom:** Different types of home Homes
2 The eco-house	1–1.5	Learn about eco-houses and the material we need to build them	4Rd.01 4Us.07	Learner's Book Lesson 3.2 Workbook Lesson 3.2 ⬇ Photocopiable 7 **Digital Classroom:** Materials Infinitives of purpose
3 Strange buildings	1–1.5	Use modal verbs and yes/no questions to talk about strange buildings	4Sc.05 4Sc.06 4Ug.10	Learner's Book Lesson 3.3 Workbook Lesson 3.3 ⬇ Photocopiable 8 **Digital Classroom:** Pronunciation practice Modal verbs
4 Famous places	1–1.5	Write a magazine article about a famous place	4Wc.02	Learner's Book Lesson 3.4 Workbook Lesson 3.4 ⬇ Photocopiable 9 **Digital Classroom:** The Eiffel Tower You're the editor! ⬇ Sample answer for Unit 3
5 *The Hobbit*	1–1.5	Read an extract from *The Hobbit*	4Rm.02	Learner's Book Lesson 3.5 Workbook Lesson 3.5 ⬇ Differentiated worksheet 3 **Digital Classroom:** *The Hobbit*
6 Project challenge	1–1.5	Project A: Create a dream home! Project B: Describe an interesting building in your town or city	4Wca.03 4Wc.03 4Rd.01 4Wc.02 4Sc.03	Learner's Book Lesson 3.6 Workbook Lesson 3.6 ⬇ Unit 3 project checklists

Cross-unit resources
⬇ Unit 3 Audioscripts
⬇ Unit 3 Progress report
⬇ End of Unit 3 test
⬇ Unit 3 Wordlist

BACKGROUND KNOWLEDGE

Typically, homes in the UK tend to be houses (detached, semi-detached, terraced and/or bungalows) or flats (also called apartments, especially in the USA). Common building materials are bricks, wood, glass and concrete.

Unit 3, however, encourages learners to think about other types of homes (tree houses, house boats, castles, etc.). Content from the geography curriculum is reinforced by inspiring curiosity about landscapes, landmarks and the key physical features of homes around the world. This is achieved by looking at types of homes in different regions, e.g. yurts and stilt houses. A yurt is a circular tent on a collapsible frame, which is traditionally used as a home in central Asia.

Stilt houses are built over water on vertical beams in various locations globally, such as Asia, South America and the Arctic.

Linking again with the geography curriculum, learners are encouraged to improve location and place knowledge, and to develop knowledge of globally significant landmarks. Learners collect, analyse and communicate a range of information to write a magazine article in Lesson 4 – skills that can be applied across the curriculum. The unit also looks at the question of energy efficiency, which is an increasing concern worldwide. Learners will find out about eco-houses, which are sustainable and environmentally friendly homes.

TEACHING SKILLS FOCUS

Metacognition

What is metacognition?

Metacognition is training learners to monitor their own progress and take control of their own learning.

How can I use it?

Metacognition can help maximise the learning potential of each unit and lesson. It can be applied to improve various skills, like listening, as well as learning factual information and new words more efficiently.

How can I find more information?

See *Getting started with Metacognition* on the Cambridge Assessment website (cambridge-community.org.uk). The article separates metacognition into three phases: Planning, Monitoring, Evaluation.

Phase 1

- Set clear learning objectives, encouraging learners to think about these and consider which strategies to use to approach tasks, for example when reading the extract from *The Hobbit* in Lesson 5. (Possible strategies are: making predictions; listening first for gist and then for specific information; and asking learners to think back to previous strategies they've used.)

- Encourage learners to pose questions about what they know about a topic. For example, in Lesson 1: *What do I know about homes around the world and the materials we need to build houses?*

- Encourage learners to summarise information as they learn, e.g. see *Differentiated worksheet 3* with exercises to develop summarising skills using *The Hobbit* extract.

- Encourage learners to make predictions, e.g. in Lesson 4: *What do I expect to learn about Peru, China, Italy, India and Saudi Arabia/eco-houses?*

Phase 2

During Phase 2, the monitoring phase, help learners implement their chosen approach and encourage reflection on progress towards the stated learning goal. Encourage learners to ask themselves questions about their progress. For example: *How am I doing? How did the listening strategies help me with the listening? What should I do next? (for example, revise the new language from the lesson).*

CONTINUED

Phase 3

During Phase 3, the evaluation phase, assess how successful the strategies were in achieving the set learning goal. Encourage learners to come up with questions about how they did. For example, for Listening Activity 3 on page 44, questions might include: *How successful were the listening strategies I used? What went well? Is there something I still don't understand? How can I further improve my listening skills?*

OK, I'd like to try! How do I know if I've been successful?

At the end of the unit/lesson, answer the following questions honestly:

1 How well were the lesson objectives stated at the beginning of each lesson? Did I check at the end of the unit/lesson that these were fulfilled?

2 Is there anything I could improve next time?

3 Was the learning potential of the learners improved?

3.1 How can we describe where we live?

LEARNING PLAN

Learning objective	Learning intentions	Success criteria
4Lo.01	• **Listening:** Recognise the opinions of the speakers when talking about their homes. • **Vocabulary:** *balcony, floor, roof; bricks, wood, wool and white canvas, chimney; ecological home, low impact on the environment, solar panels, eco-efficient; detached house, stilt house, yurt, bungalow.*	• Learners can talk about different homes.

21st-century skills

Critical thinking: Compares information about different types of homes.

Collaboration: Learners explain reasons for own suggestions in a simple way.

Materials: Learner's Book pages 43–45; Workbook pages 32–33; Pictures of homes from around the world, including eco-houses, a detached house, an apartment, a stilt house, a yurt, a bungalow and a canal boat (enter the names for each type of house into a search engine and there are lots of images)

Starter ideas

Getting started (10 minutes)

• Focus on the big question 'How are buildings important to us?' and tell learners they are going to talk about buildings in this unit. Show the pictures of the stilt house, yurt and eco-houses (see Materials).

• Learners answer questions a–c on Learner's Book page 43 in pairs.

Answers

a Clockwise from top of image: A sports stadium; apartment blocks; a hospital; office building; a school; a supermarket. Centre of image: a tower (eg. a TV or signal tower, or a tower landmark with a viewing deck).

b Learner's own answers.

c Learner's own answers.

Talking about buildings (5 minutes)

• Pre-teach/practise the words that can be used for talking about buildings. Learners will need these words for the main speaking and listening activities. There are a number of ways you can do this. For a fun activity, write the words on the board with missing letters, e.g. *b_d_oms, b_thr_ _m, k_tch_n, di_ _ng ro_m,* and encourage learners to guess the words.

Main teaching ideas

> **Digital Classroom:** Use the video 'Different types of home' to introduce the subject of different types of home around the world. The i button will explain how to use the video.

1 Read the clues and match (5 minutes)

• The aim is to pre-teach/elicit vocabulary about different parts of the house that learners will hear in the listening activity (Activity 3).

• Focus on the illustrations and ask learners what they can see. Elicit the words *bedroom, living room, kitchen, bathroom, dining room, roof* and *window*.

• Address any pronunciation issues by drilling the correct pronunciation, e.g. confusion between *bedroom/bathroom* and *kitchen/chicken*.

• Now focus on the definitions (a–g). Demonstrate the activity by eliciting the first description refers to *window*, which is picture 2.

• Give learners five minutes to complete the activity in pairs.

> **Differentiation ideas:** If learners need more support with this task, put them in mixed-ability pairs. More confident readers can provide language support.

Answers
a   window (Picture 2)

b   roof (Picture 5)

c   dining room (Picture 7)

d   bedroom (Picture 1)

e   living room (Picture 4)

f   kitchen (Picture 3)

g   bathroom (Picture 6)

2 Match the words with the pictures (5 minutes)

• The aim is to check learners know the words for the different types of houses the speakers will describe in the listening activity.

• Focus on the words and pictures. Ask learners which type of home goes with which picture.

Answers
a	detached house	b	eco-house
c	bungalow	d	apartment
e	yurt	f	stilt house

3 Listen and match the speakers to the photos (5 minutes)

CROSS-CURRICULAR LINKS

Geography: Learners find out about physical features of homes around the world.

• Ensure learners know and use strategies to help with listening. Help them make predictions about what they might hear by asking them what they can see in the pictures (building materials, size and number of floors).

• Ask learners what they like about these types of homes, so that they will have ideas about what they might hear on the recording.

• Focus on the photographs in Activity 2. Listen to the first speaker and pause the audio. Nominate a learner and ask which photo the speaker is referring to (Photo c, the bungalow).

• Repeat the procedure for the remaining photographs, without pausing the audio.

• Give feedback at the end of the activity.

• You might find it helpful to pause the audio and give feedback after every speaker.

Audioscript: Track 12

See Learner's Book page 44.

1   **Girl:** What do you think about this place to live?

Boy: Well, it looks big from the outside, but it's only got one floor, so the bedrooms are on the same floor as the kitchen, dining room and living room. Hmmm... I think I prefer to sleep upstairs.

Girl: Well I like it because you don't have to walk up and down the stairs all the time!

Boy: Now, that's a good point!

2 **Boy:** Now, this is a really different place to live. It looks quite small though.

Girl: It's called a yurt. It's a traditional home in Central Asia. Look, you can see that it's circular. In the middle of the roof there is a hole for a chimney to keep people warm and to cook the food.

Boy: I love nature and animals, so I think it's a great place to live!

3 **Girl:** This looks interesting! What are those things on the roof?

Boy: They're solar panels. They absorb energy from the sun to heat the house.

Girl: Ah! So this is an ecological home.

Boy: Yes, it is. I like it because it's modern and energy efficient.

4 **Boy:** Do you like this house?

Girl: Well it looks very big! How many bedrooms do you think it has?

Boy: I'm not sure, perhaps four or five.

Girl: It probably has more than one bathroom too and I like the garden.

Boy: I've got three brothers and sisters so I love this house because it's got a lot of space!

5 **Boy:** What do you think of this one?

Girl: Well, it looks like my home. It's an apartment.

Boy: Is your apartment big?

Girl: Yes, it's quite big. It's got three bedrooms, two bathrooms... and big balcony.

Boy: Do you like living there?

Girl: Yes, I do! I love it because it's near my school and it has great views.

6 **Boy:** Wow! This house is near the water!

Girl: Hmm, my little brother can't swim, so I don't think it's a good place to live for my family.

Boy: Well, I love fishing with my mum and dad at the weekend, so this is a perfect house for my family.

Answers

1	c (bungalow)	2	e (yurt)
3	b (eco-house)	4	a (detached house)
5	d (apartment)	6	f (stilt house)

4 **What do the children like about their homes? (5 minutes)**

- Remind learners of the predictions they made before Activity 3.

- Focus on the sentences about the homes and nominate a learner to match the speaker with one of the sentences.

- Check learners have understood the kind of information they are listening for before listening to the other speakers.

- Avoid giving feedback at this stage, as learners compare their answers in Activity 5.

Answers
1e 2c 3a 4b 5f 6d

5 **Which house do you like best? (5 minutes)**

> **Collaboration:** Learners say which house they like best and give (simple) reasons why.

- Elicit and build up a list of characteristics about the homes on the board.

- Ask learners which home they prefer and why.

- Allow learners time to ask and answer the question in pairs.

- Circulate and offer support. Give class feedback on common errors.

Answers
Learner's own answers.

6 **Describe your home to your partner (5–10 minutes)**

- Focus on the prompts on page 45.

› **Assessment ideas:** While learners do the activity, circulate and monitor, making a note of common errors with pronunciation, grammar and target vocabulary.

› **Differentiation ideas:** Extend the activity by asking more confident speakers to tell their partner what their dream house would be like, and why.

- Nominate learners to tell the class what they have just told their partners. Ask learners to report back on what their partners told them.

- Give class feedback on common errors, for example with pronunciation and possible confusion of *It's and It's got*. Ensure that this is done sensitively.

Answers
Learner's own answers.

7 **Look at the photos in Activity 8 (5–10 minutes)**

› **Critical thinking opportunity:** Learners compare information about different types of homes.

- As a class, focus on the questions and elicit some of the differences between the three places. Build up a list under three headings: *tree house, houseboat, castle.*

› **Assessment ideas:** Circulate and monitor while learners answer the questions in pairs, making a note of common errors with pronunciation, grammar and target vocabulary.

- After Activity 7, invite learners to tell the class what they have just told their partners.

- Give class feedback on common errors. Make sure you do this sensitively.

8 **Choose a word from the list to describe each photo (10 minutes)**

- To get the most out of the next listening activity, pre-teach/revise vocabulary to describe the photos, including the adjectives in the boxes.

Answers
Suggested answers:

a   Tree house: *wooden, tiny, relaxing*

b   Houseboat: *comfortable, relaxing, modern, colourful*

c   Castle: *grand, spacious, mysterious, enormous*

9 **Listen to Sam and answer the questions (5 minutes)**

- Remind learners that it is always useful to make predictions about what they will hear.

- Read the questions as a class. Then learners listen to the audioscript and answer the questions individually.

› **Differentiation ideas:** If learners need more support with this task, download the audioscript for them. Ask them to underline useful information for answering the questions, either as they listen or afterwards.

Audioscript: Track 13

See Learner's Book page 45.

Sam: Hi, my name's Sam and I live with my dad. Our house is very special because it's very modern and extremely long. It's colourful and it's got large windows so we can enjoy the view of the canal. It's more spacious and comfortable than you think! Life on the canal is very different from living in a house. I love being next to the water with the ducks and at the weekend we visit lovely places.

Answers

a   Photo b (houseboat).

b   It's very modern and extremely long. It's colourful and it's got large windows.

c   It's on the water. There are ducks and you can visit lovely places on your houseboat.

10 **Which is your favourite place to live? Tell your partner (5 minutes)**

- Before you start the activity, invite learners to tell you the meaning of the adjectives in the word boxes.

› **Digital Classroom:** Use the activity 'Homes' to revise types of homes. The i button will explain how to use the activity.

Plenary ideas

Consolidation (10 minutes)

*   Using Activity 6 as a model, ask learners to write a paragraph about their own homes. They should include what kind of home it is, a drawing, information about building materials, and why they like (or dislike) living there.

› **Assessment ideas:** When learners have finished writing their paragraph, ask them to exchange it with a partner. They give each other feedback on the use of new vocabulary, the use of *like + ing* and the connector *because*.

Homework ideas

> **Workbook**
>
> Questions 1–5 on pages 32–33.

*   Ask learners to write a email message to their English-speaking friend. They should tell their friend about their ideal home. Talk about the different rooms in the home. Talk about the view. Say where their ideal home would be.

3.2 Ecology: The eco-house

LEARNING PLAN

Learning objective	Learning intentions	Success criteria
4Rd.01 4Us.07	• **Reading:** Understand, with little or no support, the main information in a text about an eco-house. • **Use of English:** Use infinitive of purpose. • **Vocabulary:** *mud, stone, Earth, rubbish tip, water tank, tubs (to catch the rain), recycling; turn off lights/ appliances, unplug charger, heat the house, collect water, provide energy, roof, water the plants.*	• Learners can answer questions on a text about an eco-house. • Learners can use infinitive of purpose.

21st-century skills

Social responsibilities: Understand personal responsibilities as part of a group in society – use consumables wisely.

Materials: Learner's Book pages 46–47; Workbook pages 34–35; **Photocopiable 7**; Interesting pictures of eco-homes that show features of houses that help the environment, e.g. tubs that collect rainwater and homes with grass roofs – see, for example, the greenroofs.com website (look under the Projects tab)

LANGUAGE BACKGROUND

Infinitive of purpose

*   The infinitive of purpose is the focus of the Language detective in this lesson. You use the infinitive to express the reason why you do an action.

The use of the infinitive without *to* and the use of *for* instead of *to* are both incorrect:

*   *They have solar panels **to provide** energy.*
    NOT *They have solar panels **provide** energy.*
*   *They used stone and mud **to build** the walls.*
    NOT *They used stone and mud **for build** the walls.*

Common misconceptions

Misconception	How to identify	How to overcome
In the infinitive of purpose, the infinitive does not change its form. For example, it is not possible to say: • *I went to town to ~~bought~~ a book.* • *It takes 2 hours to ~~getting~~ to school.* The correct forms are: • *I went to town to **buy** a book.* • *It takes 2 hours to **get** to school.*	Check if your learners have understood how to form the infinitive of purpose. Ask questions such as: • *Why did she go to town?* • *How long does it take to **get** to school?*	Often this error occurs because the infinitive of purpose has different rules in learners' first language(s). The best way to break the habit is to practise using the infinitive of purpose. Comparing the English form with learners' first language can also help.

Starter ideas

Eco-pictures (5 minutes)

• To interest learners in the reading text, show pictures of eco-homes, focusing on environmentally friendly features, e.g. tubs that collect rainwater and homes with grass roofs. Encourage learners to describe the images and pre-teach useful language from the vocabulary list. Also revise relevant vocabulary from the previous lesson.

Main teaching ideas

1 What does eco- or ecological mean to you? (5 minutes)

• To help predict the words learners will encounter in Activity 2, ask the class what they can see in the pictures.

• Learners tick the pictures that are associated with an eco-house.

Answers
c, d and e.

2 Read and listen (10 minutes)

• As the text contains some challenging language, make it clear that, at this stage, learners only need to understand enough to answer what is good about an eco-house.

• Read and listen to the text and then ask them: *What's good about an eco-house?* If answering the question is challenging, elicit words in the text that the learners associate with an eco-house.

Answers
Learner's own answers.

Audioscript: Track 14
See Learner's Book page 46.

Key words: Environment (5 minutes)

• Read the sentences.

• Check comprehension by eliciting more examples, e.g. *I put my old bicycle in the rubbish tip.*

Language detective (10 minutes)

• Read the sentences.

• There are more examples of the infinitive of purpose in the text. Tell learners to underline them. Ask questions to check learners understand the meaning, e.g.

What did they use recycled materials for? (To build the house.)

What did they use stone and mud for? (To build the walls.)

> **Workbook**
>
> For further practice of infinitives of purpose, learners can look at the Language detective and complete Questions 1–3 on pages 34–35.

3 Complete the sentences (5–10 minutes)

- Focus on the example and check learners understand the meaning of the sentence. Allow time for learners to complete the sentences without referring to the text.

- Learners re-read the text and check. Give feedback on correct answers and pronunciation of *to*.

Answers
a to heat   b to keep   c to build   d to collect

4 Now read the text again (5 minutes)

- Demonstrate the activity by scanning the text and looking for the information needed to answer the question (*to provide energy for heating*).

- Allow learners time to scan the text and look for the other answers before giving feedback.

> **Digital Classroom:** Use the activity 'Materials' to revise materials used to build houses. The i button will explain how to use the activity.

5 Match the phrases to the correct pictures (5–10 minutes)

- In small groups, learners guess which phrase matches each picture. Give class feedback and practise the correct pronunciation.

- Learners could do **Photocopiable 7**.

Answers
1b   2a   3a   4b

6 Which actions do you do most to save energy? (10 minutes)

> **Social responsibilities:** In Activity 6, learners show to what extent they understand their personal responsibilities to use consumables wisely.

- Elicit and build up a list of things that learners do/could do and then ask them to tell the class about which actions they do the most.

Answers
Learner's own answers.

> **Digital Classroom:** Use the grammar presentation 'Infinitives of purpose' to revise the form and functions of infinitives of purpose. The i button will explain how to use the grammar presentation.

Plenary ideas

Consolidation (10 minutes)

- To consolidate the vocabulary and ideas from the lesson, write a heading or headings on the board, e.g. *Ways to save energy; Eco-home characteristics*. Give learners a suitable time limit in pairs to write as many connected words/expressions as they can remember.

- To practise the infinitive of purpose, write *to…* on the board and make up questions that can be answered using an infinitive of purpose. For example: *Why do you… come to school? go shopping? learn English?*, etc. Ask learners to answer the questions using the infinitive of purpose.

Homework ideas

> **Workbook**
> Questions 1–3 on pages 34–35.

- Ask learners to write an email to an English-speaking friend. They should answer the questions: *What do you do to save energy? What parts of your home/school are good for the environment?*

3.3 Talk about it: Strange buildings

Learning objective	Learning intentions	Success criteria
4Sc.05	• **Speaking:** Pronounce yes/no questions clearly; others may need to ask for repetition from time to time.	• Learners can form yes/no questions to talk about strange buildings.
4Sc.06	• **Speaking:** Describe buildings using a sequence of short sentences to maintain short exchanges, allowing for some hesitation, false starts and reformulation.	• Learners can describe buildings by asking and answering questions.
4Ug.10	• **Use of English:** Use *might, may, could* to express possibility. • **Vocabulary:** *library, school, house, hotel, offices, music academy, museum, amusement park, sports centre, shop.*	• Learners can use *might, may, could* to express possibility when talking about buildings.

21st-century skills

Collaboration: Make sure everyone is joining in.

Critical thinking: Sort and classify objects according to key features.

Materials: Learner's Book pages 48–49; Workbook pages 36–37; **Photocopiable 8**; Interesting pictures of strange buildings, with similar characteristics to the strange buildings in the Learner's Book (see, for example, the awesomeinventions.com website and search for 'crazy building designs').

Modal verbs of possibility

The focus of the Language detective in this lesson is the modal verbs of possibility *can't, mustn't, might, could* and *may*. You can use these modal verbs to make deductions. For example:

• *It must be a school. Must* is used because the speaker feels sure that this is true, usually because it is the only (realistic) possibility.

• *It can't be a house.* (It looks nothing like what I expect houses to look like.) Can't is used

because the speaker feels sure that this not (realistically) possible.

• *It might/could/may be a museum. Might, could* or *may* are used if the speaker considers something to be possible, but isn't totally certain. Although *may* is often considered more formal, there are only subjective differences in meaning between the three modal verbs.

Common misconceptions

Misconception	How to identify	How to overcome
Learners often do not use the correct modal verb, e.g.: • *I think Mum ~~can~~ might like her.* • *We ~~can~~ could paint a picture to put on the wall.* • *Kate ~~must~~ might not be home – the lights aren't on.*	Write examples on the board. Ask learners if they are correct / incorrect and their meaning. For example: **can** versus **might**: • It **can** be a library. (Incorrect) • It **might** be a library. (Correct, possible) For example: **must** versus **might**: • She **must** be at home. (Very probable) • She **might** be at home. (Possible)	Practise by asking learners to make example sentences that they can remember and use as a reference point, This will help them remember the correct usage and difference in meaning between modals.

Starter ideas (10–15 minutes)

Photos

- Look for photos of strange buildings to show the class (see Materials). Ask questions that are formed with the auxiliary verbs *be, do* or *have*. For example: *Is it circular/square? Is it built from bricks/canvas? Has it got a roof? Is the roof at the top of the building?* Elicit *It looks like a… / It's made of…*

> **Collaboration:** Write the questions on the board, point to each question and ask a learner to choose another learner to ask the question to.

Guess the place game

- Give pairs of learners definitions and get them to guess each place. For instance: library – you can get books here; school – you have lessons here; house – where you live; shop – you buy things here.

> **Differentiation ideas:** If learners need support with this game, photocopy the words and definitions, cut them up and ask learners to match the words to the definitions.

Main teaching ideas

1 **Look at these buildings. What's strange about them? (5 minutes)**

> **Critical thinking opportunity:** Learners look at the photos on page 48 of the Learner's Book and tell a partner what they can see and what's strange about each building.

- It may help to elicit information about the first photo together. If necessary, write suggestions/prompts on the board.

Answers
Learner's own answers.

2 **Listen to the children (5–10 minutes)**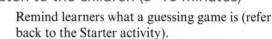

- Remind learners what a guessing game is (refer back to the Starter activity).

- Tell learners they are going to hear two girls' voices talking about one of the photos.

- Encourage learners to make predictions about what they will hear.

- Stop the audio before the answer is revealed, to encourage learners to guess the building.

Audioscript: Track 15

See Learner's Book page 48.

Girl 1: Let's play a guessing game! I think of one of the photos in Activity 1 and you ask me questions to find out which one I'm thinking of. I can answer 'yes' or 'no'.

Girl 2: OK, you start.

Girl 1: Hmm… let me see. Ok, ask me a question.

Girl 2: Is it made of books?

Girl 1: No, it isn't.

Girl 2: Is it colourful?

Girl 1: No, it isn't.

Girl 2: Is it the shape of a bag?

Girl 1: No, it isn't.

Girl 2: Is it upside down?

Girl 1: Yes, it is!

Girl 2: I know, it's photo a!

Girl 1: Yes, that's correct!

Answers

Photo a: amusement park–Wonderworks, USA

---

 3 Listen and repeat and Language focus (5 minutes)

• Focus on the information about yes/no questions. Elicit examples of similar questions.

• Focus on questions a–e in the Learner's Book.

• Learners listen to the correct pronunciation and then repeat.

• Allow learners time to circle the auxiliary verbs before checking the answers together.

• You may need to pause the audio to allow learners time to process what they hear.

Audioscript: Track 16

See Learner's Book page 49.

> **Digital Classroom:** Use the activity 'Pronunciation practice' to help learners with pronunciation when responding to yes/no questions. The i button will explain how to use the activity.

4 Play the guessing game with a partner (10 minutes)

• Tell learners they are going to play the guessing game with their partners. Check learners have understood the activity by choosing two learners. Tell one learner to think of any of the buildings from Activity 1 (but not to say which it is) and the other to ask questions about it. Encourage the class to guess the building.

• Allow learners 3–4 minutes to play the game in pairs before giving feedback on common mistakes. Do this sensitively.

• Ask several pairs to demonstrate and build up prompts on the board before learners continue the activity in pairs.

5 Language detective and Talk (10 minutes)

• Focus on the Language detective. Encourage learners to use the modals to suggest sentences speculating about the photos on page 48. Build up logical (and correct) sentences about the buildings using the modal verbs.

• **Photocopiable 8** can be used to practise making deductions about people's homes using modals of deduction.

Workbook

For further practice of modal verbs of possibility, learners look at the Language detective and complete questions 1–3 on pages 36–37.

---

6 Check your ideas (5 minutes)

• Play the audio, pausing where necessary for learners to say whether their predictions about the use of the buildings were correct. Make sure this is done in a light-hearted, fun way.

Audioscript: Track 17

See Learner's Book page 49.

a **Boy 1:** What type of building do you think photo a is?

Boy 2: It could be a museum.

Boy 1: Yes, I agree.

Teacher: Well… it's an amusement park.

Boys: Wow! Really?!

b **Girl 1:** I think photo b must be an apartment block because there are lots of windows.

Girl 2: Yes, I think you're right!

Teacher: Well it's actually a factory!

c   **Boy 1:** Hmmm… this one is difficult.

Boy 2: I think it might be a hotel because it's very big!

Boy 1: I'm not sure, it could be a cool apartment building!

Teacher: Well, it's a building with offices!

d   **Girl 1:** What about d? Well, it's a very big shoe, isn't it? It can't be a real house!

Girl 2: I think it's an art museum.

Girl 1: Yes, me too!

Teacher: Well it's actually someone's house!

e   **Boy 1:** This building is really cool!

Boy 2: Yes, I agree! It must be a library with all those books!

Teacher: Yes, it is! Well done!

7 Listen again and circle the correct modal verb (15 minutes)

- Learners complete the activity in pairs by listening to the audio and looking at the photos.

› **Differentiation ideas:** If learners need more support with this activity, download the audioscript and underline the sentences containing the modal verbs. In small groups, ask learners to refer again to the pictures. If necessary, circulate and help learners guess the meaning of the modal verbs by pointing to the photos and giving clear examples. If learners want more of a challenge, ask them to write three sentences about buildings using three different modal verbs.

Answers

a could	b must	c might
d could	e can't	f must

› **Digital Classroom:** Use the activity 'Modal verbs' to revise modal verbs of possibility. The i button will explain how to use the activity.

8 Find some photos of unusual buildings (5 minutes)

- Help learners locate the pictures (see Materials) and elicit questions that can be asked about the buildings.

- Allow time for learners to practise asking and answering questions about the buildings in pairs. Encourage learners to use modal verbs.

Plenary ideas

Consolidation (10 minutes)

- Explain that learners are going to work in pairs and write down ten words they have seen in today's lesson. Make sure they have closed their books and are ready to start. Circulate and check the words as they write.

Homework ideas

Workbook

Questions 1–3 on pages 36–37.

- Learners find a picture of a strange building. They find out what it is used for and write a dialogue about it, using questions like those in Activity 3. Encourage learners to use modal verbs.

› **Assessment ideas:** Give written feedback on the variety of questions learners use and modal verbs.

3.4 Write about it: Famous places

LEARNING PLAN

Learning objective	Learning intentions	Success criteria
4Wc.02	• **Writing:** Write, with support, a short sequence of simple sentences which describe a famous landmark. • **Vocabulary:** *mountain, peak, spectacular, hidden, trek.*	• Learners can write a magazine article about a famous place.

21st-century skills

Creative thinking: Write an article, reflecting interests.

Learning to learn: Employ practical skills for learning independently in completing a task.

Collaboration: Once the article has been written, ask learners to work through the checklist.

Materials: Learner's Book pages 50–51; Workbook pages 38–39; **Photocopiable 9**; Pictures of top 10 famous landmarks, e.g. at the kids-world-travel-guide.com website; A clickable world map, e.g. the one at the geology.com website (search for clickable world map and scroll down); Large sheets of card for displaying blogs

Starter ideas

Landmark pictures and quiz (5 minutes)

- Generate interest in the topic. Show the class images of fascinating famous landmarks from around the world (see Materials). Make sure learners can't see where the places are. If possible, and **before** opening the Learner's Book, include pictures of Machu Picchu and other landmarks learners will see on pages 50–51.

- Describe the pictures. Try to use the vocabulary and grammar from the previous lessons in the unit.

Main teaching ideas

1 **How many famous places are there where you live? (10 minutes)**

- Use a world map to elicit/pre-teach where the countries from the lesson (Peru, China, Italy, India, Saudi Arabia) are.

CROSS-CURRICULAR LINKS

Geography: Nominate learners to pin labels to a world map on the wall to indicate the places from the lesson.

- Encourage learners to start thinking about which country they would like to write about later on.

- Build up a list of famous landmarks and buildings in learners' countries.

Answers

Learner's own answers.

⟩ **Digital Classroom:** Use the video 'The Eiffel Tower' to consolidate famous places and provide a framework for the writing activity. The i button will explain how to use the video.

2 **Read and find answers (10 minutes)**

- Ask if anyone has been to Peru or knows anything about Peru or the Incas.

- Encourage learners to make predictions about what they will read in the article by asking what they can see in the pictures and looking at the labels. Check learners know the words *mountain, peak, spectacular, hidden* and *trek*.

- Read the questions. Tell learners they are going to find information in the text to answer them.

- Allow time for learners to find the answers, in pairs, which they then share with the class.

Answers

a It's in the Cusco region of Peru in South America. It is high up in the mountains above the Urubamba River.

b It was a spiritual and ceremonial Inca site.

c Hiram Bingham, an American explorer, discovered Machu Picchu.

d You can travel by train, by helicopter or by trekking.

e Learner's own answers.

3 Choose one of the landmarks and write about it (30 minutes)

> **Critical thinking opportunity:** Learners write their own article, reflecting their preferences. The first step is for learners to choose a landmark to write about. If they don't want to write about one of the suggested landmarks, they can write about a famous landmark in their own country. Ensure that not all the learners have chosen the same landmark.

> **Learning to learn:** During this task, learners use practical skills for learning independently. Support them by eliciting the four steps for writing the article in the table on page 51. Encourage learners to follow the model provided in the article about Peru.

- The research can be set for homework, or if you have access to a computer room, during the class.

- Once research has been completed, learners organise their ideas into paragraphs as suggested in the table.

- Learners follow the instructions for Steps 3 and 4.

- An alternative approach to this writing activity is for learners to work in groups. Each group decides on one landmark, and learners can do the research and planning stages together. Within the group, each learner could be assigned a role, e.g. researching location, historical facts, etc.

> **Digital Classroom:** Use the activity 'You're the editor!' to help learners edit and proofread their own work. The i button will explain how to use the activity.

> **Assessment ideas:** Print out the sample answer. Ask learners to assess it against **Photocopiable 9** before they finalise their article.

4 Present, display or publish your work (5 minutes per learner)

- There are different ways to approach this. For instance, you could put the articles on the wall and tell learners to read their classmates' work, or learners could present the article orally to the class.

> **Assessment ideas:** If learners present their article, check their use of vocabulary and interesting adjectives. Encourage learners to ask follow-up questions to check understanding/find out more.

Plenary ideas

Reflection (10 minutes)

- Have a class discussion about what learners enjoyed about writing their articles. What did they enjoy and what was difficult? Invite learners to share any interesting facts they have learned about landmarks. Is there a landmark they would particularly like to visit now?

Homework ideas

Workbook

Questions 1–5 on pages 38–39.

3.5 Read and respond: *The Hobbit*

LEARNING PLAN

Learning objective	Learning intentions	Success criteria
4Rm.02	• **Reading:** Read, with support, a fiction text with confidence and enjoyment. • **Vocabulary:** *brass knob, porthole, carpeted, comfort, tunnel, fond of, meadows, pegs, respectable, tiled.*	• Learners can answer questions on and talk about the extract from *The Hobbit*.

21st-century skills

Critical thinking: Say whether something is true or not and give reasons.

Creative thinking: Engage in reading activities with fantasy and mystery elements.

Materials: Learner's Book pages 52–55; Workbook pages 40–41; **Differentiated worksheet 3**; A copy of *The Hobbit* to show learners, or a picture of the book online; The trailer to the cartoon version of *The Hobbit* on YouTube (easily searchable online)

Starter ideas

Hobbit introduction (5 minutes)

- Focus on the picture of the hobbit house on page 53 of the Learner's Book. Revise the vocabulary from previous lessons by asking learners what they can see in the picture. There will be new words in the text, so use the picture to pre-teach the names of things they see, like *porthole, brass knob, pegs (for hats and coats), tiled, carpeted.*

- Learners can get an idea from the video trailer (see Materials) about what the Hobbit House is like inside.

Main teaching ideas

1 **Look at the pictures and answer the questions (5 minutes)**

- Discuss the questions as a class. Talk about what learners know about hobbits. If it is difficult to interest your class in literature, and you didn't do so in the Starter activity, show the Hobbit trailer (see Materials).

⟩ **Critical thinking opportunity:** Discuss what a fantasy story is. Ask: *Do you like fantasy stories? Why (not)?* Ask learners if they think *The Hobbit* is a fantasy story.

Answers
a Learner's own answers.
b Learner's own answers.

2 **Read the extract. Check and match (10 minutes)**

⟩ **Creative thinking:** The aim of this activity is for learners to engage in reading a story extract with fantasy and mystery elements.

- Explain that this famous story was written many years ago. Over time, writing styles change, so this writing style may be unfamiliar to learners and has new words. Explain that this is part of the pleasure and challenge of reading new stories.

CROSS-CURRICULAR LINKS

Literature: This activity introduces an early (1930s) children's fantasy novel, which is still extremely popular and is recognised as a classic in children's literature. Learners read both for pleasure and information, and should be starting to read with greater ease and with increasing fluency. Learners should be beginning to understand the benefits of a wide literary heritage.

- As there are high-level words in the text, discuss strategies for dealing with difficulties this may cause, like knowing the names for things that they can see in the picture.

- To demonstrate other strategies, first look at the headings in a, b, c and predict what information might be in each paragraph. Then use the picture to help discuss ideas about what the house might look like. Encourage the use of modals and words from the warm-up, e.g. *It can't have many windows.*

- Make clear that to do the task, it is not necessary to understand every word of the story.

Answers
a Paragraph 3   b Paragraph 1   c Paragraph 2

3 Are the sentences after each part true or false? (10 minutes)

〉 **Critical thinking opportunity:** In this activity, learners say whether something is true or not and give reasons.

- Focus on sentences a and b. Remind learners that it is not necessary to understand every word to decide whether the sentences are true or false. Explain that they will look at difficult words in the next activities.

- Learners re-read the first paragraph. Ask them to work in pairs and write down whether sentences a and b are true or false.

- Follow the same procedure for the remaining sentences (sentences c–f for paragraph 2, and sentences g–j for paragraph 3).

〉 **Differentiation ideas:** Learners could work in mixed-ability pairs; more confident readers could provide language support.

〉 **Assessment ideas:** Reading texts like *The Hobbit* can be challenging. While learners are talking in pairs, circulate and check how confident they are with the vocabulary and language. Give verbal feedback.

Answers
a True   b False   c True   d True   e False
f False   g False   h True   i True   j True

4 Correct the false sentences (5 minutes)

- Focus on the first two sentences. Elicit that a is true and b is false. Elicit that b is false because the hobbit's house is *comfortable*. Show learners where to find the words in the text that tell us this.

- As a class, correct Sentence B. Elicit the words in the story that tell us this sentence is false.

- Allow learners time to correct the other questions.

Answers
b   he hobbit's house is comfortable.
e   His house has only one floor (there is no upstairs).
f   There are windows on the left-hand side.
g   Most of the Baggins family were rich.

5 Find and match (10 minutes)

- Read the definitions a–f. Ask learners questions to check they have understood them.

- The first blue word in the text is *hole*. Ask questions to check learners understand *hole* is a noun. Encourage them to discard all definitions that are not nouns. Use the context and the picture to help. Read the sentence *In a hole in the ground there lived a hobbit* and elicit that the answer is c.

- Learners match the words to the meanings individually.

〉 **Differentiation ideas:** If learners want an extra challenge, extend the activity by asking them to write a new sentence using each of the blue words.

Answers
a respectable   b meadows   c a hole
d fond of   e comfort   f a tunnel

6 Read again and answer the questions (5 minutes)

- Focus on the questions. Then allow learners time to re-read and locate the answers. Circulate and offer support, particularly for question d.

Answers

a   comfort

b   a hall, bedrooms, bathrooms, cellars, pantries (small rooms to keep food), wardrobes, kitchens, dining-rooms

c   It has windows.

d   For a very long time.

e   Because the Baggins family have never had adventures before or done anything unusual or unexpected.

7   In pairs, talk about the questions (5 minutes)

- Discuss ideas as a class, before allowing learners time to answer the questions in pairs.

- At the end of the discussions, share ideas.

Answers
Learner's own answers.

8   Values: Making visitors welcome (10 minutes)

- This activity checks learners' understanding of how to make visitors feel welcome. Focus on the questions and brainstorm ideas as a class before discussing in pairs.

> **Differentiation ideas:** If learners want a challenge, ask them to write down answers to the questions in full sentences.

Answers

a   His hall was comfortable with chairs for visitors and coat pegs (hooks) to hang their coats.

b   Learner's own answers.

c   Learner's own answers.

> **Digital Classroom:** Use the activity 'The Hobbit' to reinforce the reading comprehension of the story. The i button will explain how to use the activity.

Plenary ideas

Consolidation (10 minutes)

- Revise the ideas from the lesson by inviting learners to work in groups. Tell them to write names for five rooms in the hobbit house, five of the *blue* words and three more characteristics of the house (tunnel-shaped hall, windows on the left, etc.).

> **Differentiation ideas:** Learners could complete **Differentiated worksheet 3**.

Homework ideas

Workbook
Questions 1–5 on pages 40–41.

- Learners read another interesting short extract from this text (or another literary text suitable for their age, e.g. *the Happy Prince* or *The Selfish Giant*) and focus on understanding the main ideas without looking up more than five new words. They can bring the extract to the next class and share it with their friends.

3.6 Project challenge

LEARNING PLAN

Learning objective	Learning intentions	Success criteria
4Wca.03/4Wc.03	**Writing:** Plan, write, edit and proofread a description of a 'dream home' with support. Express, with support, opinions and feelings.	• Learners can create and write about their dream home, giving reasons for why they like it.
4Rd.01	• **Reading:** Find out specific information about a building in learners' town or city.	• Learners can research an interesting building in their town or city. • Learners can write a short sequence of simple sentences which describes a building, with researched information.
4Wc.02	• **Writing:** Write, with support, a short description of a building.	
4Sc.03	• **Speaking:** Ask and answer questions to find out general information about a building.	• Learners can ask questions about a special building and respond accordingly.

21st-century skills

Critical thinking: Make a choice of activity and give reasons for the choice.

Collaboration: Work in groups, managing and sharing the tasks in the project.

Learning to learn: Portfolio opportunity: Leave work projects on display. Then consider dating and filing the projects, photos or scans in portfolios.

Materials: Learner's Book pages 56–57; Workbook page 42; **Unit 3 project checklists**; Pictures of interesting homes that could be considered dream homes, and pictures of interesting local buildings

Starter ideas

Raise interest in the projects (15–20 minutes)

- Raise interest in the projects. Show pictures of interesting homes that could be considered dream homes and pictures of interesting local buildings.

- Demonstrate the concept of a mind map to the class. Divide the board in half. On one half of the board, elicit suggestions from the class about their dream homes and use them to build up a mind map together on the board. Repeat the procedure on the other side of the board for interesting buildings.

- An alternative approach is to give each group of 3–4 learners a large sheet of paper and a marker pen, and encourage them to make their own mind map. Suggest questions to help them. For instance, for the dream home mind map: *What are the special features of my dream home? Where is it? What is the landscape like? What are the building materials?*

Main teaching ideas

Introduce projects (60 minutes)

- Encourage learners to choose one of the projects and then follow the steps for their chosen project.

- Learners work in groups, managing and sharing the tasks in the project.

Project A: Create a dream home!

- Focus on the five steps *(What?, Describe, Write, Create, Display)* in the Learner's Book. Give support by asking learners about these steps. Write ideas on the board. For example, for the first step, look at the suggestions and ask learners if they agree. Elicit a list of other features that could make homes special.

- Learners use these ideas to write about their dream home. Circulate and give help or advice.

CROSS-CURRICULAR LINKS

Art: In Step 4, learners explore their ideas by drawing a picture of their dream home.

> **Assessment ideas:** Learners use the **project checklist** to assess how well they carried out the project and make suggestions for improvement.

Project B: Describe an interesting building in your town or city

CROSS-CURRICULAR LINKS

Geography: Learners find out about interesting buildings in their geographical region and choose one to write about.

- Focus on the five steps *(Find out, Choose, Write, Draw, Talk)* in the Learner's Book. Give support by asking learners about these steps. Write ideas on the board.

- Learners use these ideas to write about an interesting building in their town. Circulate and give help or advice. Give learners support and advice while they are working.

> **Assessment ideas:** Learners use the **project checklist** to assess how well they carried out the project and make suggestions for improvement.

Plenary ideas

Reflection (10 minutes)

- After learners have completed their projects, have a class discussion about what they enjoyed about doing them, and what they would do differently next time. For Project A, what did learners enjoy about designing their dream home? For Project B, what did learners find out about buildings in their area? Was any of the information they found out surprising?

Homework ideas

Workbook

Questions 1–12 on page 42.

- Photocopy the projects (with language mistakes corrected) of the other learners and learners can read them at home.

3.7 What do you know now?

How are buildings important to us?

> **Learning to learn:** Learners have the opportunity to reflect and evaluate their own learning success.

- Reintroduce the question from the start of the unit: *How are buildings important to us?* Discuss learners' responses to the question now and compare them with their comments at the beginning of the unit. How much has changed?

- Ask learners to work through the questions in pairs.

- If learners find questions 4 and 5 difficult, encourage them to look back through the unit and find the relevant information.

- For questions 7–9, discuss the questions and build up a list to help learners celebrate what they've learnt in Unit 3.

Answers

1 Learner's own answers.

2 Five of: detached house, eco-house, bungalow, apartment, yurt, stilt house, tree house, house boat, castle; Learner's own answers.

3 Stone, metal, recycled materials, mud, wood, (concrete, bricks); Learner's own answers.

4 Suggested answers: solar panels (to heat the house); recycled materials/local materials (e.g. stone, wood, mud, metal) (to build the house); stone and mud (to build the walls); wood from trees (to build the roof); uses natural resources (e.g. water) and energy efficiently; wood burner (to heat the house); big windows (to let in natural light); a vegetable garden; earth and grass on the roof (to keep the house warm); a large tub (to collect rainwater).

5 Suggested answers: turn off lights; turn off appliances; put on a jumper (to save heating); unplug charger.

6 Learner's own answers.

Look what I can do!

- There are seven 'can do' statements. Learners read through the statements and tick the things they can do. Encourage them to reflect on how well they can do these things. Also invite them to think of ways they can improve further, e.g. what strategies they can use or learn to use.

- If learners find it challenging to read the statements, look through the unit with them and support them to find the relevant information.

- Finally, ask learners to work through the questions on page 43 of the Workbook. Encourage them to talk about what they enjoyed and also about any further support they might need.

Check your progress 1

Learners answer the ten questions.

Answers

1 a grandfather b freezing
   c space shuttle d spacious
   e bungalow f caretaker
   g rover h surfing i apartment

2 Learner's own answers.

3 Learner's own answers.

4 Learner's own answers.

5 1: My school is ~~big~~ *bigger* than my cousin's school.
   2: There is a large water tub in our school ~~collect~~ *collecting* rainwater.
   3: My country has the ~~taller~~ *tallest* mountains in the world.
   4: My friends really enjoy ~~play~~ *playing* basketball.
   5: When I am older I want *to* be a P.E. teacher.
   6: The building opposite our school ~~must~~ *might* be a library – I'm not sure.

6 Learner's own answers.

7 Learner's own answers.

8 Learner's own answers.

9 Learner's own answers.

10 Learner's own answers.

> 4 Food

Unit plan

Lesson	Approximate number of learning hours	Outline of learning content	Learning objective	Resources
1 Do we all eat the same breakfast?	1–1.5	Discover what children eat for breakfast around the world	4Lm.01 4Us.02	Learner's Book Lesson 4.1 Workbook Lesson 4.1 **Digital Classroom:** Food Food and drink: *some* or *any*?
2 All about chocolate!	1–1.5	Find out how chocolate is made Write about quantities of things	4Rd.01 4Uv.05 4Us.01	Learner's Book Lesson 4.2 Workbook Lesson 4.2 ⬇ Photocopiable 10 **Digital Classroom:** Chocolate Quantifiers
3 Grow your own!	1–1.5	Explain how to grow a vegetable using connecting words	4Us.03	Learner's Book Lesson 4.3 Workbook Lesson 4.3 ⬇ Photocopiable 11 **Digital Classroom:** Growing a bean plant
4 A fruit poem	1–1.5	Write a poem about a fruit	4Wor.03	Learner's Book Lesson 4.4 Workbook Lesson 4.4 ⬇ Photocopiable 12 **Digital Classroom:** Strawberries ⬇ Sample answer for Unit 4
5 *Charlie and the Chocolate Factory*	1.5–2.0	Enjoy a story about a magical chocolate factory.	4Rm.01 4Rm.02 4Rd.03	Learner's Book Lesson 4.5 Workbook Lesson 4.5 **Digital Classroom:** Chocolate fun: descriptive adjectives
6 Project challenge	1–1.5	Project A: Create a tasty treat! Project B: Find out about where food comes from	4Wor.02 4Wca.04	Learner's Book Lesson 4.6 Workbook Lesson 4.6 ⬇ Differentiated worksheet 4 ⬇ Unit 4 project checklists

Cross-unit resources
⬇ Unit 4 Audioscripts
⬇ End of Unit 4 test
⬇ Unit 4 Progress report
⬇ Unit 4 Wordlist

BACKGROUND KNOWLEDGE

The Big Question of the unit is *What can we discover about food?* In Unit 4, learners are encouraged to think about the different foods that are eaten around the world. The content is linked to geography, food and nutrition, and science lessons.

Learners compare different breakfasts from around the world and explore the process of making an 'international' food – chocolate. They are encouraged to explore where their food comes from and how it travels to their countries, as well as to learn how to grow, create and investigate foods.

Several different kinds of food are the focus of Unit 4: from chocolate in Lesson 2, to fruit in the poem in Lesson 4, and chocolate and sweet treats in Lessons 5 and 6.

Notes on fruits and vegetables

- Papaya is another name for the paw paw, a fruit with orange flesh containing lots of seeds.
- The fruits of the okra plant are contained in pods that are often called ladies' fingers, as they resemble long green fingers.
- Squash is a fruit, which is cooked and eaten as a vegetable. It can refer to a variety of fruits, like pumpkins or courgettes, and its meaning may be subject to local variations. *Squash* can also refer to a sugary drink.
- Cress is a quick-growing herb that is often grown in primary school science lessons, as it grows without soil.
- The durian fruit is a spiky fruit from trees that are native to Borneo and Sumatra.

TEACHING SKILLS FOCUS

Active learning

What is active learning?

General information on active learning is provided on page 14 and more information can be found on the Cambridge Assessment International Education website (search for Active learning).

Getting started with active learning

Active learning involves learners in the learning process. It should involve language output and higher order thinking skills. To facilitate learners playing an active role in learning, encourage them to:

- ask and answer questions
- make discoveries
- analyse evidence
- connect evidence to knowledge of other subjects
- draw conclusions.

There are plenty of opportunities for this in Unit 4. Here are a few examples.

- **Lesson 2:** Learners build knowledge and understanding of how chocolate is made. You could ask them to do the same for another food.

- **Lesson 6:** Learners have the chance to make their own sweet treat or investigate a food.
- Learners are regularly required to learn by reading, writing, discussion or solving problems.
- Learners are regularly asked to reflect on their learning achievements.

Look through the unit and see how many (other) examples you can see.

Questions

1 So don't I, as the teacher, have any role in active learning? Although active learning implies learner independence, learning potential can be increased with your **guidance**, **support** and **feedback**.

2 But can I really use active learning with learners of this age? Yes! But learning experiences should always be **age-appropriate**. Where necessary, **support** young learners and/or provide **scaffolding**.

3 How can I use active learning with all my learners? Give tailored and differentiated support. There are examples of differentiated support throughout the unit and resource.

4.1 Think about it: Do we all eat the same breakfast?

LEARNING PLAN

Learning objective	Learning intentions	Success criteria
4Us.02 4Lm.01	• **Use of English:** Use quantitative pronouns, *some* and *any*. • **Listening:** Understand, with support, most of the main points in speakers' comments about food. • **Vocabulary:** *papaya, nutritious, to grow food.*	• Learners can use a limited range of quantitative pronouns (e.g. *some* and *any*) to talk about food. • Learners can answer questions on the speakers' comments about food.

21st-century skills
Critical thinking: Sort objects according to key features (*countable* or *non-countable nouns*).

Materials: Learner's Book pages 61–63; Workbook pages 44–45; Pictures of interesting food from the learners' country/ies and other countries

LANGUAGE BACKGROUND

Some and *any*

In this lesson, the Language detective focuses on the use of *some* in positive sentences, *any* in negative sentences and *any* in questions.

• In positive sentences, *some* is used with plural and uncountable nouns. For example: *There's **some** jam; There are **some** oranges.*

• In negative sentences, *any* is used with plural and uncountable nouns. For example: *There isn't **any** soup; There aren't **any** vegetables.*

• In questions, *any* can be used with plural and uncountable nouns. For example: *Is there any bread? Are there any grapes?*

Although *any* is more common than *some* in this type of question, *some* would not be incorrect. However, using *some* could imply a slight change in meaning. For example, *Is there some bread?* might imply that the speaker expects a positive answer. (A2 level learners are not expected to know this.)

Common misconceptions

Misconception	How to identify	How to overcome
Learners often wrongly use uncountable nouns in the plural, e.g. *musics, informations, equipments, furnitures, homeworks.*	Build up a list of uncountable nouns that your learners use incorrectly in the plural. You could elicit these from learners, or build up your own list from learners' mistakes.	Make posters for the classroom. Under the heading *Uncountable nouns*, make a list of the uncountable nouns that learners often incorrectly treat as countable. Display these in the classroom.

Misconception	How to identify	How to overcome
Often, the determiner *some* is missing: • *I have free time* on Sunday. • *Will you give me advice?* Sometimes, the determiner *any* is missing: • *I haven't got shorts.* • *Did you buy new clothes yesterday?*	Elicit when *some* and *any* should be used and compare this with the learners' first language(s).	If possible, practise translating sentences from learners' first language, emphasising that sometimes literal translation is not possible.

Starter ideas

Food and drink game (5 minutes)

* Generate interest in the topic and pre-teach useful vocabulary for the lesson. Show pictures of interesting dishes from the learners' country/ies and other countries.

* Elicit the use of *a* for singular countable nouns and *some* for non-countable nouns.

* Write countable and non-countable food and drink nouns from Lesson 1 on the board, in random order. To encourage critical thinking, include nouns like *orange juice* that can be used as countable or non-countable nouns.

> **Critical thinking opportunity:** Learners sort words for food and drink into two categories: *countable* or *non-countable nouns*.

* If learners prefer working in groups, make cards with the names of a food on each and let learners work in their groups to sort the foods.

Getting started (10 minutes)

* Focus on the questions on page 61. Learners explore the photo in more detail. Discuss the answers to questions a–c in the Learner's Book.

Answers
Learner's own answers.

> **Digital Classroom:** Use the video 'Food' to introduce the unit vocabulary. The i button will explain how to use the video.

Main teaching ideas

1 Read and find the foods (5–10 minutes)

* Look at pictures a–d. Using modal verbs from Unit 3, ask learners to speculate about what the foods might/could be, where they might/could be from, etc.

* Allow learners time to complete the activity in pairs, before giving class feedback on the answers and pronunciation of the food words.

Answers
cheese: a
bread: a, d
banana: d
orange juice: a, d
chicken: c
onions: c
mushrooms: b
tomatoes: a
egg: a
papaya: d

2 Do you eat the same or similar food in your country? (5–10 minutes)

* Encourage groups of learners from different countries to use the structures below (from Unit 1) to find out which foods are eaten in other countries and to make comparisons.

    1 *I like eating/drinking…*

    2 Adverbs of frequency, e.g. *We don't/never/ sometimes/often eat chicken for breakfast.*

    3 Using *both* and *too* to express similarity, e.g. *We eat cheese for breakfast, too.*

* If all the learners in your class come from the same country, encourage them to compare what they eat with the photos in Activity 1.

* Speak about as many of the foods as possible to familiarise learners with words they will hear next on the audio.

3 Listen and match (5 minutes)

- Encourage learners to make predictions about the words the children might use to talk about the pictures.

- Each child mentions several foods, not just the one(s) in the pictures. If learners find this challenging, pause the audio after each speaker and replay if necessary.

Audioscript: Track 18

See Learner's Book page 62.

Lucas: Hi, my name's Lucas and I'm from Brazil. I usually have a fruit smoothie with banana or papaya, a tropical fruit. I also have a bowl of cereal with milk and yoghurt or toast with butter, but my favourite breakfast of all is Bisnaguinha, which is a type of sweet bread. It's delicious!

Nehir: My name's Nehir and I'm from Turkey. My mum always prepares me an orange juice for breakfast. I also like eggs. My favourite food is cheese. I eat it with sliced tomatoes and bread. It's very tasty!

Kuong: Hi! I'm Kuong and I'm from Vietnam. I often eat Pho for breakfast. It's a type of soup that we eat with noodles. I like to eat it with chicken, eggs, mushrooms and onions. Some people like it with lemon, chilli and herbs too. It's very nutritious and tastes really good!

Answers
Lucas – d
Nehir – a
Kuong – c

4 How does our food grow? (5 minutes)

- Elicit different places where food can grow. Pre-teach *trees, in the soil, underground* – and build up a list of examples of these foods.

- Learners match the plants and trees to a picture.

Answers
1c   2d   3b   4e   5a

5 Look at the pictures and answer true or false (5 minutes)

- In pairs, learners discuss whether the sentences about the fruits and vegetables and places they grow are true or false.

Answers
a   False – A tomato grows on a plant.
b   False – A mushroom grows on the ground.
c   True
d   False – A papaya grows on a tree.
e   False – An onion grows on the ground.

6 Read the Language detective (5 minutes)

- Before focusing on Activity 6, read the sentences in the Language detective and focus on the photo.

- To check learners know when to use *some* and *any*, ask questions such as: *When do we use 'some' in positive sentences? When do we use 'any'?*

- Ask learners to recall nouns from the audio. Ask which are countable (singular and plural) and which are non-countable. Encourage learners to apply rules. Elicit whether the nouns are negative, positive and singular or plural, and if the sentences are positive, negative or a question.

- With the help of the Language detective, learners write two more positive and negative sentences about the photo.

Workbook

For further practice, learners can look at the Language detective and complete questions 1–3 on pages 46–47.

---

7 What do you eat for breakfast? (15 minutes)

- Focus on the children's pictures of their breakfasts on page 62 of the Learner's Book.

- Demonstrate the activity by asking learners what they can see in the pictures.

- Learners draw a similar picture of their breakfast. Make sure the food and drink is labelled.

- Learners sit in groups of about six. Put the learners' pictures in the middle of the table face down. Learners take turns to choose a picture and describe it. The other learners guess whose picture it is.

- Circulate and offer feedback on common mistakes while learners are describing the pictures.

> **Digital Classroom:** Use the activity 'Food and drink: *some* or *any*?' to revise when to use *some* and *any*. The i button will explain how to use the activity.

Plenary ideas

Consolidation (5–10 minutes)

- Play the *Crazy breakfasts memory game*. Start by saying: *For breakfast I have <u>an</u> egg.* Nominate a learner to repeat and add a food/drink, e.g. *For*

breakfast I have <u>an</u> egg and <u>some</u> noodles. Repeat until learners can't remember all the foods and drinks and start again. Encourage the use of *some* and *any*, and countable/non-countable nouns.

Homework ideas

> **Workbook**
>
> Questions 1–6 on pages 44–45.

- Learners write about their breakfasts.

> **Assessment ideas:** Provide learners with written feedback on the language and vocabulary they use.

4.2 Geography: All about chocolate!

LEARNING PLAN		
Learning objective	**Learning intentions**	**Success criteria**
4Rd.01	• **Reading:** Understand the main processes involved in making chocolate.	• Learners can answer questions about the processes involved in making chocolate.
4Uv.05	• **Use of English:** Use a range of quantifiers with countable and uncountable nouns.	• Learners can write about quantities of things.
4Us.01	• **Use of English:** Use an increasing range of quantifiers, (e.g. *each, every, a few, few, a little, little*).	
	• **Vocabulary:** *roast, crush, pods, machetes, containers, paste, vanilla, cacao beans, cocoa butter.*	
21st-century skills		
Critical thinking: Collaborate with others when making choices and decisions.		
Learning to learn: Search for information on a topic; take notes about key information.		

Materials: Learner's Book pages 64–65; Workbook pages 46–47; **Photocopiable 10**; A vanilla pod, or a picture of one

---

LANGUAGE BACKGROUND

A lot of/plenty of, few/a few, little/a little

In this lesson, the Language detective focuses on quantifiers.

A *lot of* and *plenty* of can be used with countable and uncountable nouns. They have a similar meaning.

Few/a few can be used with plural countable nouns. However, a difference in meaning is implied:

- The meaning of *There are a few cakes left* is similar to *There are **some** cakes left.*

- The meaning of *There are **few** cakes left* is similar to *There aren't as many cakes as I hoped or wished for/not many at all.*

Few/a few cannot be used with uncountable nouns. The same meaning is expressed with *little* or *a little*.

- The meaning of *There is **a little** bread left* is similar to *There is **some** bread left.*

- The meaning of *There is **little** bread left* is similar to *There isn't as much bread as I hoped or wished for/not much at all.*

Common misconceptions

Misconception	How to identify	How to overcome
The use of *much* and *many* in affirmative sentences: although this is hardly seen as an error in international English, *a lot of* sounds more natural to a British English/American English/Australian English, etc. ear, e.g.: - *We played a lot of ~~many~~ games.* - *We need a lot of ~~much~~ money to go.*	Write examples of these errors on the board and elicit the use of *a lot of*. *We played ~~many~~ games.* → *We played **a lot of** games.* *We need ~~much~~ money.* → *We need **a lot of** money.*	Encourage learners to use *a lot of* in spoken English, wherever possible. Using *a lot of* is actually easier as it can be used with plurals/uncountables, positive/negative/affirmative and negative/plurals. Point this out to your learners.
Incorrectly thinking that *few/a few* can be used with non-countable nouns, or that *little/a little* can be used with countable nouns.	Brainstorm examples of countable and non-countable food words. Learners write two headings: *few/a few* and *little/a little*, and sort the foods under each list.	Make posters for the classroom with correct examples of how to use *there are few…* and *there are a few…* In groups, each learner adds one sentence to each poster.
Incorrectly using the plural verb form with *a little*, when the singular is required, e.g. *There are <u>a little furniture</u> in my room.*	Brainstorm examples of sentences with countable food words and the singular verb, e.g. *There is a little rice in my cupboard.*	Practise – write sentences on the board with a space for the verb. Ask learners for the correct verb form, e.g.: *I… (to have) a little chocolate in my bag.*

Starter ideas

Vocabulary and countability (5 minutes)

- Revise the concept of countability. Divide the class into two groups.
- Allow learners one minute to write all the nouns they remember from the last lesson. One group writes countable nouns and the other non-countable nouns.
- Build up a list of countable and non-countable nouns on the board. Add *sugar* and *milk,* if necessary.
- Pre-teach *vanilla, cacao bean, cocoa* and *butter.* Write the words on the board and show a vanilla pod (or, if possible, bring one in). Elicit that *cocoa butter* and *vanilla* are non-countable, whereas *(vanilla) pods* and *cacao beans* are countable. *Pod, machete, container* and *paste* will be taught during Activity 2.

Main teaching ideas

1 Answer the questions (10 minutes)

- Pre-teach the verbs *roast* and *crush* – write the words on the board and mime the actions.
- Ask learners the first question. Build up a list of different kinds of chocolate that are popular with your class and tell each group to discuss and decide their favourite.

> **Critical thinking opportunity:** Learners collaborate with each other to decide the class's favourite kind(s) of chocolate.

- Allow learners 2 minutes to ask and answer the questions in groups of 3–4. Don't worry if learners don't know the answers. The aim of the activity is to speak, reason and be able to make predictions about the reading text.
- Circulate and offer support. If learners are finding it challenging to answer questions b–d, encourage them to evaluate ideas by asking questions, e.g. for c: *When your parents were eight, did they eat chocolate? What about your grandparents? What about 100 years ago?*

Answers
Learner's own answers at this point (which they then check on first reading).

2 Read and listen to the text (5 minutes)

CROSS-CURRICULAR LINKS

Food and nutrition: Learners read a text about where chocolate comes from and how it is produced.

- The text contains words and expressions that will challenge learners of this level. Encourage strategies to help learners overcome these challenges.
- Focus on the pictures and write *pod, machete, container, paste* on the board. Learners match the words to a picture.
- Tell learners they are going to read a text about how chocolate is made. Encourage predictions about the process. Ask questions like: *Where do the pods grow? How can we cut the pods down? What do you think happens next to the pods? Where are the pods grown? (England? Hot countries?)* Focus on the headings if necessary.
- Learners read the text and check their predictions.

Audioscript: Track 19
See Learner's Book page 64.

Answers
Learners' check their answers to Activity 1 b–d against the text:

b Chocolate is made from cacao beans. To make chocolate: the beans are roasted in big ovens then crushed into a paste and mixed with plenty of sugar, cocoa butter, milk and a little vanilla. The mixture is then cooled.

c In 1847.

d Chocolate melts in our mouth because the melting point of cocoa butter is lower than the temperature of the human body.

3 Read the text again. Are these sentences *true* or *false*? (5–10 minutes)

- Before starting the activity, check learners understand *harvested, machetes, mixed* and *mixture.*

- Focus on the first sentence in the text *Chocolate is made…*. Ask learners questions to check they understand the meaning of *is/are + past participle* and that it is used to describe a process: *Who makes chocolate from cacao beans? Do you know their names? Is it important to know their names?* Repeat with other sentences from the text with orange verbs, until learners have understood why the present simple passive is used.

- Look at sentence **a** together. Check learners understand the meaning and ask them to identify the past participle. Then ask learners to indicate where they found this information in the text.

- Learners work in pairs to decide whether the other sentences are true or false.

> **Differentiation ideas:** If learners want an extra challenge, ask them to rewrite the false sentences to make them true.

Answers

a True

b False – The beans are usually harvested twice a year.

c False – The workers open the pods with their hands (they use machetes to cut down the pods).

d False – The chocolate is made in cooler countries, in Europe or North America.

e True

f False – The mixture is cooled to make the final product.

> **Digital Classroom:** Use the activity 'Chocolate' to revise using *is/are* + past participle to describe aprocess. The i button will explain how to use the activity.

4 Underline the information in the text (5 minutes)

- Focus on the first sentence of the text. Ask learners: *Did you know chocolate is made from cacao beans? Did you know cacao beans grow on the Theobroma cacao tree?*

- Learners put up their hands if they knew the answer to each question. Those who didn't know underline the information in the text. Make clear that this is not a test.

- Allow learners time to re-read the text and underline all the facts they didn't know before.

- Learners ask their partners which fact they thought was the most interesting.

- After the activity, build up a list of 'interesting facts' from learners and vote for *the most interesting*.

5 Find and underline examples of quantifiers and Language detective (10 minutes)

- The Language detective focuses on quantifiers: *a lot of/plenty of, few/a few, little/a little*. Learners come across these quantifiers in the reading text. This may be the first time they have seen some of them.

- Ask learners to find the quantifiers in the reading text (they are highlighted in blue).

- Then check learners understand the sentences.

- Ask questions to elicit their meaning, e.g. *What's the difference in meaning between **a lot of cacao beans** and **some cacao beans**? Which one means more cacao beans than the other? Are beans countable?* etc.

- Elicit whether the quantifiers can be used with countable or non-countable nouns (or both).

6 Circle the correct quantifier (15 minutes)

- Learners complete Activity 5 individually.

> **Differentiation ideas:** If learners need support with this activity, work with them in a separate group. Ask questions to help, e.g. for part a: *What's the difference in meaning between plenty of and a few?* For part b: *Is people singular or plural?* For part c: *Can we count sugar (here) – e.g. one sugar, two sugars?* For part d: *What's the difference between a little and few?*

- Learners could do **Photocopiable 10** to practise using quantifiers.

Answers

a a few

b Few

c A lot of/a little

d A little

> **Digital Classroom:** Use the grammar presentation 'Quantifiers' to help learners revise and practise using quantifiers. The i button will explain how to use the grammar presentation.

Workbook

For further practice of quantifiers, learners can look at the Language detective and complete Questions 1–4 on pages 48–49.

---

7 **Choose one of these foods (or one of your own) to write about (25 minutes)**

> **Learning to learn:** In this activity, learners search for information. They should take notes on the information they need to answer the questions in the Learner's Book.

- Demonstrate the activity by choosing one of the foods and drawing a mind map on the board. Write the name of the food in the centre with arrows to the answers to the questions in note form.

- Learners choose one of the foods (or a food of their own).

- If it is not practical to take learners to the school library, or search online in class, set the research for homework.

- Learners find the answers to the questions and write the information on an A4 sheet with a picture of the process, ready to be displayed.

Plenary ideas

Consolidation (15 minutes)

- In groups of 3–4, learners choose one of the foods from Activity 6 and create a poster, based on the mind map example. If time, they present their posters to the rest of the class.

> **Assessment ideas:** While learners are presenting, check for their use of food vocabulary and pronunciation. Sensitively share general feedback with the class.

Homework ideas

Workbook

Questions 1–4 on pages 48–49.

- Complete Activity 6 on page 65 of the Learner's Book (if not completed in class time).

4.3 Talk about it: Grow your own!

LEARNING PLAN

Learning objective	Learning intentions	Success criteria
4Us.03	• **Use of English:** Use connectives (e.g. *when, before, after, then*) to link parts of sentences about growing a cress plant. • **Vocabulary:** *soil, seeds, ground, okra, bok choy, mango, cress, yoghurt pot, cotton wool, grow, rinse, press, fold, cut off.*	• Learners can explain how to grow a cress plant using connecting words.

21st-century skills

Critical thinking: Make predictions by looking at pictures.

Materials: Learner's Book pages 66–67; **Photocopiable 11**; For the Starter: pictures of any of the following that learners aren't familiar with – soil, seeds, ground, cotton wool, yoghurt pot; Pictures of okra, squash, bok choy and mangoes for Activity 1

Common misconceptions

Misconception	How to identify	How to overcome
In some languages, e.g. German, word order is altered when certain connecting words are used. However, this is not the case in English.	If word order is determined by connecting words in learners' first language(s): • Refer to the highlighted connectors on the audioscript. • Cover up the connectors and elicit that the word order is the same, with or without the connectors. • Discourage literal translation. Use examples to demonstrate that, in this case, translating literally doesn't work.	Encourage learners to complete sentences with connecting words about themselves. Try to use questions that learners can relate to and remember. For example: • *Before I come to school, I…* • *When I finish school, I…* • *Then I…* • *After that, I…*

Starter ideas

Guess what you need to grow a plant (5 minutes)

• Revise the quantifiers from the previous lessons. Elicit things that might be needed for growing plants (seeds, soil, cotton wool, ground, water and yoghurt pot).

• Elicit and write on the board quantifiers learners know (*some/any, a lot of/plenty of, few/a few, little/a little*).

• In groups of 3–4, learners make predictions about the quantity of the objects that are needed to grow a plant.

• Demonstrate the activity by writing *seeds* on the board and elicit which quantifier(s) is/are more appropriate.

Main teaching ideas

1 How do fruit and vegetables grow? (5–10 minutes)

• If you completed the Starter activity, the vocabulary in the questions shouldn't cause difficulties.

• Check learners know the fruit and vegetables in the quiz. Show pictures of fruits and vegetables learners don't know, preferably growing on the plants.

• Allow learners time to try the quiz before comparing their answers with a partner.

• Give class feedback on the answers.

Answers

1b	2a	3b	4c	5b

6 Suggested answers: Fruit and vegetables are healthy and contain lots of vitamins and fibre. We can learn what vegetables need to grow into healthy plants. It is cheaper to grow your own fruit and vegetables than to buy them in the supermarket. Often plants we grow ourselves are healthier and taste better than food in the supermarket.

2 Find these objects (5 minutes)

• Check learners know the correct pronunciation of the new words, then look for them in the pictures.

• Have a vote on which vegetable from Activity 1 is being grown (cress), but don't confirm the answer just yet.

Answers

cotton wool – f
a plastic bottle – c
a paper towel – d
plastic container – a, b, c, d, e, f
coloured pens b
seeds – f

3 Listen to Rosa (10 minutes)

> **Critical thinking opportunity:** The new words in the audio recording may make the re-ordering activity challenging. To overcome this and practise thinking critically, learners make predictions about what they will hear by looking at the pictures.

- Invite learners to describe what the pictures show and encourage speculation about the order in which they might be discussed.

- If necessary, replay the audio and pause after each step. You could also download the audioscript and highlight the words to help identify each picture.

Audioscript: Track 20

See Learner's Book page 67.

Girl: Cress is a leaf that you can eat and it's really good for you. You don't need soil, you can grow it in your classroom. Here's how…

Before you start, clean a recycled plastic container – a yoghurt pot, for example – and rinse it with water. Then draw a face on it with coloured pens – you'll see why later! Then fold a paper towel, put water on it and put it at the bottom of the container. After that, put water on some cotton wool and put it on top of the paper towel. Then put some cress seeds on the cotton wool and press them down carefully. Put your pot in a warm, sunny place. After that, ask an adult to cut the top off a clear plastic bottle, then put it over your pot. The inside of the bottle gets warm and humid and this helps the cress to grow. When there are green leaves on your cress plant you can eat them! Try them in sandwiches, pitta bread or a salad, or with fish or eggs.

Answers
Correct order: a, b, d, f, c, e
Because the cress looks like hair

Language detective (5 minutes)

- Elicit that the connectives used in the audio (*before, when, then, after that*) are used to show the order that something happens. Check learners know the meaning of the connectives.

- If useful for learners, you could highlight sentences with the connecting words in the audioscript.

- Using these connectives in sentences is relatively simple compared to some other languages, where the use of certain connecting words affects word order. If this is the case in your learners' language, please see the suggestions in *Common misconceptions.*

- Learners are more likely to remember the connectives if they practise using them to write sentences: see Plenary suggestion.

4 Put the sentence parts in the correct order (5 minutes)

- Ask learners to try and remember the order of the sentences from the audio. They then listen and check.

Answers
b   d   a   e   c

5 Check the meaning of the verbs (10 minutes)

- Learners work in pairs and check the meaning of the verbs in their dictionaries.

- Demonstrate the miming activity. Ask a learner to mime the process of growing a plant.

- Allow about 5 minutes for learners to continue the activity in pairs.

6 Listen and underline and Speaking tip (5 minutes)

- Ask learners to suggest which words on the audio weren't very clear. If necessary, listen to the audio again.

- Focus on Activity 6. Listen again to Rosa's phrases. Encourage learners to underline words that are weak and practise imitating Rosa's pronunciation. Elicit that linking words together makes you sound more natural.

- Re-play the audio and ask learners if they can understand more now that they know about the *weak* words.

Audioscript: Track 21

See Learner's Book page 67.

Answers

a   Grow <u>it</u> in your classroom…

b   Before <u>you</u> start…

c   …rinse <u>with</u> water…

d   …press <u>them</u> down…

e   …put <u>your</u> pot…

f   …ask <u>an</u> adult…

7 Work in pairs and describe how to grow a cress plant (5 minutes)

- Elicit and build up a list of useful language on the board (connecting words from the Language detective and phrases from Activity 5).

- Allow learners time to revise the process in pairs.

- Invite learners to tell the class about the process.

〉 **Digital Classroom:** Use the activity 'Growing a bean plant' to revise the use of connectives: *before, when, then, after that*. The i button will explain how to use the activity.

8 Which fruit and vegetables do you like? (10 minutes)

- Brainstorm names of fruit and vegetables. Ask learners the first question (*Which fruit and vegetables do you like?*). Ensure that they use the plural for countable nouns.

- Ask learners the second question (*Have you ever grown a fruit or vegetable plant?*). In the case of a *yes* answer, help learners describe how they grew the plant. Build up a list of useful expressions on the board. Check they know the simple past of the verbs used in today's lesson: *grew, put, rinsed, cleaned, etc.*

- Learners practise asking and answering the questions in pairs.

- Circulate and support learners.

Plenary ideas

Consolidation (10 minutes)

- Help learners remember new vocabulary by creating a word puzzle for them to solve. Using the Puzzlemaker website, create your word search puzzle with new words from the lesson.

- Learners complete **Photocopiable 11.**

Homework ideas

CROSS-CURRICULAR LINKS

Science: Learners follow the instructions and grow their own cress or other plant.

4.4 Write about it: A fruit poem

LEARNING PLAN		
Learning objective	**Learning intentions**	**Success criteria**
4Wor.03	• **Writing:** Use, with support, appropriate layout for a poem. • **Vocabulary:** *spiky, smooth, sweet, salty, juicy, smell like, taste like, feel like, sound, hold on tight.*	• Learners can write a poem about a fruit using the appropriate layout.

21st-century skills

Critical thinking: Sort words according to what they are used for; say which adjective is best and give reasons.

Creative thinking: Respond to a poem and write a poem to reflect personal likes.

Collaboration: Encourage other learners and give simple feedback.

Materials: Learner's Book pages 68–69; Workbook pages 50–51; **Photocopiable 12**; Similar poems written by other young learners, for example search for fruit poems on Pinterest

Starter ideas

Rhyming words and adjectives (10 minutes)

- Generate interest in rhyming verse and revise vocabulary from Lesson 3. Write words from the last lesson and words that might come in useful for the poem, e.g. *sweet, hard, soft, crunchy, fresh, delicious, natural, round, juicy, fruity, full, free, soil, cotton wool, mango, potato, tree, oil, ground, seed, eat, grow, feed, fold, hold, sound.*

- Focus on *sweet* and ask learners to think of words that rhyme with it (even if not exactly), e.g. *eat, seed, feed.*

- Encourage suggestions about other words that rhyme, for example: *ground, round; mango, grow, potato; cotton wool, full; tree, free; fold, hold; juicy, fruity.*

- Check learners use the correct pronunciation, especially *sweet, juicy, fruity, wool,* etc.

- Write: *A sweet juicy orange* on the board and elicit that the function of the adjectives is to describe the noun.

- Ask learners to identify the noun and adjectives (*orange* is the noun and *sweet* and *juicy* are the adjectives).

- Revisit the words you identified at the start of the activity. Ask learners to sort them into adjectives and nouns. Which ones might describe an apple and which a potato?

Main teaching ideas

1 Talk about the questions (10 minutes)

- Have a quick class discussion about the characteristics of an apple based on the questions in the Learner's Book. Make sure learners understand the verbs *smell, taste, feel* and *sound.*

- Build up a mind map of suggestions that will come in useful later in the lesson, when learners are writing their poems.

Answers

Suggested **Answers**

a   big, round

b   sweet, fresh

c   sweet, delicious, fresh

d   hard

e   crunchy

---

2 Read and listen (5 minutes)

- Tell learners that they are going to read a poem about a child eating an apple.

- Look at the picture and encourage predictions about what the child does in the poem.

- Learners read the poem and check their ideas from Activity 1.

Audioscript: Track 22

See Learner's Book page 68.

3 Listen again (5 minutes)

- If learners have completed the Starter activity, this activity shouldn't present any difficulties.

- Focus on Verse 1. Elicit and circle the rhyming words.

- Allow learners a minute to find and circle the other rhyming words.

Answers
Verse 1: ground, round
Verse 2: tight, bite
Verse 3: sweet, eat

4 Adjectives and senses (5 minutes)

> **Critical thinking opportunity:** Nominate a learner to remind the class what an adjective is. Look at the adjectives from the poem together (they are highlighted in bold). Encourage critical thinking by asking learners which adjectives they like best and why.

- If learners find it hard to say which adjective they like best, make suggestions like: *Do you like the sound(s) of the adjective? Do you like the meaning?*

- Now move on to the five senses. Demonstrate by miming them.

- Focus on the example in the table together and then elicit suggestions for the other four senses.

Answers

Sight	Touch	Smell	Taste	Hear
big	hard	sweet	sweet	crunchy
round		delicious	delicious	
		fresh	fresh	

5 Find the meaning and write (5 minutes)

- This is a continuation of the previous activity. Learners will need to look up some words in their dictionaries.

- Learners work together in pairs to decide on the correct answers.

Answers

Sight	Touch	Smell	Taste	Hear
long	smooth	spicy	juicy	crispy
colourful	spiky		salty	
large	soft		creamy	
spiky	sticky		spicy	
			chewy	
			bitter	
			crispy	

> **Digital Classroom:** Use the activity 'Strawberries' to help learners choose the best adjectives to describe different fruits. The i button will explain how to use the activity.

6 Read the sentences (5 minutes)

- Check learners understand the activity by checking their answer to part a about the durian fruit.

- Learners continue the activity in pairs. Give class feedback about the answers.

Answers
a   spiky
b   soft
c   colourful
d   sweet
e   juicy

7 Write a poem (20 minutes)

> **Creative thinking:** Learners respond to the poem and write their own poem reflecting their personal likes, by following Steps 1–3.

- The poem should be about a fruit grown in their country. Learners use the poem on page 68 as a model.

> Differentiation ideas: If learners need support with this task, ask them to work in small groups to brainstorm the answers to the questions. This should help them build up a list of ideas to work from. Circulate and give support where needed.

- When learners have completed Steps 1–3, refer them to the Writing checklist on **Photocopiable 12**.

> Assessment ideas: Print out the sample answer. Ask learners to assess it against **Photocopiable 12** before they finalise their poem.

8   Read your poems aloud in small groups (5 minutes)

- Demonstrate the activity. Re-read the poem in the Learner's Book. Elicit and build up a bank of useful compliments about it on the board, e.g. *I like the sound of the adjectives. I like this rhyme.*

> **Collaboration:** Encourage learners to give feedback. Learners read their poem to a small group, who compliment them using expressions like those in Step 4.

Plenary ideas

Reflection (20 minutes)

- Ask learners what they enjoyed about writing a poem. Was it easier or harder than they expected? Has the experience made them want to read and/or write more poetry? Encourage them to read or listen to other age-appropriate poetry and share any good examples in the next lesson.

Homework ideas

> **Workbook**
>
> Questions 1–5 on pages 50–51.

- Learners could write a simple poem about a favourite food, e.g. chocolate.

> Assessment ideas: Write a short checklist as a class so that learners can self-assess their work before handing it in. For example: *Have I used interesting adjectives? Have I used rhyming words?*

4.5 *Charlie and the Chocolate Factory*

LEARNING PLAN

Learning objectives	Learning intentions	Success criteria
4Rm.01 4Rm.02 4Rd.03	• **Reading:** Understand, with support, some of the main points of short, simple texts. • **Reading:** Read, with support, an increasing range of short, simple fiction and non-fiction texts with confidence and enjoyment. • **Reading:** Deduce meaning from context, with little or no support, in short, simple texts.	• Learners can understand, with support, some of the main points of short, simple texts. • Learners can read, with support, an extract from a story, with confidence and enjoyment. • Learners can deduce the meaning of 'swudge' from context, with little or no support.
	Vocabulary: food, landscapes: *meadows, valley, river, steep cliffs, waterfall, whirlpool, muddy, trees, bushes, grass, buttercups;* adjectives: *generous, helpful, greedy, selfish, mean*	

21st-century skills
Learning to learn: Learners look at pictures to guess the storyline.

Materials: Learner's Book pages 70–73; Workbook pages 52–53; a copy of *Charlie and the Chocolate Factory*; pictures of a chocolate factory – real photos, film sets or cartoon pictures

Starter ideas (10 minutes)

- Have a competition in groups to try and remember the stages of making chocolate.

- If groups forget any stages, mime or show the pictures to remind them.

Main teaching ideas

1 **Talk: Would you like to visit a chocolate or sweet factory? What do you think it would be like inside? (5–10 minutes)**

- To generate interest in the text about the chocolate factory, show the pictures you have brought. Ask learners what they can see.

- Learners ask and answer questions in pairs before telling the class about their ideas of what a chocolate factory would look like inside.

> **Learning to learn:** Learners look at pictures to guess the storyline. Before reading Extract 1, focus on the photos. Ask learners what they can see in the photos and tell them to guess how they might be connected to the story.

Answers
Learner's own answer.

2 **Read and listen to the first extract from the story. (10 minutes)**

- Focus on the questions and encourage learners to make predictions about what they are going to read.

- Learners read and listen to the first extract from the story and check their ideas.

Note: There are some high-level expressions in the extract, for example *screwed the little caps on to the tops of the tubes of toothpaste* and *they could afford.* Tell learners to focus on the words they *do* know, especially for question a. For example, they should understand the family is poor because of *is never paid much* and *there wasn't enough money.*

> **Audioscript:** Track 23
> See Learner's Book page 70.

Answers
a The family are very poor. There is not enough money to feed everyone properly and Charlie lives in a house that is too small for the family to live in comfortably.

b He eats bread and margarine for breakfast, boiled potatoes and cabbage for lunch and cabbage soup for supper.

c It is the largest and most famous chocolate factory in the world.

d He wins an invitation to visit the chocolate factory and enough sweets and chocolate to last a lifetime.

3 **Read and listen to the next extract about what was inside the Chocolate Factory. (10 minutes)**

- Before learners read and listen to the second extract about what was inside the Chocolate Factory, read questions a–d together.

- Learners read and listen to the text and check their ideas.

> **Differentiation ideas:** Work with learners who are struggling in a smaller group. For question b, help to elicit synonyms for the words and encourage learners to scan the text for the green words if necessary. For question d, read the sentences around the word 'swudge' and help learners predict which meaning is most likely. Learners could work in pairs to check words in a dictionary.

> **Audioscript:** Track 24
> See Learner's Book page 71

Answers
a Learner's own answers.

b type = *kind of*   best = *finest*   high = *steep* very big = *enormous*

c Two verbs from: *mixes; churns; pounds; beats; makes it light and frothy.*

d *Swudge* is a type of sugar with the flavour of mint / a minty flavour.

4 **Read and listen to Augustus Gloop's accident and answer the questions. (10 minutes)**

- Tell learners that Augustus Gloop had an accident at the Chocolate Factory. Read questions a–c together and elicit ideas about what might have happened to him.

- Play the recording and tell learners to read as they listen.

- If learners struggle with questions, replay the relevant parts of the recording.

Audioscript: Track 25
See Learner's Book page 72

Answers

a Augustus touches the chocolate in the chocolate river when Mr Wonka tells him not to.

b He falls in the chocolate river and disappears.

c Learner's own answer.

5 **Vocabulary: Which adjective best describes Augustus? Which adjectives are positive and negative? (10 minutes)**

- Check learners know what an adjective is and its function in a sentence. Focus on the adjectives and check learners know their meaning.

- As a class, discuss whether the adjectives are positive or negative.

- Learners then consider which adjective best describes Augustus.

- If there is time, elicit the negative versions of the positive adjectives and the positive versions of the negative adjectives.

Answers

Positive adjectives: generous, helpful, kind.

Negative adjectives: greedy, selfish, mean.

Adjective that best describes Augustus: learner's own answer, but likely answer is greedy / selfish.

6 **Talk: Use the adjectives to talk about people you know. (10 minutes)**

- Encourage learners to be positive about the other class members. Elicit and write up example sentences from more confident learners.

- Circulate and offer support while learners write their own sentences.

- Give class feedback and build up more sentences on the board.

〉 **Digital Classroom:** Use the activity 'Chocolate fun: descriptive adjectives' to revise adjective-noun combinations from the story. The i button will explain how to use the activity.

Answers
Learner's own answer.

7 **Put the sentences in order. Now act out what happens in the story! (10 minutes)**

- Allow learners time to read the sentences.

- Circulate and offer support as learners discuss the order the pictures go in.

- Time permitting, have a fun drawing game. Ask artistic learners to draw pictures of the sentences and get the class to guess what the picture shows.

- Time permitting, put learners in pairs and have them act out the scenes after they have established the correct order.

Answers
Sentence order: e, b, a, d, c

8 **Choose an adjective from Activity 6 to complete this description. (10 minutes)**

- Elicit and build up a list of adjectives from the story.

- Allow learners time to read the text and choose the adjective and its opposite.

- Give class feedback.

Answers
greedy.
The opposite of greedy is *generous*.

9 Values: Being generous (10 minutes)

- Read the suggestions in the Learner's Book and elicit more examples. Build up a list on the board.

- Circulate and offer support while learners tell their partners about times when they have been generous to someone else and/or when someone has been generous to them.

Answers
Learner's own answer.

Plenary ideas (10 minutes)

- Learners write a summary of the story (maximum 80 words).

- Take the 60-second challenge! Learners work in pairs. Allow 60 seconds for each learner to recall the new words from today's reading text.

> **Workbook**
>
> Learners do Activities 1–5 on pages 52–53.

Homework ideas

Learners write a paragraph about why they would like to visit a chocolate factory. Support less confident learners by writing questions, such as: *What would you like to do there? Who would you like to go with? What would you like to take home with you?*

4.6 Project challenge

LEARNING PLAN		
Learning objective	**Learning intentions**	**Success criteria**
4Wor.02	• **Writing:** Link, with support, a short sequence of simple sentences using a limited range of connectives to create a paragraph.	• Learners can create a paragraph about a cake using a limited range of connectives.
4Wca.04	• **Writing:** Use simple grammatical structures and sentence patterns correctly, allowing for some mistakes.	• Learners can make a poster describing a food process, using sentences with **is/are + past participle**.

21st-century skills

Creative thinking: Based on a model, develop a new cake.

Collaboration: Participate actively in a group activity.

Learning to learn: Take notes about key information and leave work projects on display. Date and file the projects, photos or scans of work in portfolios.

Materials: Learner's Book pages 74–75; Workbook page 54; **Differentiated worksheet 4**; **Unit 4 project checklists**; Pictures of interesting novelty cakes and other foods that your learners like; Recipes for cakes that you think your learners will choose for Project A; Use of the internet for Project B

Starter ideas

Raise interest in the projects (10–15 minutes)

- Raise interest in the projects *Create a tasty treat* and *Find out about where food comes from.*

- Show pictures of interesting novelty cakes. Encourage learners to think about which ones they like and a cake they would like to make.

- Then show pictures of popular foods that are available in the learners' country/ies.

⟩ **Collaboration:** In groups of 3–4, learners ask questions comparing the foods. For example: *Are they all produced or made in your country? Which food travels the furthest? How are the foods transported? Are any of them for a special occasion? Do you know what you need to make any of the foods? Which do you like best?* Ask groups to tell the class their answers.

Main teaching ideas

Introduce projects (60 minutes)

- Encourage learners to choose one of the projects and then follow the steps for their chosen project.

- Learners work in groups, managing and sharing the tasks in the project.

Project A: Create a tasty treat!

- Allow learners time to answer in pairs. Then use the photos from step 1 and the Learner's Book to build up a list of different kinds of sweet treats and their characteristics.

- Make sure learners have chosen a cake and a person to make it for.

- Elicit occasions the cake might be for.

- Pre-teach any cooking verbs that learners might need. Show learners recipes you have brought or search on the internet so they can see what ingredients are needed.

- Support learners by making suggestions about their invented names for the cakes.

- Learners follow the instructions and produce their description.

- Circulate and offer assistance. Make sure learners use *before*, *when*, *then* and *after that.*

⟩ **Assessment ideas:** Learners use the **project checklist** to assess how well they carried out the task and make suggestions for improvement.

Project B: Find out about where food comes from

⟩ **Learning to learn:** Learners follow the steps below to research and take notes about where their favourite food comes from.

- Build on the information in step 1 and add any other popular foods or drinks that learners could find out about.

- Check learners have chosen their favourite food and allow them time to draw a picture of it.

- Focus on one food, e.g. chocolate, and elicit example notes for Step 2. Elicit what they remember about the production of chocolate, and look up the answers to the other questions on the internet, so learners have a model to work from.

- Use the internet to find the information needed to answer the questions. If this isn't practical in class, see the Homework suggestion.

- Before learners tell their partners about their food, focus on the advice about using is/are + past participle. Make sure learners can do this by eliciting examples from the class.

- Circulate and offer assistance while learners tell their partners.

⟩ **Assessment ideas:** Learners use the **project checklist** to assess how well they carried out the project and make suggestions for improvement.

Plenary ideas

Consolidation (5 minutes for each group)

- Learners present their projects to the class.

⟩ **Assessment ideas:** While learners are presenting, check their use of vocabulary and pronunciation. Encourage learners to ask follow-up questions to check understanding/find out more.

⟩ **Differentiation ideas:** Learners could complete **Differentiated worksheet 4.**

Homework ideas

Workbook

Questions 1–2 on page 54.

- Learners could find out about their food for Project B for homework, if it is not practical to use the internet in class.

- Photocopy the projects (with language mistakes corrected) of the other learners and learners can read them at home.

4.7 What do you know now?

What can we discover about food?

> **Learning to learn:** Learners have the opportunity to reflect and evaluate their own learning success.

- Reintroduce the question from the start of the unit: *What can we discover about food?* Discuss learners' responses to the question now and compare them with their comments at the beginning of the unit. How much has changed?

- Ask learners to work through the questions in pairs.

Answers

1 Learner's own answers.

2 Learner's own answers.

3 Learner's own answers based on Lesson 4.2 text.

4 Suggested answer:

- *You can grow cress in your classroom (without soil).*

- *Before you start, clean a recycled plastic container.*

- *Then rinse the container with water.*

- *Draw a face on it with coloured pens.*

- *Then fold a paper towel, put water on it and put it at the bottom of the container.*

- *After that, put water on the cotton wool and put it on top of the paper towel.*

- *Then put some cress seeds on the cotton wool and press them down.*

- *Put your pot in a warm, sunny place.*

- *After that, ask an adult to cut the top off a clear plastic bottle.*

- *Then put it over your pot.*

5 Learner's own answers.

6 Charlie found a 'Golden Ticket' in the wrapping of a chocolate bar. (Two from) A lovely valley; green meadows; a chocolate river; a huge waterfall; enormous glass pipes; 'swudge' grass.

Look what I can do!

- There are six 'can do' statements. Learners read through the statements and tick the things they can do. Encourage them to reflect on how well they can do these things. Also invite them to think of ways they can improve further, e.g. what strategies they can use, or learn to use.

- If learners find it challenging to read the statements, look through the unit with them and support them to find the relevant information.

- Finally, ask learners to work through the questions on page 55 of the Workbook. Encourage them to talk about what they enjoyed and also about any further support they might need.

> 5 Adventures

Unit plan

Lesson	Approximate number of learning hours	Outline of learning content	Learning objectives	Resources
1 Creating an adventure story	1.5–2	Talk about what makes a good adventure story	4Lm.01 4So.01	Learner's Book Lesson 5.1 Workbook Lesson 5.1 **Digital Classroom:** Why do we love stories? Features of stories
2 Create a superhero	1–1.5	Use instructions to draw a superhero Use different words to describe personal qualities	4Ug.03 4Sc.04 4Rd.02	Learner's Book Lesson 5.2 Workbook Lesson 5.2 **Digital Classroom:** Describing people How to draw a superhero Giving instructions
3 Telling a story	1.5–2	Create and act out a story in the past tense	4Rd.01/4Ug.05 4Sc.07/4So.01	Learner's Book Lesson 5.3 Workbook Lesson 5.3 ⬇ Photocopiable 13 ⬇ Differentiated worksheet 5 **Digital Classroom:** Past simple
4 Story adventures	1–1.5	Write our own story adventures	4Wca.03/ 4Wor.03/ 4Wor.01	Learner's Book Lesson 5.4 Workbook Lesson 5.4 ⬇ Photocopiable 14 **Digital Classroom:** Punctuation practice ⬇ Sample answer for Unit 5
5 *The Seekers*	1–1.5	Enjoy an adventure story	4Rm.02/4Rd.01 4Ld.04 4Us.05	Learner's Book Lesson 5.5 Workbook Lesson 5.5 ⬇ Photocopiable 15 **Digital Classroom:** *The Seekers*: True or false?
6 Project challenge	1–1.5	Project A: Create your own comic strip Project B: Write the ending to *The Seekers* story.	4Wca.03/ 4Wca.04 4Wor.02/ 4Wor.03 4Sc.02	Learner's Book Lesson 5.6 Workbook Lesson 5.6 ⬇ Unit 5 project checklists

(continued)

Cross-unit resources

⬇ Unit 5 Audioscripts

⬇ End of Unit 5 test

⬇ Progress test 2

⬇ Unit 5 Progress report

⬇ Unit 5 Wordlist

BACKGROUND KNOWLEDGE

Unit 5 focuses on a variety of adventure stories. A children's adventure can be a story or anecdote about any unusual experience that is daring or exciting. Although adventures can be dangerous, they don't have to be.

In Britain, as in other countries, adventure stories are very popular with children of this age. Examples include traditional classics such as *The Jungle Book* (Rudyard Kipling) and modern classics like *Stig of the Dump* (Clive King), as well as more modern stories such as the *Harry Potter* series (J. K. Rowling) and shorter illustrated stories like *The Gruffalo* by Julia Donaldson and Axel Scheffler.

Readers and authors are enthralled and inspired by international classics such as the *Voyages of Sinbad the Sailor*, which is part of the *Arabian Nights* compilation of traditional stories. The story of a Chinese girl escaping from a tiger is said to have provided the inspiration for the popular children's story *The Gruffalo*.

The reading in Lesson 5, called *The Seekers*, is based on a story by Valerie Bloom, a Jamaican-born writer who writes in both English and Jamaican.

Learners will also share one of their own adventures, like getting lost, a (first) trip on a boat, plane or train, a (first) camping trip.

TEACHING SKILLS FOCUS

Skills for Life

What are skills for life?

The *Cambridge Framework for Life Competencies* is a response to research on how different approaches to life skills, knowledge and attitudes relate to English language programmes. The framework helps equip learners with the required competencies to meet the fast changing demands of the 21st-century. These competencies have been divided into seven areas: *Creative thinking, Critical thinking, Learning to learn, Communication, Collaboration, Social responsibilities* and *Emotional Development*.

A number of *Can Do* statements have been devised for each age and competency. These *Can Do* statements will help you to assess your learners' grasp of each of the life competencies. More information and a list of the *Can Do* statements for each level can be found in the Cambridge Competency Booklets, available on the cambridge.org website.

Your challenge

In each unit of the Learner's Books, opportunities to practise and develop these skills are highlighted.

Download the seven Life Competency booklets and tick off the *Can Do* statements that apply to your learners at the end of the unit. Look through Unit 5 and highlight the suggested opportunities for practising these competences. As you continue with the following units, tick off the relevant *Can Do* statements. Can you think of any more of these skills that your learners have developed in this or other units?

5.1 Think about it: Creating an adventure story

Learning objective	Learning intentions	Success criteria
4Lm.01 4So.01	• **Listening:** Understand, with support, most of the main points in the story descriptions. • **Speaking:** Express, with support, opinions and feelings. • **Vocabulary:** *character, dilemma, title, setting, detective, solve a crime, catch bad guys, come back, possession, science kit, big trouble, on fire, are lost, danger.*	• Learners can talk about and answer questions on the three story descriptions. • Learners can express their opinions and feelings about what makes a good adventure story.

21st-century skills
Creative thinking: Draw pictures to represent a familiar story and partners guess what happens. **Critical thinking:** Compare different book covers and use them to predict what happens in the stories; Decide which story to read.

Materials: Learner's Book pages 77–79; Workbook pages 56–57; Trailers for an engaging adventure film, e.g. Smallfoot, or adventure books/comics, etc., that your learners will find interesting

Starter ideas

Getting started (5 minutes)

- Focus on the Big question for this unit: *What makes an adventure story?* Elicit names of adventure stories learners have read (and, hopefully, enjoyed). Elicit a variety of different kinds of adventures – traditional stories and classics, as well as stories by contemporary authors, not just stories that involve superheroes. Elicit what learners liked and disliked about the stories, and the answers to questions b and c on page 77.

- You could show learners colourful books and/or comics containing adventures. You could also elicit suggestions about adventure stories from enthusiastic readers.

- Interest learners in the subject of the adventure genre by showing a trailer for an engaging adventure film, e.g. Smallfoot. If you cannot access this in your region, any adventure that is suitable for this age will do.

Answers

a   Learner's own answers.

b   Adventure stories usually have a dangerous or difficult situation that needs to be solved by the characters in the story. This is usually the main theme of an adventure story. Other types of stories might have mystery, romance or horror as their main theme. Adventure stories usually contain action scenes and often include a journey or settings in places away from the characters' home.

c   Learner's own answers.

Favourite adventure story (5 minutes)

- Give each group of 3–4 learners a piece of paper to write the names of their favourite adventure stories. Circulate and offer suggestions for translations into English, where necessary. Build up a list of stories on the board for the next activity.

Answers

Learner's own answers.

> **Digital Classroom:** Use the slideshow 'Why do we love stories?' to discuss the importance of stories and storytelling, and to introduce vocabulary around adventure story genres. The i button will explain how to use the slideshow.

Main teaching ideas

1   Think of an adventure story (5–10 minutes)

> **Creative thinking:** Encourage learners to choose a familiar story and to (quickly) draw three things from it for their partners to guess what happens in it. If learners find it difficult to think of a story, refer them to the names of the stories on the board from the Starter activity.

• Circulate and take advantage of opportunities to pre-teach useful words to describe the pictures.

• Learners guess their partners' stories.

Answers
Learner's own answers.

Listening tip (5 minutes)

• Elicit that we can make predictions about a story by looking at the pictures. Show learners large pictures from colourful illustrated children's books like *The Gruffalo*. Ask: *What's happening?* – and then read the page to confirm predictions.

2   Look at the book covers (5 minutes)

> **Creative thinking:** Learners compare different book covers and use them to make predictions about what happens in the stories.

• Take the opportunity to pre-teach useful words for the listening activity.

Answers
Learner's own answers.

 ### 3   Listen to three story descriptions (5–10 minutes)

• Learners may find the vocabulary in this listening activity challenging. There are strategies to overcome this. Firstly, make it clear that learners don't need to understand every word to complete the task. However, if learners don't know the key words (see Vocabulary), create a fun matching

exercise. Learners match each word/expression with a definition, e.g. *detective* (noun): *A person who investigates bad people.*

• Learners match Speaker 1 with a book cover. Ask learners which words helped them make their choice. Do not worry about learners understanding every word – there is the chance to listen in more detail in Activity 6.

• Repeat for the other two speakers.

Audioscript: Track 26

See Learner's Book page 78.

1   Leila wants to be a hotshot detective just like her dad. She wants to solve crimes and catch the bad guys just like he does. But one day Dad goes out and doesn't come back. Leila must become a real detective to find him. She soon realises that you must be careful what you wish for…

2   Felix lives for science! His most precious possession is his home science kit. Everyone thinks he's a little…strange! But now Felix has discovered a magic liquid… suddenly he can have any superhero power that he wants. But he soon finds out that superhero powers get you into big trouble…

3   It's the year 1414 and 10-year-old Kai is running for his life. His village is on fire and his family are lost. Running deep into the forest, he is stopped in his tracks by a beautiful wolf. The animal says she can help him find his family. But can Kai trust her? Or will he find himself in greater danger than ever?

Answers
Description 1: Cover b

Description 2: Cover c

Description 3: Cover a

4   Match the parts of stories to the descriptions (10 minutes)

• Learners do the matching activity in pairs.

> **Differentiation ideas:** If learners need support with this task, provide examples from the listening activity in a worksheet, e.g. *Leila and Felix are* **characters.** *Leila's* **dilemma** *is whether to become a*

detective. Avoid Speaker 3, as this is the focus of Activity 7.

Answers
a title   b setting   c characters   d dilemma

> **Digital Classroom:** Use the activity 'Features of stories' to revise the parts of stories: characters, dilemma, title, setting. The i button will explain how to use the activity.

5 Use 'parts of a story' words to describe your pictures (5–10 minutes)

- First, demonstrate using an example that learners are familiar with, e.g. a well-known adventure story. Draw a mind map on the board. In the centre, put the heading *Title* and the name of the story. Create a bubble for each of the other headings – *Characters, Dilemma, Setting* – and elicit the missing information.

- Allow learners 5 minutes to describe their Activity 1 pictures. The mind maps can be displayed in the classroom.

Answers
Learner's own answers.

6 Listen again: true or false (5 minutes)

- First, check learners understand Sentence a.

- Listen to Leila speaking again and check learners understand that Sentence a is true.

- Replay speakers 1 and 2. Learners decide whether the other sentences are true or false.

- Learners correct sentences c and d.

- If necessary, replay the audio and pause after the relevant part of the story description

Audioscript: Track 27

See Learner's Book page 79.

1   **Be careful what you wish for:** Leila wants to be a hotshot detective just like her dad. She wants to solve crimes and catch the bad guys just like he does. But one day Dad goes out and doesn't come back. Leila must become a real detective to find him. She soon realises that you must be careful what you wish for…

2   **Felix's experiment:** Felix lives for science! His most precious possession is his home science kit. Everyone thinks he's a little…strange! But now Felix has discovered a magic liquid… suddenly he can have any superhero power that he wants. But he soon finds out that superhero powers get you into big trouble…

Answers
a   True
b   True
c   False – When Leila's father doesn't come home, Leila goes to look for him herself.
d   False – Felix does science experiments at home (with his 'home science kit').
e   True

7 Read the sentences and match to the story parts (5 minutes)

- Demonstrate the activity by matching 1 to b.

- Before learners match the other story parts in pairs, check that they understand the sentences, writing key words on the board if necessary.

- Allow learners time to match the remaining story parts.

Answers
1b   2c   3d   4a

8 Which adventure story would you like to read? Why? (5–10 minutes)

> **Creative thinking:** Learners decide which story they would prefer to read and share their thoughts with a partner.

> **Differentiation ideas:** Learners could work in mixed-ability pairs and more confident speakers could give language support to their partners.

Answers
Learner's own answers.

9 Describe an adventure story (10 minutes)

- Briefly revisit the list of adventure stories that your learners like from the Starter.

- Learners choose a story and write a short description under suggested headings (*Characters, Setting, Dilemma, Why I like it*).

- Learners read their description to another pair who tries to guess the story.

Answers
Learner's own answers.

Plenary ideas

Consolidation (10 minutes)

- If your learners like to watch adventure stories, you could choose a short film (or extracts from a longer film) that is suitable for their age and interests. For example, *The Highway Rat* by Julia Donaldson, or an extract from one of the *Cars* or *Planes* series. Try watching with English subtitles.

- If you let learners choose, make sure the clip is suitable for their age and culture.

Homework ideas

> **Workbook**
> Questions 1–6 on pages 56–57.

- Learners look for an easy-to-read children's adventure story (in English) to present to the class. For example, search for the Cambridge Reading Adventure book series. Also look in the (school) library and (second-hand) bookshops.

> **Assessment ideas:** As a class, write a short checklist so that learners have a model for their presentation and can self-assess it before the next lesson. For example: *Who are the main characters? What happens in the adventure? Have I used adventure words? Have I said what I think about the book?*

5.2 Art and Design: Create a superhero

LEARNING PLAN		
Learning objective	**Learning intentions**	**Success criteria**
4Rd.02 4Sc.04 4Ug.03	• **Reading:** Read and follow instructions. • **Speaking:** Give, with support, a short sequence of instructions. • **Use of English:** Use imperative forms [positive and negative] of an increasing range of verbs to give a short sequence of commands and instructions. • **Vocabulary:** *add, create, describe, draw, (don't) press, guideline, rub out, think about.*	• Learners can read and follow instructions for drawing a superhero. • Learners can give, with support, a short sequence of instructions for drawing a superhero. • Learners can use imperative forms of a range of verbs to give a short sequence of commands and instructions for drawing a superhero.
21st-century skills		
Creative thinking: Interpret characters in games and drama.		

Materials: Learner's Book pages 80–81, Workbook pages 58–59; Pictures/video clips of popular children's superheroes, like *The Incredibles* or *Big Hero 6* – these are easy to find, by entering the name of the film and trailer into a search engine; try searching for clips with subtitles

Common misconceptions

Misconception	How to identify	How to overcome
When using imperative forms, learners may wrongly inflect verbs, adding the present participle, past simple or present simple forms, e.g.: *Please waiting for me.* *Please sent them to my address.* *Please wears a thick jacket.* *Don't forgot to write to me.*	Write plenty of examples on the board, e.g. *stand up, sit down, jump.* Ask concept check questions to check learners understand, e.g. *Who is the instruction for?* *Why don't I use a subject?* *Why doesn't the verb end in –ing / –s / ed?*	Practise, e.g. by playing a game. Give instructions like those from the previous section and the last person to follow is 'out'. Keep going until only one learner (the winner) is left. Encourage learners to spot their own mistakes and to peer-correct mistakes.

Starter ideas

Find the *bravest* superhero(es) (10 minutes)

- To gain interest in superheroes, show pictures or video clips. If you show a compilation, like the one suggested in Materials, elicit the meaning of *bravest* and have a vote for *The bravest superhero.*

- If you watch the video, you could prepare the class for the first activity by pausing it and eliciting the name for each character's special power, e.g. *She can fly* or *He's very good at acrobatics.*

Main teaching ideas

1 Talk about your favourite superheroes or story characters (10 minutes)

- Tell learners to think for a few moments about their favourite superheroes.

- Ask learners about their favourite superheroes' special skills.

- On the board, build up a list of superheroes, and special powers and skills. This list will be useful for Activity 3.

Answers
Learner's own answers.

2 Match the personal quality adjectives (5 minutes)

- Demonstrate the activity by eliciting the definition of *brave.*

- Allow learners time to complete the activity, using a dictionary if necessary. Check their answers and drill the correct pronunciation.

Answers
1d   2e   3a   4f   5c   6b

3 Which adjectives describe your favourite superheroes or story characters? (5–10 minutes)

> **Creative thinking:** Learners interpret characters in games and drama.

- Demonstrate the activity by writing adjectives on the board about a superhero. Elicit suggestions about who the superhero is.

- Learners work in pairs. One of them chooses a superhero but doesn't tell their partner. Allow them time to write down two or three adjectives about their superhero. Their partner listens to the adjectives and guesses the name of the superhero. Then the partners swap roles.

Answers
Learner's own answers.

Key words: drawing (5 minutes)

CROSS-CURRICULAR LINKS

Literature: Before reading the text, learners look at the words in the box to help them understand the instructions.

> **Digital Classroom:** Use the activity 'Describing people' to revise personal qualities adjectives. The i button will explain how to use the activity.

4 Read and listen to the text (5 minutes)

- Before listening, elicit suggestions from learners about what the text will include. Encourage the use of the drawing words.

- Play the audio and answer the questions as a class. Re-play the audio, if necessary.

Audioscript: Track 28

See Learner's Book pages 80–81.

Answers

First thing to draw: the superhero's head.

Last thing to do: rub out the guidelines and add some colour.

> **Digital Classroom:** Use the video 'How to draw a superhero' to take learners through the stages of drawing a superhero. The i button will explain how to use the video.

5 Read the Language detective and underline instruction words (5 minutes)

- The Language detective focuses on giving instructions. Point out the three examples of imperatives.

- Focus on the instructions in Activity 4 (from 'Draw your superhero's head' to 'boy or a girl'). Ask learners to underline the instruction words. Check they have done so correctly.

Answers

- <u>Draw</u> your superhero's head.

- <u>Draw</u> a simple stick person with a circle for a head. These are your guidelines.

- <u>Don't press</u> too hard on your pencil.

- <u>Use</u> a light pencil line, then you can <u>rub out</u> the guidelines later.

- <u>Decide</u> now if your superhero is a boy or a girl. Is he/she wearing a mask? What is the expression on his/her face?

- <u>Draw</u> your superhero's body.

- <u>Add</u> the rest of your superhero's body. <u>Use</u> the guidelines to draw arms and legs.

- <u>Think about</u> your superhero's clothing. What is he/she wearing? Boots? Armbands? A cape? A belt? Does he/she have a special symbol or logo? Is he/she holding anything?

- Your cartoon superhero is complete! <u>Rub out</u> the guidelines and <u>add</u> some colour!

Workbook

For further practice of instructions, learners can look at the Language detective and complete questions 1–3 on pages 58–59.

---

6 Find five words to describe things a superhero wears (5 minutes)

- Look back at the text in Activity 4. Point at what the superhero in the illustration is wearing and elicit suggestions. Find the things superheroes wear in the text.

Answers

a mask, boots, armbands, a cape, a belt

---

7 Draw and talk about your own superhero (10–15 minutes)

CROSS-CURRICULAR LINKS

Art and design: Learners explore ideas and produce creative work.

- Learners work in pairs. Without showing their partners, they each draw and colour their own superhero, using the instructions from Activity 4.

- Learners give their partners instructions to draw their superhero. Encourage them to use imperatives, the Activity 4 text, and the Language detective to help them.

- Their partner uses the instructions to draw the superhero. Then learners compare them and discuss any misconceptions.

- Allow learners time to give instructions for their partners to draw their superhero.

> **Digital Classroom:** Use the activity 'Giving instructions' to revise vocabulary about instructions and rules. The i button will explain how to use the activity.

Answers
Learner's own answers.

Plenary ideas

Reflection (15 minutes)

- Have a class discussion about the lesson. Go over anything that learners have found challenging and also talk about Activity 7. Did they enjoy drawing their own superhero? How difficult was it for them to give instructions? Is there anything they would do differently next time?

Homework ideas

Workbook

Questions 1–3 on pages 58–59.

- Learners write instructions about how to draw something, e.g. a character from a book. Encourage learners to use imperatives for the instructions and vocabulary from the lesson. If learners are not interested in drawing they can write instructions for something else, like playing their favourite game/sport.

5.3 Talk about it: Telling a story

LEARNING PLAN

Learning objective	Learning intentions	Success criteria
4Rd.01	• **Reading:** Understand specific details of a short simple story.	• Learners can answer questions and talk about Tom's story.
4Ug.05	• **Use of English:** Examine the use of past simple regular and irregular forms in a short simple story.	• Learners can use past simple forms to describe Tom's story.
4Sc.07/4So.01	• **Speaking:** Use simple grammatical structures and sentence patterns correctly, allowing for some basic mistakes, to tell a short simple story with feeling and expression.	• Learners can retell and act out Tom's story with feeling and expression.
	• **Vocabulary:** *bush, campsite, hide, stare, black bear, sniff, exciting.*	

21st-century skills

Communication: Change sound levels or pitch when doing drama or acting a role.

Materials: Learner book pages 82–83; Workbook pages 60–61; **Photocopiable 13**; **Differentiated worksheet 5**; Children reading a story, e.g. *The Gruffalo's Child* (there are examples online)

LANGUAGE BACKGROUND

Past simple

In this lesson, the Language detective focuses on the past simple.

The past simple tense is commonly used to talk about finished actions that happened in the past. Its use is especially common for storytelling or when you specify a finished time period, like *last year* or *three years ago*.

Regular verbs end in *-ed*. The auxiliary verb *did* is used for negatives and questions, and short answers. For example: *What **did** you do yesterday? I watched a film.* *Did* should not be used with *can* or *be*.

Remember, you don't usually use the *past simple*:

- if the action isn't finished; instead use the present perfect, e.g. *I've been at this school for three years and I have one more year left*

- with the adverbs *just*, *yet* or *already*; instead use the present perfect.

If you want to emphasise the duration of an activity, instead use the past continuous/present perfect, e.g. *I **was eating** dinner when she called; I **have been studying** English for ten years*

- if you want to emphasise an experience/ action as opposed to *when* you did it; e.g. *I've watched that film five times!*

Common misconceptions

Misconception	How to identify	How to overcome
Many common errors at this level are with the form of the affirmative, e.g.: • treating irregular verbs as regular e.g. **gave** written **gived** • 'inventing' irregular forms, e.g. **wroten** for **written** • adding *d* to irregular forms, e.g. **broked**.	To elicit the past simple form of common irregular verbs, write the past simple verbs on the board and encourage learners to guess which verbs they are from.	• Practice will help learners get used to using the correct forms. See Photocopiable 13 and 15 for examples of fun ways to practise the correct forms. • Encourage learners to read (graded) readers with stories that are narrated in the past simple.
Learners often mispronounce regular verbs, e.g. *opened* as *openéd*. Or they misspell past forms, e.g. *opened* spelt *opend*.	Make a list of common regular and irregular verbs and pronounce them for your learners.	Divide irregular past simple verbs into three columns and drill pronunciation, i.e. 'd' / 't' / 'éd' *opened / walked / waited* See also **Differentiated worksheet 5: Language for telling stories 1.**

Starter ideas (5 minutes)

Adventures

- Interest learners in the subject of adventures. Build up a list of adventures that learners of this age enjoy and may have experienced personally. Make it clear that an adventure can be any unusual, exciting or daring experience. Suitable ideas include visiting a theme park, exploring a nature reserve, going camping, going on a boat, a steam train, a plane, etc.

Main teaching ideas

1 **Think of a time when you had an adventure (10 minutes)**

- Start the activity by asking the class if anyone has had an adventure like the ones in the Starter. Elicit suitable answers to the two questions in the Learner's Book. These answers can be used as a model for learners.

- Pre-teach the word *exciting* by voting for the *most exciting adventure*.

- Build up a list of time expressions to help learners answer the question about *when* the adventure happened.

Answers
Learner's own answers.

2 Find the words in the pictures (5 minutes)

- To pre-teach the six words from the reading, point at the first picture and elicit that it is the *black bear*. Drill the correct pronunciation. Repeat for the other pictures and words.

- You could pre-teach difficult vocabulary in a fun way. For instance, for *sniff* write _n_f_ on the board. Learners guess the missing letters.

Answers
a: black bear

b: campsite, stare

c: hide, bush, black bear, sniff

d: bush, black bear

3 Read and listen to the introduction (5 minutes)

- There are a number of past simple tense verbs in the text. However, learners shouldn't have too much difficulty identifying the correct picture if you make it clear that, to do this, it is not essential to understand every word.

- Play the audio and match it to the correct picture. Ask learners which words helped them make their choice.

- If necessary, re-play the audio.

- Generate interest in the subject of camping by asking learners if they have ever been camping and other simple questions such as: *Where did you go? What did you see?*

Audioscript: Track 29
See Learner's Book page 82.

Answers
Introduction – Picture b

4 Read and listen to the next part of Tom's story (5–10 minutes)

- Demonstrate the activity by playing the next part of the audio. Elicit which picture is described first. Ask learners which words helped them to identify this.

- Learners listen to and read the rest of the story, putting the remaining pictures in order.

- Read the story again as a class and give class feedback about the correct answers.

Audioscript: Track 30
See Learner's Book page 82.

Answers
b d a c

5 Why do you think the bear stopped and sniffed the air? (5 minutes)

- Elicit as many reasons as possible for the bear stopping and sniffing the air. Encourage creativity.

- Tell learners that to help understand a text, it is useful to make predictions before reading or listening. Discuss as a class what could happen next.

- Help learners make predictions by asking questions. For example: *Was Tom scared? What did the bear want to eat? Was it interested in Tom? Did Tom and Jack take a photo of the bear?*

Answers
Learner's own answers.

6 Listen to the final part of Tom's story and check your predictions (5–10 minutes)

- Before you play the audio, tell learners to listen to see if their predictions are correct. If you asked questions about what happened next, tell learners to listen for the answers to these questions.

- Play the audio. Afterwards, ask learners to work in pairs and compare their predictions with what happened.

- Replay the audio if necessary.

- As a class, discuss what happened compared to predictions.

Audioscript: Track 31

See Learner's Book page 83.

The bear grunted loudly. It turned to the bush. My heart was beating fast…Too scared to move, we stared at the bear. It sniffed the air again. Time seemed to stand still!

Then slowly the bear turned and looked ahead. It ran over to the side of the road, to a big rubbish bin. It stood up again, pushed open the lid, put its enormous paw inside and grabbed a leftover hamburger with great enthusiasm.

The bear wasn't interested in us after all. The hamburger was far more exciting! 'Take a photo!' I whispered. Jack pulled his phone from his pocket. 'Otherwise no one will ever believe us!'

Answers

The bear ate a leftover hamburger from the rubbish bin and didn't see the boys. (The bear could smell the leftover food in the rubbish bin and wasn't interested in the boys at all!)

Language detective (5 minutes)

- Learners probably know some past simple forms already. They have also read and heard some past simple forms in this lesson.

- Write the heading *Past simple* on the board. Brainstorm as many past simple forms as possible. Elicit which are regular and which are irregular.

7 Read and underline the past simple verbs (5 minutes)

- Learners underline the past simple verbs in the introduction to Tom's story, on page 82. Use two different colours – one for regular and one for irregular. If necessary, go through the text together.

- Check that learners know which is the base form of the past simple verbs.

Answers

Last year I <u>went</u> on an adventure holiday with my family. We <u>stayed</u> at a campsite by a huge lake in the mountains. It <u>was</u> far away from any cities and there <u>were</u> lots of wild animals and birds. My dad <u>said</u> that a few black bears <u>lived</u> in the forests by the lake. Every day we <u>looked</u> for black bears. But we <u>didn't see</u> one…until…

Regular verbs: *stayed* (stay), *lived* (live), *looked* (look).

Irregular verbs: *went* (go), *was/were* (be), *said* (say), *saw* (see).

Workbook

For further practice of the past simple, learners look at the Language detective and complete Questions 1–3 on pages 60–61.

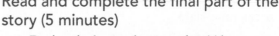

8 Read and complete the final part of the story (5 minutes)

- During the lesson, learners should have become familiar with the past tense. However, check that learners remember the correct meaning and pronunciation.

- Learners could do **Photocopiable 13** at this point.

- Demonstrate the activity by doing one answer together. Learners complete the exercise in pairs. Listen again to the audio and check the answers and pronunciation. Re-listen if necessary.

Answers

1 turned

2 sniffed

3 looked

4 ran

5 stood

6 was

7 pulled

9 Listen and repeat the lines from the story and Speaking tip (5–10 minutes)

- Read the lines from the story without any expression and then play the audio. Elicit from learners that reading with expression makes a story more interesting.

- Learners practise reading *with expression* in pairs.

> **Communication:** Learners change sound levels or pitch when doing drama or acting a role.

Audioscript: Track 32

See Learner's Book page 83.

Then we saw it. A strange black shape on the road…

'Look Jack! What's that?' I said. The black shape moved towards us, getting bigger and bigger. Jack stopped, 'Tom, it's a bear! We need to hide and fast!'

Answers
To reflect the excitement or fear in the situation, the narrator reads with *expression*, emphasising key words, reading different sentences at different speeds, making the voice higher then lower. These techniques reflect the emotions the boys were feeling in the story.

---

10 In groups, practise retelling and acting out the story (15–20 minutes)

- Demonstrate the activity by assigning the role of Tom, Jack, the bear and a narrator to four learners.

- Encourage the four learners to read out the text with as much expression as possible.

- Learners work in groups of four. Make sure each learner has been given a role and allow time to practise reading.

11 Present the story to the class (5 minutes for each group)

- Allow each group time to present to the class. Encourage them to imitate the sound effects on the audio.

> **Digital Classroom:** Use the grammar presentation 'Past simple' to revise past simple regular and irregular forms. The i button will explain how to use the grammar presentation.

Plenary ideas

Consolidation (20 minutes)

- Learners write an adventure story. Give them ideas by asking questions such as: *Where were you? Why were you there? What animal did you see? What did the animal do?*, etc. Encourage learners to use the past simple tense.

> **Differentiation ideas:** Learners could complete **Differentiated worksheet 5**.

Homework ideas

Workbook

Questions 1–3 on pages 60–61.

- Find a book in the library and learners listen to children reading the story, e.g. *The Gruffalo's Child*.

5.4 Write about it: Adventure stories

LEARNING PLAN

Learning objective	Learning intentions	Success criteria
4Wca.03 4Wor.03 4Wor.01	• **Writing:** With support, plan, write, edit and proofread a short story using punctuation with some accuracy and an appropriate layout. • **Vocabulary:** *skyscraper, jungle, experiment, twin brother/sister.*	• Learners can plan, write, edit and proofread their own adventure story, with support, using punctuation for dialogue with some accuracy and paragraphs.

21st-century skills

Creative thinking: Plan and write a new story, based on a model.

Learning to learn: Make corrections after making mistakes; Present a story to the class before displaying in the classroom or putting in a portfolio.

Collaboration: Collaborate with others when making choices and decisions.

Materials: Learner's Book pages 84–85; Workbook pages 62–63; **Photocopiable 14**; For Activity 5: one dice per pair of learners

Starter ideas (5 minutes)

Stories

- Revise the names for parts of stories (lesson 5.1) and elicit related ideas for writing a story for Activities 5–7.

- Write *Setting: time, Setting: place, Character* and *Problem/dilemma* on the board. Elicit the places, times, characters and dilemmas from the chart in Activity 5.

- Learners who are interested in reading could tell the class about the setting, character and dilemma of a story they enjoyed.

Main teaching ideas

1 **What can you remember about Tom's story? (5 minutes)**

- Learners read sentences a–d. Elicit predictions about which sounds they will hear (e.g. a bear sniffing, birds singing and boys running).

- Play the first sound and ask learners to match it with a sentence.

- Play the rest of the sounds and give class feedback on correct answers.

> **Audioscript:** Track 33
> See Learner's Book page 84.
> 1 birdsong
> 2 scrambling, rustling sounds
> 3 bear grunting, sniffing
> 4 bear slurping and chomping

Answers
a – sound effect 3
b – sound effect 4
c – sound effect 2
d – sound effect 1

2 Match the sentences (5 minutes)

- Check learners understand the story parts.
- In pairs, learners match the story parts to the sentences.

Answers
1d   2a, c   3b

3 Read the sentences again (5 minutes)

- Learners highlight the three time expressions in the text.
- Extension: Learners work in groups of 3–4. Allow a minute to see which group can come up with the longest list of past simple time expressions.

Answers

Sentence c: *One evening*

Sentence d: *Last year; Every day*

Learner's own answers.

4 Add the correct pronunciation and Writing tip (5–10 minutes)

- Note: This activity extends beyond the curriculum framework so may be challenging for some learners.
- First, focus on the examples of punctuation in the Writing tip. Elicit the rules for speech marks, commas, question marks, exclamation marks and full stops.
- Elicit the correct punctuation for the first sentence in Activity 4.
- Learners work individually on sentences b to d.

> **Differentiation ideas:** If learners need support with this task, work with them in a separate group. Underline parts of the sentence, e.g. *You did really well*, and ask questions like: *What do we need to add at the beginning and end? Do we need to add a comma or a full stop?*

Answers

a   'You did really well,' he said.

b   'Can you see that bear?' she asked.

c   'That's amazing!' he shouted.

d   'Be quiet!' she whispered.

> **Digital Classroom:** Use the activity 'Punctuation practice' to revise the punctuation of direct speech. The i button will explain how to use the activity.

5 Work in pairs and follow the instructions (10 minutes)

- Before starting the activity, allow learners time to read the chart.
- Check learners understand all the vocabulary by asking concept check questions, e.g. A twin brother or sister: *Mark is 9. He has a twin sister. How old is she?* You got caught in a huge storm: *Could you escape from the storm?*
- Make sure learners understand that these are suggestions for the stories they are going to write, and they are going to roll a dice to choose their story parts.
- Demonstrate this fun activity by rolling a dice to find the parts of *your* story plan.
- Allow learners time to roll the dice to create their own story plan.

6 Writing tip and Use your ideas to write your story (15 minutes)

- Focus on the Writing tip and elicit reasons why planning your writing can make it much easier.
- Focus on the chart and demonstrate the activity by eliciting information for your story plan from Activity 5.
- Ask learners to find examples of long sentences, short sentences and dialogue in the text on page 82 and 83.

> **Collaboration:** Learners work in pairs to plan the different elements of the story. Less confident writers can collaborate with more confident writers when making choices and decisions about details, and the writing of the story.

- Allow learners time to write their stories. Circulate and help learners as needed.
- Once the story has been written, focus on the writing checklist on **Photocopiable 14**.

> **Assessment ideas:** Print out the sample answer. Ask learners to assess it against **Photocopiable 14** before they finalise their story.

- Display learners' stories in the classroom.

> **Assessment ideas:** Give written feedback on the stories, focusing on how well learners have incorporated the four elements of the story, the use of short and long sentences, and the use of punctuation, particularly for dialogue.

Plenary ideas

Consolidation (10 minutes)

• If you have time, learners could present their stories to the class.

Homework ideas

Workbook

Questions 1–5 on pages 62–63.

• Story writing competition: Learners plan, write and illustrate a new adventure story. In the next lesson, learners read all the stories and vote for the most exciting adventure.

> **Assessment ideas:** Write a short checklist as a class so that learners can self-assess their work before handing it in. For example: *Have I included the four elements of the story: time, place, character, problem/dilemma? Have I used longer sentences to start the story? Have I used short sentences to describe the exciting bits? Have I included dialogue?*

5.5 Read and respond: *The Seekers*

LEARNING PLAN		
Learning objective	**Learning intentions**	**Success criteria**
4Rm.02/4Rd.01	• **Reading:** Read an adventure story with confidence and enjoyment, and understand, with little or no support, most specific information and detail.	• Learners can discuss and answer questions about *The Seekers*. • Learners can order pictures to show the sequence of events in the story.
4Ld.04	• **Listening:** Understand, with little or no support, most specific information and detail of short talk.	
4Us.05	• **Vocabulary:** *wicked tribe, captured, peaceful, kingdom, brave, guardians, sword, magic powers to protect, paths, valley, narrow mountain track, ravine, flash of light, beasts, intelligent, honest, loyal, athletic, powerful.*	
21st-century skills		
Creative thinking: Engage in activities with fantasy or mystery elements.		
Learning to learn: Use pictures to follow a storyline.		

Materials: Learner's Book pages 86–89; Workbook pages 64–65; **Photocopiable 15**

Starter ideas

Literary language (5 minutes)

*   Like most stories, *The Seekers* contains words that are used in literature to make descriptions sound more exciting, louder or more dangerous, e.g. *seekers* instead of searchers. Such words are less common in everyday language.

*   To introduce learners to this concept, and to pre-teach new words from the story, write 'Everyday' and 'Literary' on the board. Then write some everyday words (e.g. *shine, narrow valley, animal, afraid, jumped*) with their literary equivalents (*blaze/ burn, ravine, beast, terrified, leapt*). This activity extends beyond the curriculum framework so may be challenging for learners.

*   Using the words as prompts, and looking at the illustrations, make predictions about the story.

Main teaching ideas

1 Talk (5 minutes)

*   Tell learners they are going to read an adventure story called *The Seekers*. Although there is a lot of new vocabulary in the story, there are reading tips to help make reading an enjoyable process.

*   Focus on the three questions and encourage learners to give their suggestions. If learners find part b difficult, explain that *seek* (the verb) is similar to the verb *search*, and that *-er* is added to make the noun, i.e. a person who *seeks* or *searches*.

Answers
Learner's own answers.

---

2 Read and listen to the introduction and Reading tip (5 minutes)

> **Creative thinking:** Learners read *The Seekers*, an exciting story with fantasy or mystery elements. To help them read more fluently, give the following tips. Discourage learners from trying to understand every word of the story. Explain that it is not necessary to fully understand a story. The aim, at this stage, should be to grasp the general ideas, i.e. the information asked for in questions from Activity 1. Explain that there will be the chance to focus on details later.

*   If you think learners may find this activity hard, photocopy the first part of the story and cross out about ten words that are not vital to understanding the general idea. Ask learners to re-read the text with the crossed-out words, proving they can still get the gist even though they can't see the crossed-out words.

*   Pre-teach the verb *capture* and explain that the story is set in the *Kingdom of Raban*.

*   Learners listen to and read the introduction (once only) for gist, then check their answers for Activity 1.

Answers
a   Kehan, Bariel and Horaf (Learners should be able to establish that Bariel is the girl. By listening to Track 33, it will become clear that Kehan is the boy in the white shirt.)

b   Because they have been chosen to look for something.

c   Three magic stones.

Audioscript: Track 34
See Learner's Book page 86.

---

3 Read and listen, and answer the questions (5–10 minutes)

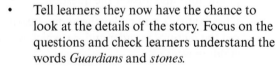

*   Tell learners they now have the chance to look at the details of the story. Focus on the questions and check learners understand the words *Guardians* and *stones*.

*   Allow learners a few minutes to re-read the introduction and answer the questions before giving feedback.

Answers
a   It was captured by a wicked tribe called the Digons.

b   They could save Raban.

c   Learner's own answers.

d   They chose a special boy or girl to go on a journey to find the stones.

e   His good friends, Bariel and Horaf.

---

4 Look at the pictures (5 minutes)

> **Learning to learn:** Learners use the pictures to understand new words and to predict (and then follow) the storyline. Explain that looking at pictures is a useful strategy for understanding a story.

- Find the four things in the pictures.

- If you did the Starter activity, learners shouldn't have difficulty with this activity. If you didn't have time for the Starter, explain that the story contains words that are often used in stories, but are less common in everyday language. Give examples, like the nouns *seekers* and *beasts*.

- Use these words and other things the learners can see to make predictions about what happens next.

Answers

a   *a ravine* – picture g
    a sword – all pictures
    a flash of light – pictures e and f
    the beasts – pictures b, e, f and g

b   Learner's own answers.

 ## 5 Listen to the next part of the story (5–10 minutes)

- Play the audio so learners can check their predictions and answer the question.

- Give feedback and replay the audio. Learners put the pictures in order and say which way the children went.

- If necessary, pause the audio after each part that corresponds to a picture and offer feedback.

Audioscript: Track 35

See Learner's Book page 88.

Suddenly the children heard a terrible sound. The sound was like the scream of a human and the howl of a crazy dog. 'I knew they would find us in the valley,' Horaf said quietly. Kehan looked around quickly. He was very frightened. There was nowhere to hide. 'Here they come!' Bariel shouted. The three friends crouched down. Three beasts appeared in front of them. They had heads like dogs, tongues like snakes and bodies like cats, but their bodies were covered in green scales, like fish. They had large feet with huge claws. Their eyes burned like fire. 'What are they?' whispered Bariel. 'They are called Mistraals,' Kehan said.

The beasts crouched down, ready to attack. The children were terrified. Suddenly, Kehan knew what to do. 'Put the swords together!' he shouted, as the animals leapt. The children fell down hard on the rocky valley path. They were very close to the edge of the ravine. As they fell, Bariel's sword clashed with Kehan's. There was a flash of light and the Mistraals backed away. The three children jumped up. 'The swords!' Kehan shouted. 'Bring them together.' The swords blazed as they clashed together. Snarling, the Mistraals backed away. 'We must lead them to the ravine,' Kehan said. 'Walk slowly towards them. Then, when I give the signal, turn and run. Stop at the edge of the ravine and jump.' He looked at the faces of his friends. They looked confused and worried. 'Trust me,' Kehan said. The friends moved towards the terrible beasts. They could feel the hot breath of the Mistraals on their faces. Kehan shouted, 'Run!' They ran quickly towards the ravine. Then, as they came to the edge, Kehan shouted, 'Jump!' The swords lifted them high into the air. Bariel gasped. 'We're flying!'

Answers

Correct order: b c g d e f.

They went left through a thick forest down to the valley.

---

6 Listen again and match the sentence halves (5 minutes)

- Learners read the first halves of the sentences (1–5) and the mixed-up second halves (a–e).

- Replay the audio and tell learners to listen out for the key words in the related sentence halves. You could also pause the audio between each related sentence. Note that some of the sentences are not exactly the same as the audio.

- Ask the class what they think happened to the beasts.

Answers

1d 2e 3c 4b 5a

Learner's own answers.

> **Digital Classroom:** Use the activity 'The Seekers: True or false?' to reinforce reading comprehension of the story 'The Seekers'. The i button will explain how to use the activity.

7 Find six examples of the past simple in the story (5 minutes)

- Demonstrate the activity by pointing out the two examples in the table. Tell learners to find them in the introduction to the story.

- Check learners understand the difference between regular and irregular verbs.

- Allow learners time to scan the text and find the remaining verbs. Ask learners to copy and complete the table from Activity 7 and categorise the verbs into regular and irregular.

- Give class feedback, checking learners know which verbs the irregular forms come from.

Answers

Learners should be able to provide six of the examples in the table.

Regular	Irregular
captured (capture)	gave (give)
called (call)	chose (choose)
wanted (want)	came (come)
passed (pass)	said (say)
finished (finish)	found (find)
	can (could)
	has (have)
	was (were)

8 What do you think happened next? (10 minutes)

- Learners discuss their predictions about what happened next in groups of 3–4. Encourage the use of past tense forms from the story.

> **Differentiation ideas:** If learners need support with this task, give them a worksheet with some prompts. Write down some of the past tense verbs, for example *captured; didn't capture*. Add possible subjects or objects of the verbs, e.g. *The Mistraals; the beasts; the children; Bariel; Kehan*, and encourage suggestions. Write question words like *How? What? Why?* to encourage more predictions.

Answers

Learner's own answers.

9 Which children in the story do these adjectives describe? (5 minutes)

- Check learners understand what each adjective means. Focus on the first adjective and discuss which child(ren) it describes.

- Encourage learners to create sentences, using the sentence in the Learner's Book as a model.

- Repeat for the other adjectives.

Answers

Learner's own answers.

10 Values: Being brave (5 minutes)

- Build up a list of jobs on the board where people do brave things. Encourage learners to talk about people they know who do one of these jobs.

- Elicit reasons for this, e.g. *A police officer is very brave because he stops dangerous people.*

Answers

Suggested answers: *firefighter, soldier, sailor, pilot, police officer*, and learner's own answers.

11 Read the sentences about being brave (5 minutes)

- Read the sentences and encourage learners to tick those that describe someone they know or have read about. Help them with new words and expressions, e.g. *stands up for, faces something difficult.*

Answers

Learner's own answers.

12 Tell your partner about the sentences you have chosen (5 minutes)

- Allow learners time to tell their partner about the sentences they have ticked. Offer help with pronunciation of the new vocabulary.

Answers
Learner's own answers.

Plenary ideas

Consolidation (10 minutes)

- Revise vocabulary from the lesson by creating a word search or crossword at the Puzzlemaker website.

- Using the sentences in Activity 11 as a starting point, learners write a paragraph describing someone they know who is brave.

- Learners could do **Photocopiable 15**.

Homework ideas

> **Workbook**
>
> Questions 1–5 on pages 64–65.

- Learners write their own adventure story based on *The Seekers* (maximum of 100 words). Remind learners to use the simple past.

> **Assessment ideas:** Choose one of the learners' adventure stories that is particularly effective and read it to the class. Give verbal feedback to the class about what the learner has done well.

5.6 Project challenge

LEARNING PLAN

Learning objective	Learning intentions	Success criteria
4Wca.03/4Wca.04	• **Writing:** Plan, write, edit and proofread a comic strip, with support and allowing for some mistakes, using simple grammatical structures and sentence patterns correctly.	• Learners can plan, write, edit and proofread their comic strip or an ending to their story, with support.
4Wor.02 /4Wor.03	• **Writing:** Link, with support, a short sequence of simple sentences using a limited range of connectives to create a comic strip, using an appropriate layout.	• Learners can use some simple grammatical structures and sentence patterns correctly in their comic strip or story endings, for example the past simple, different adjectives, time expressions and dialogue in speech bubbles. • Learners can use, with support, a storyboard for their comic strip.
4Sc.02	• **Speaking:** Describe people, places and objects, using a short sequence of sentences.	• Learners can present their ending to *The Seekers* story or their comic strip, using a short sequence of sentences.

21st-century skills

Learning to learn: Participate in shared writing activities.

Communication: Share thoughts with others to solve problems and use polite forms to make and respond to suggestions.

5 ADVENTURES

Materials: Learner's Book pages 90–91; Workbook page 66; **Unit 5 project checklists**; Comics or pictures of comics that are suitable for this age can be shown on-screen; comic strip projects (these can be found by entering *kids' cartoons* into a search engine and clicking on images or videos)

Optional: short videos explaining how to create comics, e.g. the cartoonist Dave McDonald has a number of related videos (enter *cartoonist Dave McDonald* into a search engine); A large piece of card or poster paper for each group's cartoon storyboard; 6–8 small pieces of paper per cartoon; Glue for sticking cartoons onto the storyboard

Starter ideas

Raise interest in the projects (10–15 minutes)

- Tell learners they are going to either create their own comic strip or write an ending to 'The Seekers' story.

- Brainstorm adjectives from the unit and useful sequencing words for learners to use in their stories.

- Revise the past tense from Lesson 5.3. Write the infinitives of the verbs used to narrate the key events from 'The Seekers' on the board and elicit the past forms.

- See which group of 3–4 learners can recall most past simple verbs (regular and irregular). Build up a list on the board.

Main teaching ideas

Introduce projects (60 minutes)

- Encourage learners to choose one of the projects and then follow the steps for their chosen project.

- Learners work in groups, managing and sharing the tasks in the project.

Project A: Create your own comic strip

> CROSS-CURRICULAR LINKS
>
> Art and design: Following the steps in the Learner's book, learners explore their ideas and use their creativity to produce a comic strip.

- Focus on Step 1. Raise interest by showing similar projects by other learners, or look online (see Materials). Refer learners back to the 'Roll and Write' game on page 85 of the Learner's Book. Allow a few minutes for them to think of ideas in pairs or groups.

> **Communication:** In pairs/groups, learners share thoughts with others to decide on a title and plan the comic strip. Allow 5–10 minutes for this. If necessary, pre-teach polite forms to make and respond to suggestions.

- If learners have trouble planning or choosing a title, build up a list of suggested titles and an example plan on the board.

- Next, focus on Step 3. Allow learners time to write their own comic stories using the past tense, time expressions and adjectives. Offer assistance and encourage them to look back over the unit. Make sure each story has 6–8 sentences.

- Learners divide the finished story into 6–8 parts (each part must be at least one sentence). Make sure each group has 6–8 pieces of paper. Learners draw one picture for each story part.

- Next, learners write what is happening under each picture. Then they add dialogue next to the characters in speech bubbles. Tip: to ensure the sentences fit, write the speech before drawing the speech bubble around it.

- Distribute the card or poster paper and the glue. Learners stick their pictures onto the card to create a storyboard.

- Ask each group to present their comic strip to the class.

> **Assessment ideas:** Learners use the **project checklist** to assess how well they carried out the task and make suggestions for improvement.

Project B: Write the ending to *The Seekers* story

- As a class, read and listen to the story again. Briefly discuss the story so far. Then learners work in small groups.

- Support learners by eliciting suggestions to questions about the ending, e.g. *Did the children find the stones? What happens to the Mistraals? How do the children get back to Raban? Did the people of Raban get their freedom? What happens to the Digons?*

> **Communication:** In pairs/groups, learners share thoughts with others to decide on an ending to the story. Allow 5–10 minutes for this. If necessary, pre-teach polite forms to make and respond to suggestions.

121 >

Allow 5 minutes for each group to decide on their preferred ending.

- Encourage learners to use the suggestions on page 85 (Lesson 5.4) in the Learner's Book to plan their endings.

- Circulate and offer guidance about how to plan and what to include.

- In groups, learners write their stories. Circulate and give advice about using the past simple, adjectives, time expressions, dialogue and punctuation.

- Allow learners time to type up their stories then decorate them. If this is not practical in class, it can be done for homework. Continue to circulate and offer support and encouragement where necessary.

- Invite each group to the front of the class to present their story ending.

- Learners vote for the most exciting ending by writing their favourite ending on a piece of paper.

> **Assessment ideas:** Learners use the **project checklist** to assess how well they carried out the task and make suggestions for improvement.

Plenary ideas

Reflection (10–15 minutes)

- Have a class discussion about how the projects went. What did learners enjoy about them? What would they do differently next time? If there wasn't much time earlier in the lesson, encourage learners to ask other groups questions about their presentations to check understanding/find out more.

Homework ideas

> **Workbook**
>
> Questions 1–4 on page 66.

- Photocopy the projects (with language mistakes corrected) of the other learners, and learners can read them at home.

5.7 What do you know now?

What makes an adventure story?

> **Learning to learn:** Learners have the opportunity to reflect and evaluate their own learning success.

- Reintroduce the question from the start of the unit: *What makes an adventure story?* Discuss learners' responses to the question now and compare them with their comments at the beginning of the unit. How much has changed?

- Ask learners to work through the questions individually or in pairs.

Answers
1 Draw your superhero's head.

Draw a simple stick person with a circle for B-head.

Don't press too hard on your pencil.

Use a light pencil line.

Decide now if your superhero is a boy or a girl.

Draw your superhero's body.

Add the rest of your superhero's body. Use the guidelines to draw arms and legs.

Think about your superhero's clothing.

Rub out the guidelines and add some colour!

2 Adjectives: brave; intelligent; powerful; honest; loyal; athletic.

Possible synonyms: fearless, courageous (brave); clever, smart (intelligent); strong (powerful); fit (athletic).

Possible opposites: weak (brave/powerful); stupid (intelligent); dishonest (honest); disloyal (loyal); unfit (athletic).

3 Learner's own answers.

4 Title, characters, setting, dilemma, solution (or resolution).

5 Five from: (give) gave; (choose) chose; (come) came; (say) said; (find) found; (could) can; (have) has; (were) was.

6 Learner's own answers.

Look what I can do!

- There are seven 'can do' statements. Learners read through the statements and tick the things they can do. Encourage them to reflect on how well they can do these things. Also invite them to think of ways they can improve further, e.g. what strategies they can use, or learn to use.

- If learners find it challenging to read the statements, look through the unit with them and support them to find the relevant information.

- Finally, ask learners to work through the questions on page 67 of the Workbook. Encourage them to talk about what they enjoyed and also about any further support they might need.

> 6 Going places

Unit plan

Lesson	Approximate number of learning hours	Outline of learning content	Learning objectives	Resources
1 Getting around	1–1.5	Compare ways of getting to school	4Lm.01 4Rd.01/4Rd.03	Learner's Book Lesson 6.1 Workbook Lesson 6.1 **Digital Classroom:** Getting around: types of transport
2 Road safety	1–1.5	Find out about road safety	4Rd.01 4SC.02 4Ug.04	Learner's Book Lesson 6.2 Workbook Lesson 6.2 ⬇ Photocopiable 16 **Digital Classroom:** Tips for travelling safely Present simple
3 Getting around cities	1–1.5	Design town maps to practise giving directions	4Uv.02 4Ld.01 4Sc.04	Learner's Book Lesson 6.3 Workbook Lesson 6.3 ⬇ Photocopiable 17 **Digital Classroom:** Places on a map Prepositions of direction
4 Travel experiences	1.5–2	Write a description of a special journey	4Wc.02 4Rd.03 4Uv.01	Learner's Book Lesson 6.4 Workbook Lesson 6.4 ⬇ Photocopiable 18 **Digital Classroom:** Descriptive words ⬇ Sample answer for Unit 6
5 *Lost in the Desert*	1–1.5	Read a short story	4Rm.02 4Ug.07 4Sc.05	Learner's Book Lesson 6.5 Workbook Lesson 6.5 ⬇ Differentiated worksheet 6 **Digital Classroom:** Past continuous
6 Project challenge	1–1.5	Project A: Design your own safety poster Project B: Plan a visit to your town or city for two visitors	4Ug.04/4Wca.04 4Wca.01/4Wca.02 4Sc.06/4Uv.02	Learner's Book Lesson 6.6 Workbook Lesson 6.6 ⬇ Unit 6 project checklists

(continued)

Cross-unit resources

⬇ Unit 6 Audioscripts

⬇ End of Unit 6 test

⬇ Unit 6 Progress report

⬇ Unit 6 Wordlist

BACKGROUND KNOWLEDGE

The themes of Unit 6 are types of travel (especially for getting to school), safety when travelling, and getting lost (the focus of the reading in Lesson 5). The vocabulary focus is on types of transport, products that keep us safe when travelling (Lesson 2), places in cities (Lesson 3), the desert and the jungle.

In the UK, typical types of transport used to get to school are cars, buses, trains and trams. Walking is also common. Unit 6 also looks at more extreme and exciting ways of getting to school around the globe, such as zipwire, motorbikes and tuk-tuks. A zipwire (Lesson 1) is a long rope or wire attached between two points that people can slide down. In the UK, zipwires are used for entertainment rather than for travelling. A tuk-tuk is a three-wheeled motor vehicle often used as a taxi in Thailand.

Note: As well as its literal meaning, *going places* is a common expression, which can be used to imply that a person is likely to become successful.

TEACHING SKILLS FOCUS

Cross-curricular learning

What is cross-curricular learning?

Cross-curricular learning is also known as interdisciplinary learning (or teaching). It is an integrated learning framework where learners are encouraged to apply/contrast knowledge from two or more subject areas at the same time. For example, a modern English language textbook will not just focus on rules about the English language. It will contain reading and listening activities that draw on knowledge from a variety of subjects, as well as projects that require learners to combine knowledge and skills from several disciplines.

The Global English Learner's Book doesn't just focus on aspects of the English language. So far, learners have read, listened and discussed texts about communities, Earth and space, homes, food and adventures, drawing on knowledge and skills from other subjects like citizenship, art, literature, science and creative writing. There are cross-curricular links throughout the teacher's resource to help signpost/support teachers with CCL.

Although cross-curricular learning requires more planning and collaboration between teachers, it can offer a number of benefits. Learners will be more motivated by projects on subjects and issues that interest them than if they just studied English grammar rules. This increased motivation will make it easier to engage learners, which has been shown to improve their performance in tests. As learners look at information from a variety of different sources, there is also the opportunity to approach each subject from a wider perspective. Cross-curricular learning can be a way to address fragmentation of knowledge and skills, and to give extra support for achieving learning objectives.

Your challenge

When using Global English, consider links between activities and other subjects in order to differentiate between learners. For example, if your learners have studied road safety in another class, it can be an opportunity to create more learner-centred activities, to let them demonstrate what they already know.

Have a look through Unit 6 and make a list of all the cross-curricular learning links with different subjects studied in your country.

6.1 Think about it: Getting around

LEARNING PLAN

Learning objective	Learning intentions	Success criteria
4Lm.01	• **Listening:** Understand, with support, most of the main points in a listening text about different ways to travel to school.	• Learners can discuss and answer questions about the good and bad points of different ways to travel to school.
4Rd.01/4Rd.03	• **Reading:** Understand specific details and deduce the meaning of key words from context, with little or no support, in a short, simple text.	• Learners can talk and answer questions about a text on travelling by zipwire.
	• **Vocabulary:** *ferry, tuk-tuk, tram, hike, zipwire, canyon, cable, harness.*	

21st-century skills

Communication: Participate with appropriate confidence and clarity – using simple connecters such as 'and', 'but' and 'because'.

Learning to learn: Answer *who, where, what, where, why, how* questions after listening.

Materials: Learner's Book pages 93–95; Workbook pages 68–69; A video showing dangerous journeys to school: search for 'On the way to school trailer Tiff kids 2014'

Starter ideas

Different ways to travel (5 minutes)

• Ask the class about different ways to travel. For example, how does everyone get to school? Then show children going to extremes to reach school, for example by watching the video or looking at the photos from *Materials*. Discuss which ways of travelling are safe and which might be unsafe.

Getting started (5 minutes)

• Answer questions a–c as a class.

Answers

a   Four different ways of travelling: on foot, by bike, by car, by train. Differences: some transport types use fuel; large/small numbers of passengers; fast/slow; traditional/new; ticket needed; public/private transport.

b   City map, pedestrian crossing, helmet, seatbelts. Learner's own answers.

c   Learner's own answers.

> **Digital Classroom:** Use the video 'Getting around' to introduce the vocabulary of the unit. The i button will explain how to use the video.

Main teaching ideas

1   Quick quiz! (5 minutes)

• Generate interest in the subject of transport by making the quiz as fun as possible. Learners can do the quiz in pairs as a competition. Give feedback and see who has the most correct answers.

Answers

1   c
2   a
3   Trains that travel under the ground in a city.
4   Possible answers: trams, buses, cars, electric bikes, electric scooters, hoverboards.
5   b

---

2 Look at the photos (5 minutes)

- The aims of this activity are to ask and answer questions about the different methods of transport. Don't worry about learners not knowing the names of the types of transport, they will find out in the next activity.
- Practise the activity as a class before allowing 2 minutes for learners to ask and answer the questions in pairs.
- Encourage learners to ask extra questions. For example: *How long did the journey take? How often do you travel by ferry? How many times have you travelled by ferry?*

Answers
Learner's own answers.

3 Find the types of transport (5 minutes)

- If learners find *tuk-tuk* challenging, encourage them to match the names they know and guess using the process of elimination.
- Ask learners to report back to the class about their partners' answers in Activity 2. For example: *Luisa has travelled by ferry and tram, but she has not travelled by tuk-tuk because there aren't any tuk-tuks in Lima.*

Answers
ferry d, motorbike e, tuk-tuk f, tram b, train c, car a

4 Match the speakers to the photos (5 minutes)

- Learners will hear the speakers use vocabulary and expressions that may be new to them. Before listening, make it clear that, for this activity, it is only necessary to listen for the name of the method of transport that is used. Tell learners they will have the chance to listen again to understand the details.
- Focus on the pictures in Activity 2. Play the audio and match the first speaker to a picture. Play the rest of the audio for learners to match the photos to the speakers.

Audioscript: Track 36
See Learner's Book page 95.

1: I live in Bangkok, in Thailand. There are a lot of cars in my city and the roads are very busy. That's why I go to school by tuk-tuk. It's faster than walking and you don't get stuck in traffic jams! The tuk-tuk driver can drive between cars, so we don't have to wait behind them. The only problem is that tuk-tuks are open on each side, so you breathe in the traffic fumes!

2: I live near Madrid, in Spain, and I always go to school by car with my best friend. We take it in turns … sometimes her parents drive us to school and sometimes we go with my dad. I like going to school by car because you don't get wet when it rains. The only problem is that sometimes we get stuck in traffic and then we are nearly late for school!

3: My dad takes me to school on his motorbike. I live in Ho Chi Minh City, in Vietnam, and everybody here travels by motorbike! I like it because it's fast and I get to spend time with my dad. But sometimes it rains really hard and then it's not so much fun. We wear waterproof clothing but we still get wet!

4: I live on a small island close to Hong Kong and I get the ferry to school every day. When the weather is good I like travelling by ferry because you can stand on the deck and look at the lovely views of the harbour. But during the winter it gets really cold, even if you sit inside in the cabin.

5: I live in Hiroshima in Japan and I go to school by tram. It's quite fast and it stops right outside my school, so I don't have to walk far. But it often gets really crowded and sometimes I don't get a seat.

Answers
1f   2a   3e   4d   5b

5 Listen again (5–10 minutes)

- Before playing the audio, make predictions about good and bad points of each type of transport and elicit/pre-teach necessary/new vocabulary, which can be seen in the answer box.
- Listen to the first speaker. Elicit ideas from learners. Repeat for the other speakers.

- If necessary, repeat the recording. Give feedback after each speaker. Download the audioscript and underline the words that help with the answers.

> **Learning to learn:** Invite learners to ask and answer *who, where, what, where, why* and *how* questions after listening, e.g. *Why is the tuk-tuk faster than a car?*

Answers

Transport	Good points	Bad points
Tuk-tuk	Good fun. It's faster than walking. You don't get stuck in traffic jams! You don't have to wait behind cars.	Open on both sides, so you breathe in traffic fumes.
Car	You don't get wet when it rains.	Sometimes we get stuck in traffic and are nearly late for school.
Motorbike	Fast. Gets to spend time alone with his dad.	You get very wet when it rains hard.
Ferry	Can look at lovely views.	Very cold in winter.
Tram	Quite fast. Stops right outside school.	Often really crowded. Sometimes don't get a seat.

6 Talk about how you get to school (5–10 minutes)

- Ask the class how they travel to school (recap the Starter activity if needed). Elicit suggestions about good and bad points of their journeys. For example: *It's fast; It takes a long time!*

- Allow learners time to talk to their partners before asking learners to report back to the class.

Answers
Learner's own answers.

7 Read the article quickly (5 minutes)

- Elicit strategies for reading for specific information. If necessary, remind learners that they don't need to understand every word and tell them they will have the chance to ask about new words later.

- Have a fun competition. See who can find the two answers most quickly. Make a note of how long this takes.

Answers
She takes a ride on a zipwire. It takes one minute.

8 Work out the meaning of the words in blue (5–10 minutes)

- Focus on the first two blue words, *hike* and *zipwire*. Read the whole sentence and ask questions that help learners guess the meaning. For example: *Which takes longer: the hike or the zipwire ride? Is there a big difference? So what could a hike be?* Learners work in pairs to work out the meaning of the other blue words.

> **Differentiation ideas:** If learners need support with this task, make a matching exercise. For each pair, photocopy (and enlarge) the answers below. Cut out each of the words and separate from their definitions. Learners match each word to a definition.

Answers
Hike – a long walk, usually in the countryside.

Zipwire – a long thick wire between two points. You can travel along it by hanging onto a small wheel on the wire (see photo).

Canyon – a large valley with very steep sides.

Harness – something you wear with straps and belts that stops you falling (see photo).

Cable – a thick strong wire (see photo).

9 Read and answer the questions (5 minutes)

- Tell learners they now have more time to read the article. Allow them time to look at the text carefully and answer the questions. Give class feedback on the answers.

Answers
a   She could take a two-hour hike through the jungle. She probably takes the zipwire because it is much faster.

b   She helps her brothers get safely to the other side by fixing them into their harnesses first (before she travels).

c   Nearly 50 kph.

d   She feels nervous.

10 Find other phrases that use *get* and Language focus (5–10 minutes)

- Discuss the two uses of *get* in the Language focus box.

- Learners re-read the text and look for the other uses of *get*. Encourage learners to guess the meanings of each from the context.

Answers

Get to school (×2) / get safely to the other side / it never gets any easier / gets nervous.

---

11 Can you think of safer ways for Daisy and her brothers to get to school? (5 minutes)

- Write useful discussion expressions on the board, for example: *She could get there by…; How about getting…? No, that's too…*

- Brainstorm ideas with the class before giving learners time to discuss in pairs.

> **Digital Classroom:** Use the activity 'Getting around: types of transport' to revise transport vocabulary. The i button will explain how to use the activity.

Plenary ideas

Consolidation (10 minutes)

- Learners write five sentences using *get/gets*. Build up a list of these sentences on the board.

Homework ideas

Workbook

Questions 1–7 on pages 68–69.

- Learners write a paragraph about their journeys to school. Write prompts on the board to encourage the use of *get* expressions. Encourage learners to write about the good and bad points of the type of transport they use.

> **Assessment ideas:** Give written feedback on the paragraph, focusing on learners' use of *get* expressions and vocabulary from the lesson.

6.2 Health and safety: Road safety

LEARNING PLAN

Learning objective	Learning intentions	Success criteria
4Rd.01	• **Reading:** Understand, with little or no support, most specific information and detail in a short text about road safety.	• Learners can answer questions on a simple text about road safety.
4Sc.02	• **Speaking:** Describe people, places and objects, and routine past and present actions and events, using a short sequence of sentences.	• Learners can describe road safety signs and their purpose, using a short sequence of sentences.
4Ug.04	• **Use of English:** Use present simple regular and irregular forms to describe routines, habits and states.	• Learners can use present simple regular and irregular forms to describe road safety habits.
	• **Vocabulary:** *lorries, helmet, reflective (armbands), reverse, pedestrian crossing, seatbelt.*	

21st-century skills

Creative thinking: Based on a model, develop a new road sign.

Materials: Learner's Book pages 96–97; Workbook pages 70–71; **Photocopiable 16**; Products that learners use for improving road safety on their way to school, e.g. a helmet, high-visibility clothing – if learners don't have these with them, show a road safety video, such as *Road safety for 7–11-year-olds* at the ni direct government services website (see Motoring, Road safety, Road users); Simple home-made road signs

LANGUAGE BACKGROUND

Present simple

The Language detective in this lesson focuses on the main use of the present simple: to talk about routines/habits and states (things that are always the same). For example, for habits: *I **ride** my bike to school and I always **wear** a helmet.* For states: *In the winter here, it **gets** dark really early.*

In standard English, the 's' is always required for the third person singular (*she, he* and *it*). For questions, negatives and short answers, the auxiliary verb *do* should be used with all persons except *she, he* and *it*, which require *does*. Although

it is not uncommon to hear native speakers using *don't* as a third person negative, especially in informal situations, this is grammatically incorrect, and you should discourage it.

Some present simple verbs are irregular, for example **be** and **have**.

Remind learners **not** to use the present simple:

- to refer to the future, except when talking about something that is fixed, like a timetable, or in an *if* clause
- to make or invite suggestions.

Common misconceptions

Misconception	How to identify	How to overcome
Learners forget to add the third person singular *s*.	Learners underline present tense verbs in the text. Practise saying them out loud and elicit which verbs end in 's' and *why*.	Practise. Use Photocopiable 16: **My school journey**, which practises *Does she/ Does he* questions.
Learners often incorrectly use the third person singular with the irregular plural noun *people*.	Write *person* on the board. Elicit that the plural is (usually) *people*. Elicit that *one people* is incorrect as this is (an irregular) plural.	Allow 2 minutes to write interesting sentences, e.g. *People are… People in my country like…/eat… People don't… etc.* Learners choose the two sentences they like best and memorise them.

Starter ideas

60-second transport challenge (5–10 minutes)

- Elicit common ways of travelling. Focus on one and elicit products/way of keeping safe. Allow groups 60 seconds to write down as many ways/products as they can. At the end of the minute, make a list of these on the board. Don't worry about making sentences about these, as learners will do this in Activity 1.

Main teaching ideas

1 **How do you usually travel? What can you do to travel safely? (5 minutes)**

- The aim of this activity is to elicit/pre-teach vocabulary for Activity 2 and to make predictions about what learners might read.

- Look at the pictures. Elicit/pre-teach *lorries, helmet, reflective (armbands), to reverse, pedestrian crossing, seatbelt* and other useful words. Build up a list on the board. If learners walk, cycle, skateboard or similar to school, ask them to talk about objects they use to stay safe or mime what they do, e.g. *putting on a helmet/ seatbelt/high-visibility clothing/armbands.*

- Alternatively, show a video, like the one suggested in *Materials.* Ask learners what they can see that can improve road safety.

Answers

Learner's own answers.

 2 Read and listen (5–10 minutes)

- Learners use their discussions and the vocabulary from Activity 1 to make predictions about what they will read and hear.

- They scan the text to see if they were correct.

Audioscript: Track 37

See Learner's Book page 96.

> **Digital Classroom:** Use the slideshow 'Tips for travelling safely' to add to the road safety advice given in the Learner's Book. The i button will explain how to use the slideshow and activity.

3 Complete the table and Giving advice (10 minutes)

- Learners copy the table into their notebooks. Allow time for them to make notes about the specific information in the text.

- Give class feedback on the answers.

- Look at the Key words: Giving advice box. Find *should* and *mustn't* in the text and elicit the difference in meaning.

Answers

What keeps you safe?	When?
a helmet	when you ride your bike
reflective armbands	when you walk home from school when it's dark
not going near lorries	at any time
use pedestrian crossings	when crossing busy roads
wear seatbelts	in a car

Language detective (5 minutes)

- Look at the Language detective box, which focuses on the present simple. Learners will already be using the present simple, so a good starting point is to ask them to give statements about their transport routines and habits. Refer to the Road safety reading text and ask about the formation of the third person singular and affirmative. Elicit the use of the 's' for *he, she* and *it*.

- Elicit which two common verbs are irregular. If learners aren't sure, ask them to check by looking at the box.

4 Complete the sentences (5 minutes)

- Learners should now be ready to complete the sentences in Activity 4 by putting the verbs into the present simple.

Answers

a isn't   b wears   c rides   d travel

Learner's own answers (ticking sentences).

> **Digital Classroom:** Use the grammar presentation 'Present simple' to revise the present simple. The i button will explain how to use the grammar presentation.

Workbook

For further practice of present simple, learners look at the Language detective and complete activities 1–3 on pages 70–71.

5 What do the signs mean? (10 minutes)

- Look at the road signs on page 97. Elicit what the signs mean and also simple descriptions to give learners ideas for the next activity. For example: *It's triangular. The people are black… They are walking/crossing…* (present continuous). *It means 'Don't…', 'You mustn't…', 'Be careful because…'*

- Also support learners by asking questions to elicit descriptions, e.g. *What shape is the sign? What is in the middle? How many people are there? Who are the people? What colour are the people/is the border/is the background? What are the people doing? What does it mean?*

Answers

a   It is safe to cross the road.

b   Drive carefully because children might cross the road.

c   You must not drive over 40 mph.

6   Design a sign (20–25 minutes)

> **Creative thinking:** Based on a model, learners follow the instructions in the Learner's Book to develop a new road sign.

- Show learners pictures of simple homemade road signs and build up a list of related dangers for drivers, cyclists and pedestrians.

- Encourage pairs of learners to choose an idea for their sign.

- Ask each pair which idea they have chosen and why.

- Allow learners time to design the sign, and make notes about what the sign is and why their neighbourhood needs it.

- If there is time, learners present their signs to the class.

Plenary ideas

Consolidation (10 minutes)

- To reinforce what has been learnt, play the *Minute memory game*. After the presentations, nominate pairs to speak for one minute about their favourite sign(s). The pairs say as much as they can remember about one or more of the other signs.

- Learners could do **Photocopiable 16**.

Homework ideas

Workbook

Questions 1–4 on pages 70–71 of the Workbook.

- Learners write a paragraph about what they do to keep safe when travelling. Encourage them to use the present simple and to discuss road safety for at least two types of transport.

> **Assessment ideas:** As a class, write a short checklist so that learners can self-assess their work before they hand it in. For example: *Have I used the present simple? Have I discussed at least two types of transport? Have I used new vocabulary?*

6.3 Talk about it: Getting around cities

<table>
<tr><td colspan="3">LEARNING PLAN</td></tr>
<tr><th>Learning objective</th><th>Learning intentions</th><th>Success criteria</th></tr>
<tr>
<td>4Uv.02

4Ld.01

4Sc.04</td>
<td>
• Use of English: Use prepositions of direction (e.g. into, out, of, from, towards).

• Listening: Understand, with support, instructions for getting to a place.

• Speaking: Give, with support, a short sequence of instructions.

• Vocabulary: from, go out, on, across/up, towards, to, a pier, a bridge, metro stations, main roads, entertainment.
</td>
<td>
• Learners can use prepositions of direction, to give directions for places on a town map.

• Learners can answer questions about a range of instructions for getting to a place.

• Learners can give, with support, a short series of instructions to find places on a town map.
</td>
</tr>
<tr><td colspan="3">21st-century skills</td></tr>
<tr><td colspan="3">Critical thinking: Sort and classify places according to key features; Explain choices to put places in locations on a map of an imaginary town.</td></tr>
</table>

Materials: Learner's book pages 98–99; Workbook pages 72–73; **Photocopiable 17**; Interesting pictures to demonstrate vocabulary for places your learners may not know: for example, for *pier*, enter *Brighton Pier* or *Huntington Beach Pier* into a search engine; Photocopiable map symbols, e.g. search for 'map symbols' on the Vecteezy website

Common misconceptions

Misconception	How to identify	How to overcome
Learners often use the wrong prepositions, e.g. • *in front of* for *opposite* • ~~at~~ on the corner • ~~in / at~~ /on the third floor • go ~~through~~ up Bear Street	Write sentences from the audio on the board. Demonstrate that literal translation is not always useful by encouraging learners to translate from their own language(s). Elicit that literal translation often causes learners to make mistakes.	For cases where prepositions cannot be translated literally, encourage learners to memorise whole phrases, e.g.: *the school is on the corner; my classroom is on the third floor.*

Starter ideas

Town vocabulary (5 minutes)

• Explain that in this lesson, learners are going to design a town map and practise giving directions.

• To start with, revise the names of places in a town by making the words in Activity 2 into anagrams. Write the anagrams on the board and see which learner(s) can unscramble them first.

• Brainstorm more places in your learners' town(s).

Main teaching ideas

1 Best places to visit (10 minutes)

• Start by revising types of transport. Build up a list on the board and ask learners questions like *Where do you get to by train? How do you get to…?*

• Give learners time to write down the five best places to visit in their town/city and how they get there.

• Learners tell a partner their choices.

Answers

Learner's own answers.

2 **Which of these places did you talk about in Activity 1? (5 minutes)**

- Briefly look at each of the places in the box. Nominate learners to report back to the class. For example: *I talked about…in Activity 1, but Emily thinks the best places are…* Insist on the correct use of the third person singular *s*.

- Nominate learners and ask them a '*Did you see…?*' question about two or three of the places.

- Learners identify the places in the photos.

Answers

Learner's own answers.

3 **Put the places into categories (5 minutes)**

- Check learners know the meanings of the four headings before they do the activity. Allow learners time to put each place under a heading before giving feedback. Elicit other places that could come under each heading.

Answers

Sports and activities	Entertainment	Eating	Sleeping
swimming pool, beach, sports centre, playground, park	museum, cinema, theatre, theme park	picnic site, restaurant	hotel

(Plus Learner's own answers.)

 4 **Listen (5 minutes)**

- Tell learners they are going to hear a conversation in the tourist office. Briefly look at the questions. Make sure learners know they should only focus on hearing the specific information that the questions ask for.

- Before you listen, encourage predictions about the types of transport a family might use on a day trip to London and the kind of special places they might like to visit.

Audioscript: Track 38

See Learner's Book page 98.

Dad:	Hello, could you give us some information about places to visit in central London? We are looking for somewhere interesting to spend the afternoon…and somewhere inside, I think, because it's going to rain.
Tourist information officer:	OK…How about the Natural History Museum? There is something for everyone there…amazing exhibitions and films, and a wonderful wildlife garden which you could visit if the rain stays away.
Dad:	That sounds perfect – how do we get there?
Tourist information officer:	Ok, let's look at the map. You take the underground to this station here; it's called South Kensington. From here you can walk to the museum – it's not very far – about five minutes…
Dad:	And where's the nearest underground station from here?
Tourist information officer:	Go out of this office at the exit on the left. Then turn right and walk across the road towards the theatre. Turn left just after the theatre and walk up that street. The entrance to the underground station is on the right, it's called…

Answers

a Underground, walking.   b Museum

5 **Guess the missing words and Listening tip (5 minutes)**

- First, look at the Listening tip. Then read the notes together and encourage predictions about the missing words. Play the audio and check learners' predictions.

Answers

1 Museum 2 garden 3 walk 4 right 5 left 6 on

6 Find and talk about (5 minutes)

- Check learners understand the meanings of the words in the box, e.g. *a pier*, by showing them images (see *Materials*). Ask and answer questions, e.g. *Is there a … in your town? Are there any …s in your city?*

- Then elicit and write questions (or question prompts) that can be used for further discussion. For example: *What's the pier/ bridge/metro station/main road like? How old is the…? How big is it? Where…? How many…? …like it/them…? Why?*

Answers

Learners identify the places on the map on page 99.

Learner's own answers.

7 Match the map symbols (10 minutes)

- Encourage learners to guess what the symbols represent. Then ask them to match each symbol to a place in Activity 2.

- Elicit suggestions about why symbols are used on maps instead of words.

Answers

a   swimming pool   b   restaurant

c   hotel   d   playground

> **Digital Classroom:** Use the activity 'Places on a map' to revise vocabulary of places. The i button will explain how to use the activity.

8 Work in pairs to design a town map (20 minutes)

- Explain to learners that they are going to design their own town map.

- First, ask the pairs to choose six places from Activity 2. Or they can choose their best places to visit from Activity 1, if they're different from the places in Activity 2. On the board, demonstrate how to *quickly* draw **simple** map symbols. Learners can also use the symbols from Activity 7.

- Encourage learners to answer the questions in the Learner's Book to establish the most logical locations for their chosen places.

Circulate and ask learners to explain their choice of location.

> **Critical thinking opportunity:** Learners explain why they have chosen to put places in the locations on the map of the imaginary town they have created.

> **Differentiation ideas:** Instead of drawing the symbols, you could provide learners who need more support with photocopiable map symbols (see *Materials*).

CROSS-CURRICULAR LINKS

Geography: Learners can read and understand maps.

Answers

Learner's own answers.

Language detective (5 minutes)

- The Language detective concentrates on prepositions of direction. Learners should be familiar with at least some of them. Start by eliciting the ones that they already know.

- If learners don't recognise all of the prepositions of direction, show them the audioscript and tell them to look for examples. Write the examples on the board.

- Practise repeating the phrases in the Language detective, using the correct pronunciation, including intonation.

> **Digital Classroom:** Use the activity 'Prepositions of direction' to revise prepositions of direction. The i button will explain how to use the activity.

Workbook

For further practice of prepositions of direction, learners can look at the Language detective and complete activities 1–5 pages 72–73.

9 Give your partner directions (5 minutes)

- Ask learners to work in their pairs. Demonstrate by using an example or examples with the whole class. Monitor and support learners while they are giving directions. Learners can use the Language detective to help them. Give feedback on common mistakes.

Plenary ideas

Consolidation (5–10 minutes)

- Learners practise giving instructions to and from places in their towns.
- Learners could work through **Photocopiable 17**

Homework ideas

> **Workbook**
>
> Questions 1–5 on pages 72–73.

- Learners write down directions from their house to school or another place.

6.4 Write about it: Travel experiences

LEARNING PLAN

Learning objective	Learning intentions	Success criteria
4Wc.02	• **Writing:** Write a description of a special journey using powerful sentences.	• Learners can write a description of a special journey.
4Rd.03	• **Reading:** Deduce meaning from context, with little or no support, in a short, simple text.	• Learners can deduce the meaning of 'strong' verbs and adjectives from context in a description of a special journey.
4Uv.01	• **Use of English:** Use *like*, as a preposition, to describe and compare things.	• Learners can use *like* to describe and compare things in their description of a special journey.
	• **Vocabulary:** *giggle, sparkle, stare, rise, huge, enormous, tiny, amazing, skyscraper, thousand.*	

21st-century skills

Communication: Share ideas with a peer before the writing task.

Creative thinking: Substitute words in a text.

Materials: Learner's Book pages 100–101; Workbook pages 74–75; **Photocopiable 18**; Images or videos of London, e.g. search for 'English London sightseeing with subtitles' for an informative video that lasts 2 minutes 53 seconds

Starter ideas

London (5 minutes)

- Generate interest in London and the London Eye by showing images or a video like the one in *Materials*. Show a variety of different places and landmarks to demonstrate that London is a fascinating city with something to interest everyone.

Main teaching ideas

1 Look at the photos (5 minutes)

- Focus on the photos. Elicit why the panoramic wheel is called the London Eye, and ask the other questions.

- If any learners have been on a similar panoramic wheel, write question prompts on the board and ask other learners to make questions for them to answer, e.g. *...see a famous castle?* → ***Did you** see a famous castle?*

Answers
The London Eye is probably called this because you can see so much of London as you travel around its circuit.

2 Imagine travelling on the London Eye (5 minutes)

- Encourage learners to give as many suggestions as possible. The main purpose of this activity is to predict what Mia might say in the reading text. The suggestions could be the name of London's famous landmarks or places from the previous lesson, e.g. *bridges* and *parks*.

Answers
Learner's own answers.

3 Read Mia's description (5 minutes)

- Learners should only skim the text to check their ideas. Allow a minute for this and make it clear that it is not necessary to understand every detail. Learners should just look for words and phrases for the sights that Mia saw from the London Eye.

- Ask learners to work in pairs and point out the things that Mia mentioned, which are the same as their ideas.

Answers
Learner's own answers.

4 Match the descriptive words (5–10 minutes)

> **CROSS-CURRICULAR LINKS**
>
> English: In Activity 6, learners start to appreciate that words can have different shades of meaning.

- Focus on the first blue verb in the text, *huge*. Encourage learners to use the words around it, 'from floor to ceiling', to guess the meaning. If they find this hard, narrow down the possibilities by looking at the suggestions in Activity 6.

- Learners use the suggestions in the box to match the other blue words. It should be possible to guess the meanings without referring to a dictionary.

- Ask learners to identify which of the 'blue words' are verbs and which are adjectives. If learners are finding this difficult, elicit the difference between verbs and adjectives and give one example of each to get learners started.

Answers
very big (x2): *huge, enormous*

laugh: *giggle*

very small: *tiny*

shine: *sparkle*

very interesting: *amazing*

look (for a long time): *stare*

go up: *rise*

Verbs: *giggle, sparkle, stare, rise*

Adjectives: *huge, enormous, tiny, amazing*

5 Why do you think the writer uses the descriptive words? (5 minutes)

- To start this discussion, read out words from the first two sentences: *'the glass capsule...had **huge** windows from floor to ceiling'*. Emphasise and mime *huge*. Then re-read the text, substituting *huge* with *very big*. Elicit the fact that *huge* makes the glass capsule more interesting than *very big*.

Answers

The 'strong' words are more interesting and help the reader imagine more clearly what it is like to travel on the London Eye.

> **Digital Classroom:** Use the activity 'Descriptive words' to revise the descriptive words in the lesson. The i button will explain how to use the activity.

6 **Make the underlined phrases more interesting and Writing tip (10 minutes)**

- Write the blue words and the words from Activity 6 on the board. Also add *skyscraper* and *thousand*. Elicit possible answers for the first sentence.

- Allow learners time to rewrite the other sentences, making them sound more interesting.

- Look at the Writing tip, which focuses on the sentences from the reading that contain expressions with the preposition *like*.

- Ask learners questions to elicit more sentences with the preposition *like*. For example: *What did you feel like on your first day of school (and other special occasions)? What do buildings look like from a plane?*

Answers

Suggested answers:

a We were on the 60th floor of an <u>enormous glass skyscraper</u>.

b I <u>stared</u> out of the <u>huge, tall</u> <u>windows.</u>

c The view was <u>amazing</u> – I could see lots of palaces, skyscrapers, towers and churches, and <u>thousands of streets</u> below.

7 **Make a paragraph (10 minutes)**

- Elicit linking words like *and, then* and *because*, which learners can use to link the ideas in the sentences. Then encourage suggestions about what learners might hear or feel looking out of the window of the skyscraper.

- Allow learners time to write their paragraphs.

Answers

Learner's own answers.

8 **Have you ever been on a special journey? (5 minutes)**

- Build up a list on the board of journeys that could be considered special.

- Make sure everyone has a 'special journey' to talk to their partner about before allowing learners time to ask and answer the questions with a partner.

- Offer learners support by telling them the English for words they need to talk about their journeys.

9 **Write a description of your special journey (20 minutes)**

- Allow learners time to read the questions and examples in the mind map. Then check they understand by asking the same questions about their special journeys.

- Allow learners time to make their own mind maps. Offer support to learners during this process.

- When you are satisfied that the learners can answer all the questions, go through the advice under the mind map together, before allowing them time to write their descriptions.

- Once the description has been written, focus on the writing checklist on **Photocopiable 18**.

> **Assessment ideas:** Print out the sample answer. Ask learners to assess it against **Photocopiable 18** before they finalise their description. Once learners have made any changes, ask them to swap their descriptions with a classmate. They should give each other feedback on the use of interesting verbs and adjectives and the past simple tense.

10 **Present, display or publish your work**

- If you have time, learners could present their descriptions to the class.

- You could display the descriptions in the classroom, put them in a portfolio or on a school blog/website.

Plenary ideas

Consolidation (5 minutes)

- Ask learners questions about other learners' descriptions using the past simple forms. For example: *What did Ann/Ahmed do first? She/He climbed into the glass capsule. What could she/he see? Then what did she/he do? What could she/he hear? What did she/he do next? How did she/he feel?*

Homework ideas

> **Workbook**
> Questions 1–5 on pages 74–75.

- Learners write a paragraph about a place that tourists visit in their own country. Encourage them to use interesting verbs and adjectives, describe what tourists can hear and how they feel when they're there, and to use the past simple tense.

6.5 Read and respond: *Lost in the Desert*

LEARNING PLAN

Learning objective	Learning intentions	Success criteria
4Rm.02	• **Reading:** Read, with support, a short story with confidence and enjoyment.	• Learners can talk and answer questions on a short story about being lost in the desert.
4Ug.07	• **Use of English:** Use the past continuous to describe background actions.	
4Sc.05	• **Speaking:** Pronounce some familiar words and phrases clearly; others may need to ask for repetition from time to time.	• Learners can use the past continuous to describe interrupted actions in the story.
	• **Vocabulary:** *dropped, arid, sprout up, parched, shade, hide, back and forth, unaware, cobra, flickering, coiled up, reddish, bushy tail, scurry off, hung her head, skipped, leapt, jumped, hopped, plodded, run away, advice.*	• Learners can pronounce some past simple endings for regular verbs.

21st-century skills

Critical thinking: Make predictions from given information.

Learning to learn: Use pictures to follow a story line.

Materials: Learner's Book pages 102–105; Workbook pages 76–77; **Differentiated worksheet 6**

Common misconceptions

Misconception	How to identify	How to overcome
Learners of this level often forget to use the *–ing* form of the verb. For example: *She **was walk** along* instead of *She **was walking** along.* Learners conjugate the main verb incorrectly, adding *–ed* instead of *–ing*. For example: *She was jump**ed** over the bushes* instead of *She was jumping over the bushes.*	• Write sentences from the story on the board and highlight the correct form. Re-read and listen to the story to get learners used to hearing the correct form. • Elicit the differences in meaning and use between *walk, walked,* and *walking*.	• If learners keep making these mistakes, encourage them to memorise whole phrases in their context. The most effective phrases are ones learners might use, e.g. *I was playing football when I fell and hurt my knee.* • Encourage learners to read stories that contain examples of the past continuous form.

Starter ideas

Story introduction (5–10 minutes)

• Elicit that in this lesson, the setting of the story is a desert.

• Ask learners to describe what it's like to be in a desert (elicit words like *hot, arid, dry, parched, no landmarks, not much water/shade, wild animals, cobra,* etc.).

• Then introduce the meaning of 'getting lost' – mime it and/or give a simple example. Tell learners that in this story a girl gets lost in the desert. Briefly discuss how the girl must feel when she realises she is lost.

Main teaching ideas

1 Talk about being lost (5–10 minutes)

• Ask learners if they have ever got lost. Elicit the short answer *Yes, I have/No, I haven't.* Build up a list of places that learners have been lost on the board.

• Ask learners to work in pairs and talk about what they did to find their way home using the past simple.

Answers
Learner's own answers.

2 Look at the pictures (5–10 minutes)

> **Critical thinking opportunity:** Before reading, elicit learners' predictions about what happens and how the girl gets lost in the desert by looking at the pictures.

• The vocabulary and the length of the story will challenge learners, so it is important to use strategies to make reading the text enjoyable and satisfying. For example, using the pictures or scanning the text to get the main ideas, before reading in detail.

Learner's
Learners' own answers.

3 Read and listen to the story (10 minutes)

• Before reading the first part of the text, tell learners to read questions a and b and guess the answers. If they find this difficult, ask questions like *Do you think Rabin lives in a skyscraper? A tent?* Make clear that it is not necessary to understand every word. Learners must just find the specific information to answer the questions.

• Learners read and listen to the first part of the story and check their predictions.

• Repeat this process for the other parts of the story.

Audioscript: Track 39
See Learner's Book page 102–104.

Answers
a She lived in a small village in the desert, southwest of Cairo.

b She lived in a tent.

c   She wanted to follow a rabbit.

d   No

e   No

f   She noticed a lot of bees.

g   She jumped up and ran as fast as she could/She ran into the bushes and realised she was lost/She sat down on a rock and started to cry.

h   She saw a cobra.

i   She was very frightened.

j   She hopped off the rock and started running back to the riverbed./She really began to cry.

k   She felt tired, hungry and afraid.

l   It was evening (the sun was setting).

m   She lay down and fell asleep.

n   The rabbit showed her the way to go.

o   He was worried and angry that Rabin had wandered off the path.

p   She looked for the rabbit, smiled and then walked back home with her father.

Language detective (5 minutes)

- The Language detective looks at the past continuous for interrupted actions. Learners encounter examples in Rabin's story.

- First, read the sentence in the Language detective. Elicit how to form the past continuous, and the difference in meaning and form between the past simple and past continuous.

4   Match sentences from the story (5 minutes)

- After learners have attempted to match the sentence halves, read and listen again to check. Practise repeating the sentences from Rabin's story using the correct pronunciation.

Answers
1b   2d   3a   4c

5   Find the verbs of movement (10 minutes)

- Point out the first of the blue words from the first paragraph of text: *skipped*. Repeat the whole sentence and encourage learners to guess

the meaning of *skipped*. Look in a dictionary to check learners' guesses. If the dictionary gives more than one meaning, look again at the context to choose the most appropriate.

- Repeat for the other blue words.

Answers

a   'Plodded' is the odd one out because it is a slow movement (all the other verbs are quick movements).

b   Learner's own answers.

6   Listen to the verbs from the story (5 minutes)

- Write the verbs *dropped, raised* and *landed* on the board. Elicit and drill the correct pronunciation. Ask learners to come up with more verbs that are pronounced in the same way.

- Ask learners to copy the table in their notebooks. Learners listen to the verbs and write each one in the correct column.

Audioscript: Track 40

See Learner's Book page 105.

dropped / landed / raised / laughed / looked / skipped / loved / wanted / jumped / listened / started / watched / hopped / arrived / moved / stopped

Answers

/t/	/d/	/ɪd/
dropped	raised	landed
laughed	loved	wanted
looked	listened	started
skipped	arrived	
jumped	moved	
watched		
hopped		
stopped		

7 Values: Taking advice (5 minutes)

- Check learners understand *advice* by asking them what sort of advice their teachers give them and *why*. Ask and answer the questions as a class.

Answers

a   They told her not to leave the path because it was very dangerous.

b   She got lost and met dangerous animals.

c   She felt tired, hungry and afraid.

d   She said she would never leave the path again.

8 Ask and answer questions (5 minutes)

- Ask learners about the advice that their parents or family members give them. Build up a list on the board.

- Allow learners time to ask and answer the questions in pairs. Tell them to try to remember their partners' answers (for the plenary activity). Circulate and offer support, for example by giving learners useful vocabulary to use.

Answers

a   Learner's own answers.

b   Learner's own answers.

> **Digital Classroom:** Use the activity 'Past continuous' to revise the past continuous with past simple interrupted actions. The i button will explain how to use the activity.

Plenary ideas

Consolidation (10 minutes)

- Using the present simple, learners report back to the class about what their partners told them, e.g. *Rakesh's mum tells him not to cross the road on the corner.*

- Learners ask and answer questions using the past continuous (*What were you doing…?*) for various times and days – yesterday at 5 p.m., last Sunday at 12.30 p.m., etc.

Homework ideas

Workbook

Questions 1–5 on pages 76–77 of the Workbook.

> **Differentiation ideas:** For further practice of the past continuous, use **Differentiated worksheet 6**.

6.6 Project challenge

LEARNING PLAN

Learning objective	Learning intentions	Success criteria
4Ug.04/4Wca.04	• **Use of English/Writing:** Use present simple regular and irregular forms and some simple grammatical structures and sentence patterns correctly, allowing for some mistakes, to describe road safety habits.	• Learners can use the present simple and other simple grammatical structures and sentence patterns on their poster or presentation.
4Wca.01/4Wca.02	• **Writing:** Use legible handwriting and spell most high frequency words correctly when writing independently.	• Learners can use legible handwriting and spell high frequency words accurately when creating their poster or presentation.
4Sc.06/4Uv.02	• **Speaking/Use of English:** Produce a short sequence of sentences to maintain short exchanges, allowing for some hesitation, false starts and reformulation, using prepositions of direction (e.g. *into, out, of, from, towards*).	• Learners can maintain short exchanges using prepositions of direction during their presentation.

21st-century skills

Communication: Share ideas with peers before a writing/speaking task.

Critical thinking: Say if something is true and give a reason.

Materials: Learner's Book pages 106–107; Workbook page 78; **Unit 6 project checklists**; Examples of similar projects (for example, search for 'poster contest' on the National Association for Pupil Transportation website); Magazines (for the safety poster)

Optional: Pictures/photos of interesting places in your town or city; Card for making posters, or PCs, if you decide to design slides using presentation software

Starter ideas

Raise interest in the projects (10–15 minutes)

- Tell learners that they are either going to design a safety poster or plan a visit to their town or city for two visitors.

- Raise interest in the projects by showing children's work on a similar topic from other classes or the Internet. For example, for the safety poster project, try sites like the **NAPT** website, or look for road safety campaign posters.

- Revise vocabulary for the challenges in a fun way. For instance, for Project B, draw map symbols on the board and learners guess what they are as you are drawing.

Main teaching ideas

Introduce projects (60 minutes)

- Encourage learners to choose one of the projects to work on in pairs or in a group.

- Learners work in groups, managing and sharing the tasks in the project.

Project A: Design your own safety poster

- Step 1: Encourage learners to share ideas with peers, using the suggestions about keeping safe when not at home. Build up a mind map on the board.

- Step 2: Learners choose 6–8 of these ideas and make a statement about each one.

- Step 3: Encourage learners to check their statements for errors by answering the questions.

- Step 4: Distribute card and magazines for learners to use to create their posters. If learners can't find any photos, encourage them to draw their own pictures. Circulate and check that learners' handwriting is clear.

- Step 5: Learners read the checklist before presenting their poster.

> **Assessment ideas:** Learners use the **project checklist** to assess how well they carried out the task and make suggestions for improvement.

Project B: Plan a visit to your town or city for two visitors

- Step 1: Brainstorm places to visit in your town or city. Elicit and build up a list of places in your city/town/village on the board.

> **Critical thinking opportunity:** Learners have a class vote on which places are the most interesting to visit. Ask learners if they agree and elicit reasons for this.

- Step 2: Learners choose three places for visitors to visit on Day 1. Elicit which types of transport could be used to travel between places and useful words for giving directions from Lesson 3. Decide how many days the visitors will stay in your town or city.

- Step 3: Learners make slides using presentation software, to show the places to visit and stay. If creating slides is not practical, distribute photos of the places in their city and card, for learners to

create posters. Demonstrate by choosing a photo and writing examples of things learners could write, e.g. why the place is interesting and directions to get there. If you don't have any photos, encourage learners to draw the places.

- Allow time for learners to create the slides or poster. Circulate and offer support, and check that the learners are all working together as a group.

- Step 4: Learners read the checklist before listening to the other groups' presentations.

> **Assessment ideas:** Learners tick the boxes if they think learners have carried out each task. Also encourage them to give constructive and sensitive feedback if they think the presentation could be improved.

Plenary ideas

Consolidation (10 minutes)

> **Assessment ideas:** Encourage learners to ask other groups questions about their presentations/posters to check understanding/find out more.

Homework ideas

> **Workbook**
>
> Questions 1–10 on page 78.

- Photocopy the projects (with language mistakes corrected) of the other learners and learners can read them at home.

6.7 What do you know now?

How can we travel safely?

> **Learning to learn:** Learners have the opportunity to reflect and evaluate their own learning success.

- Reintroduce the question from the start of the unit: *How can we travel safely?* Discuss learners' responses to the question now and compare them with their comments at the beginning of the unit. How much has changed?

- Learners work through the questions individually or in pairs. Circulate and offer support as needed.

Answers
1 Learner's own answers.
2 Learner's own answers.
3 Learner's own answers.
4 Learner's own answers.
5 Learner's own answers.
6 /t/, /d/, /Id/
7 Learner's own answers.

Look what I can do!

- There are eight 'can do' statements. Learners read through the checklist and tick the things they can do. Encourage them to reflect on how well they can do these things. Also invite them to think of ways they can improve further, e.g. what strategies they can use, or learn to use.

- If learners find it challenging to read the checklist, look through the unit with them and support them to find the relevant information.

- Finally, ask learners to work through the questions on page 79 of the Workbook. Encourage them to talk about what they enjoyed and also about any further support they might need.

Check your progress 2

Learners answer the eight questions.

Answers

1   Crossword answers:

Across:

2. sweet

5. amazing

8. delicious

10. character

Down:

1. athletic

3. banana

4. playground

6. helmet

7. hide

9. seeds

2   Unit topics:

- Food (Unit 4): *sweet, delicious, banana, seed*

- Adventures (Unit 5): *character, athletic, hide*

- Going places (Unit 6): *playground, helmet, amazing*

  Learner's own answers.

3   Learners correct statements as follows:

1 There isn't ~~some~~ any bread.

2 There is a ~~few~~ little milk in the fridge.

3 ~~Not~~ Don't press too hard on your pencil.

4 ~~Draws~~ Draw a simple stick person.

5 Go ~~in of~~ out of the door and turn right.

6 I ~~ride~~ was riding my bike when it started to rain.

7 The shop is ~~in~~ on the left.

8 There are ~~any~~ some tomatoes.

9 ~~You add~~ Add some colour.

4   Learner's own answers.

5   Learner's own answers.

6   Student A: *see – saw / go – went / run – ran / look – looked / be – was/were / have – had / say – said / stay – stayed.*

Student B: *live – lived / do – did / make – made / try – tried / give – gave / want – wanted / can – could / finish – finished.*

7   Learner's own answers.

>7 Australia

Unit plan

Lesson	Approximate number of learning hours	Outline of learning content	Learning objectives	Resources
1 Weather around the world	1–1.5	Talk about extreme weather around the world	4Ld.03 4Ld.04	Learner's Book Lesson 7.1 Workbook Lesson 7.1 **Digital Classroom:** What country is it? Extreme weather (video and activity)
2 Australia	1–1.5	Discover amazing facts about Australia	4Rm.02 4Rm.01	Learner's Book Lesson 7.2 Workbook Lesson 7.2 **Digital Classroom:** Facts about Australia
3 Animal matters	1–1.5	Give a presentation about a special animal	4Sc.02 4Ug.08	Learner's Book Lesson 7.3 Workbook Lesson 7.3 ⬇ Photocopiable 19 **Digital Classroom:** Present perfect with *for* and *since*
4 Taking a trip	1–1.5	Talk about future plans Write a blog post	4Wca.03 4Ug.06	Learner's Book Lesson 7.4 Workbook Lesson 7.4 ⬇ Photocopiables 20 and 21 ⬇ Differentiated worksheet 7 **Digital Classroom:** Future plans ⬇ Sample answer for Unit 7
5 *Why the Emu Can't Fly*	1–1.5	Read a traditional Aboriginal Australian story	4Rm.02	Learner's Book Lesson 7.5 Workbook Lesson 7.5 **Digital Classroom:** *Why the Emu Can't Fly*: a review
6 Project challenge	1–1.5	Project A: Make an endangered species 'flip-up' class poster Project B: Be international weather reporters!	4Wca.03 4Sc.02	Learner's Book Lesson 7.6 Workbook Lesson 7.6 ⬇ Unit 7 project checklists

(continued)

Cross-unit resources
- ⬇ Unit 7 Audioscripts
- ⬇ End of Unit 7 test
- ⬇ Unit 7 Progress report
- ⬇ Unit 7 Wordlist

BACKGROUND KNOWLEDGE

Unit 7 is about Australia. It covers different types of weather, geographical features and Australian animals.

Learners will talk about (or hear speakers talking about) extreme weather, e.g. a blizzard, drought, flooding, a tropical cyclone (known as a hurricane or typhoon in other parts of the world) and a tornado. They will use adjectives like *blustery*, *thundery*, *turbulent*, *crashing*, *cutting*, *violent* and *fierce*.

Australia is a unique and fascinating country with a variety of rare geographical features. Learners will hear about *deserts, mountain ranges, a coral reef, rock formations, coasts, tropical rainforests,* Uluru, Mount Kosciuszko and the Perth Canyon.

Mount Kosciuszko, in the Kosciuszko National Park, New South Wales, is the highest mountain in mainland Australia. The Perth Canyon is a similar size to the Grand Canyon. It is a submarine canyon that was cut into the seabed by the Swan River, near the coast of Perth. Uluru is the Aboriginal name for Ayers Rock, the famous monolith in central Australia.

The adjective *Aboriginal* is used to refer to inhabitancy or existence in a place since the earliest known time, in particular like Australia.

The reading in Lesson 5 is a traditional Aboriginal Australian tale about why the emu can't fly. The emu is a flightless bird that is native to Australia. Other typical Australian animals are the kangaroo, the kookaburra, the wombat, the dinosaur ant and koala bear.

TEACHING SKILLS FOCUS

Language awareness

What is language awareness?

Language is a vehicle for learning new knowledge. It is therefore vital for you to ensure that language doesn't become a barrier that could limit learners' learning potential. It is recommended that you make yourself aware of the language challenges that learners might face. This is essential in all learning situations, but especially when learners are learning new knowledge through a second or third language. Becoming *language aware* can help you understand how to support learners and maximise knowledge acquisition.

What can I do?

Watch the Cambridge Assessment International Education introductory video called *What is Language Awareness?* The video affirms that language is the key element in communication and, consequently, language awareness should be a high priority for you. To keep learners interested and motivated in the classroom, you should understand how their use of language can affect their understanding, for example knowing when to use conversational language and when to use academic language.

Scaffolding provides the necessary support to help with the language demands of the activities and materials that you use in a lesson. First, you need an idea of your learners' skills and what they already know and understand. Then you can guide learners towards achieving their goals, thereby improving their learning potential. A longer-term objective of scaffolding is making learners more confident and independent.

CONTINUED

Your challenge

How you approach language awareness will depend on your particular learning situation. It may be easier for you to understand the importance of language awareness if you speak other languages in addition to your own. If English isn't your first language, remember the challenges that you (or your peers) faced when learning English. This is especially useful if your first language is also your learners' first language. If English is your first language, but you have acquired other languages, a good starting point could be thinking about the challenges you faced learning other languages.

Look at one of the reading or listening activities in Unit 7 from the perspective of someone with the same knowledge (and skills) as your learners. Try to predict the areas of language that may challenge your learners. Think of ways you could support your learners. For example, if there are lots of new words in the reading, you could create a vocabulary matching pre-reading exercise, or an activity after reading to encourage learners to infer meaning from context.

7.1 Think about it: Weather around the world

LEARNING PLAN

Learning objective	Learning intentions	Success criteria
4Ld.03	• **Listening:** Deduce meaning from context, with little or no support, in a weather report.	• Learners can talk about extreme weather.
4Ld.04	• **Listening:** Understand, with little or no support, specific detail given about the weather in a news report.	• Learners can talk and answer questions about a weather report.
	• **Vocabulary:** *tornado, flood, blizzard, drought, humid, frosty, turbulent, blustery, crashing, cutting, violent, fierce.*	

21st-century skills

Learning to learn: Memorise key phrases.

Materials: Learner's Book pages 111–113; Workbook pages 80–81; Pictures from the internet or large pictures from a book about Australia; Pictures or videos of extreme weather

Starter ideas

Weather words (10 minutes)

- In pairs, ask learners to write six weather words. Share the vocabulary and build up a list of weather words on the board.

- Revise the names of months and seasons (to prepare for Activity 2). Learners ask and answer questions about the weather in particular months/seasons in their country/ies. Check they use the preposition *in* with months (and seasons). For example: *Does it rain/snow in January/in winter? (Yes, it does/No, it doesn't.)*

> **CROSS-CURRICULAR LINKS**
>
> **Geography:** Help learners develop knowledge about climate zones by asking them what they know about weather in different countries. If learners come from different countries, ask them about the weather in their countries.

Getting started (10 minutes)

- Look at the photos on page 111 in the Learner's Book and see if learners can identify them. On the board, build up a list of other famous landmarks in Australia.

- Give clues to help learners guess which country it is.

- Encourage learners to use comparative adjectives to compare Australia with their own country/ies. Write the base form of adjectives on the board as prompts, e.g *big, small, hot, dry, sunny*. Encourage statements like *Australia is smaller than China. It's sunnier than…*

- Allow volunteers 30 seconds to make comparative statements orally. The learner who makes the most statements is the country comparison challenge champion!

Answers

a Sydney Opera House, Uluru (Ayers Rock), the Great Barrier Reef

b Learner's own answers.

> **Digital Classroom:** Use the video 'What country is it?' to introduce the subject of Australia. The i button will explain how to use the video.

Main teaching ideas

1 Adjectives to describe the weather (5 minutes)

- Ask learners what an adjective is. If they are unsure, remind them. Write weather nouns and verbs on the board from the Starter activity, e.g. *rain, raining*. Elicit the adjective *rainy*.

- Allow pairs of learners a minute to write down as many weather adjectives as they can.

- Build up a list of adjectives on the board.

Answers
Learner's own answers.

2 Choose the phrases (5 minutes)

- Ask learners to look at the phrases – check they understand the meaning of each one.

- Elicit example sentences on the board. For example: *…January it's….; …spring it's…* Encourage the use of adverbs of frequency: *In Malaga it's always hot in summer.*

- Learners choose the phrases that describe their weather and write sentences that include the month(s).

Answers
Learner's own answers.

3 Describe the weather (5 minutes)

- Learners imagine they are talking to someone from another country. They should use the sentences they wrote in the previous activity to describe the weather. Invite learners to demonstrate.

Answers
Learner's own answers.

> **Digital Classroom:** Use the video 'Extreme weather' to explore the subject of extreme weather. The i button will explain how to use the video.

4 Match the words to the pictures (5 minutes)

- The aim of this activity is to pre-teach vocabulary for the listening activity, and to encourage learners to make predictions about what they will hear.

- Ask learners if there are any words that they can match, before looking at the activity together.

Answers

a   a blizzard

b   a drought

c   a flood

d   a cyclone

e   a tornado

5 Listen and answer the questions (5 minutes)

- There is lots of information in the recording. Two main strategies can help overcome the challenges this could cause learners. Before listening, encourage learners to make predictions about the extreme weather words they might hear. Also, make clear that learners do not have to understand every detail, just the general idea. Don't worry about the difficult adjectives because there is an activity about these later.

- If helpful, pause and repeat the recording. You could also download the audioscript and underline the words; this will help learners understand the answers. Although the answer about weather is *tropical storm*, offer learners praise and encouragement even if they only identify part of the answer, e.g. *strong wind*.

Audioscript: Track 41

See Learner's Book page 113.

Male weather reporter: Good morning, I'm Brad Neilston reporting from the south-western coast of Australia. Well, as you can see there are thundery skies today and a blustery wind is howling – as you can probably hear too! 80 kilometres-per-hour winds have been recorded this morning and they are getting stronger and stronger. The sea is really turbulent – just look at the waves crashing onto the shore. Most boats and ships are now in port, but as you can see, some boats are rocking violently out at sea.

Weather experts report that this violent storm could become a tropical cyclone in a short time, which could blow down trees and power lines. So, the authorities are recommending that everyone stays in their houses and all schools will be closed until the storm passes. You mustn't go out on the streets because it's very dangerous right now. I can hardly stand up because of the fierce and cutting wind, so I'm going back to the studio to shelter until the storm passes because it's quite frightening out here right now!

Brad Nielston reporting for Channel 6 news.

Answers
A tropical storm, in Australia, on the south-western coast.

6 Match the adjectives and nouns (5–10 minutes)

- Explain that there are some words that we often use together (usually an adjective with a noun), and that we call pairs of words like these *collocations*. Tell learners that learning *collocations* is a useful way to build their knowledge of vocabulary.

- Elicit or give examples (from the audio or elsewhere), e.g. *blustery wind*.

- In groups of 3–4, learners try to match the adjectives and nouns they heard on the audio. Don't reveal the answers just yet. Give learners the opportunity to re-listen and check.

7 Listen again and check (5 minutes)

- Re-play the audio, pausing where necessary, for learners to check their answers.

- Practise repeating and trying to memorise the collocations from the audio.

Answers

blustery/cutting/violent/fierce/strong wind

thundery sky

turbulent sea

crashing waves

8 Use the adjectives to complete the sentences (5 minutes)

- Focus on the first sentence and elicit the correct adjectives.

- Allow learners time to fill in the other four adjectives in pairs before giving feedback.

Answers

a We have **thundery** skies today and a **blustery** wind is howling.

b The sea is **turbulent** and I can see waves crashing onto the shore.

c Weather experts report that this **violent** storm could become a tropical cyclone in a short time.

d I can hardly stand up because of the **fierce** and **cutting** wind.

9 What is the worst weather you have ever seen? (10 minutes)

- Learners talk in pairs about the worst weather they have seen in their countries. Encourage the use of comparative adjectives and the adjectives from Activities 6 and 7.

> **Differentiation ideas:** If learners need support with this task, give them a worksheet with prompts. Include questions like: *Have you ever seen a big thunderstorm? What happened? How long did it last? Where were you? Were you afraid? Did the lightning hit anything?*

10 Safety advice (5 minutes)

- Write *You shouldn't…* and *You should…* on the board and elicit suggestions.

> **Digital Classroom:** Use the activity 'Extreme weather' to revise extreme weather vocabulary. The i button will explain how to use the activity.

Plenary ideas

Consolidation (10–15 minutes)

- Learners write a short paragraph about the worst weather they have seen in their country, using the weather vocabulary from the lesson and superlative adjectives.

> **Assessment ideas:** When learners have finished their paragraph, ask them to exchange it with a partner. They give each other feedback on punctuation, the use of superlative adjectives and weather vocabulary.

Homework ideas

Workbook

Questions 1–5 on pages 80–81.

- Learners find out about one of the extreme weather conditions shown in the photos on page 112 and write a paragraph about it.

7.2 Geography: Australia

LEARNING PLAN

Learning objective	Learning intentions	Success criteria
4Rm.02 4Rm.01	• **Reading:** Read, with support, a non-fiction text with confidence and enjoyment. • **Reading:** Understand with support, some of the main points in a factual text about Australia. • **Vocabulary:** *desert, mountain range, coral reef, rock formation, coast, tropical rainforest, length, width, depth, height.*	• Learners can talk about and answer questions on a factual text about Australia. • Learners can answer questions on the main numerical points in the factual text about Australia.

21st-century skills

Critical thinking: Explain preferences to visit some places more than others and rank the places from 1–5 according to how interesting they are.

Critical thinking: Compare information on two separate countries.

Materials: Learner's Book pages 114–115; Workbook pages 82–83; Pictures or videos about Australia that are suitable for young learners, from the internet or library: try the National Geographical kids' website as a starting point – go to the home page and search for 'Australia'

Starter ideas

Would you like to visit…? (10 minutes)

- Generate interest in Australia by showing pictures or videos (see Materials). To pre-teach the vocabulary for Lesson 7.2, include a variety of different places and scenery, including a desert, a mountain range, a coral reef, a rock formation, the coast and a tropical rainforest. If possible, show pictures of the landmarks that are mentioned in the text (Uluru, Mount Kosciuszko and the Perth Canyon).

- Learners ask and answer questions using *Would you like to visit…?* about different places of interest.

- You could ask two learners to demonstrate the activity.
  For example:
  Speaker A: *Would you like to visit Uluru?*
  Speaker B: *Yes, I'd love to.*
  Speaker A: *Why?*
  Speaker B: *It looks fantastic! It sounds like the coolest place in Australia!*

❯ **Critical thinking opportunity:** Learners explain why they would like to visit some places more than others and rank the places from 1–5 according to how interesting they are (1 = the most fascinating, 5 = the most boring).

Main teaching ideas

1 Talk about the questions (10 minutes)

CROSS-CURRICULAR LINKS

Geography: Elicit the location of Australia on a world map. Ask learners if they know the names of the nearest countries to Australia.

- The aim of this activity is to see what learners already know about Australia and to elicit/pre-teach vocabulary for the reading task by making predictions about what learners might read. For example, 1a asks about the size of Australia. Pre-teach the vocabulary in the text by encouraging guesses about *how many million square kilometres* Australia occupies, and if it is the *second/third/etc. biggest country* in the world. Repeat for the other questions, but don't reveal the answers; learners will read the text to confirm their ideas later.

Answers
Learner's own answers.

2 Geographical features (10 minutes)

- If you have already shown pictures of these features in the Starter activity, learners should be able to match them to the pictures on the map. If not, encourage them to guess before giving the correct answers.

Answers
(See the map on Learner's Book page 114.)

3 Read and listen and Reading tip (10–15 minutes)

- Look at the Reading tip together. Then focus on the number in the first sentence of the fact file: *The population of Australia is 25 million.* Ask for estimates of the populations of learners' own country/ies. Discuss whether Australia has a relatively large or small population. (**Note:** In some countries, e.g. the UK, a comma is used to separate large numbers. In other countries a point is used. In the UK a point is used in decimals, whereas other countries use a comma.)

- Allow learners 10 minutes to read the fact file and find the answers to Activity 1.

- Give class feedback on the answers.

〉 **Differentiation ideas:** If learners need support to find the answers, give them a copy of the fact file with the relevant sentences underlined. For example: *Australia is the sixth largest country in the world…* Circulate and, if necessary, elicit suggestions about the answers.

Audioscript: Track 42
See Learner's Book page 114.

Answers
a   Yes, it's the sixth-largest country in the world.
b   Many types of people. The Aboriginal people are the only people native to the country.
c   Kangaroos and blue whales.
d   The Perth Canyon, the Great Barrier Reef, Mount Kosciuszko, Uluru (Ayers Rock)

4 Measurements and Match the numbers (10 minutes)

- Focus on the measurement words. Demonstrate their meaning by miming measuring these dimensions using a classroom object, like a desk. Practise the pronunciation, especially the difference between the 'th' and 'ht'.

- Demonstrate the activity to the class. Focus on the first number and elicit how to say it (*25 million*). Match it to the population of Australia (b). If necessary, repeat for the other numbers.

Answers
25,000,000 people; 6th largest country in the world; 7.7 million square kilometers land mass; 1/5 people who live in Australia were born in other countries

5 Types of natural environment (10–15 minutes)

- Ask learners to recall the natural environments mentioned in Activity 2 (*desert, mountain range, coral reef, rock formation, coast, tropical rainforest*). Elicit that the most likely place to find this information is in the *Geography* section. Re-read and look for the words about natural landscapes.

Answers
Three of: desert, mountain range, tropical rainforest, coral reef, coastline.

6 Similarities and differences (5 minutes)

> **Critical thinking opportunity:** Learners use the fact file to help them compare information about their country/ies and Australia, by finding two differences and two similarities.

- Support learners by asking questions. For example: *Which is bigger/drier? Which has a bigger population? Are there any mountain ranges/coral reefs in your country? Does your country have a coastline? How long is it?*

> **Digital Classroom:** Use the activity 'Facts about Australia' to reinforce reading comprehension of the Australia fact file. The i button will explain how to use the activity.

Plenary ideas

Big number bingo (5 minutes)

- Write about fifteen big numbers on the board in figures, e.g. 22,000,000, and practise saying them. Learners choose five of the numbers and write

them down. Call out the numbers for learners to cross off. The winner is the learner who crosses off all their numbers first.

Homework ideas

| **Workbook** |
| Questions 1–6 on pages 82–83. |

- Learners write a paragraph comparing Australia to their own country. Tell them to include some facts and figures.

> **Assessment ideas:** Give written feedback on the paragraph, focusing particularly on how well facts and figures, comparatives and link words like *and*, *both* and *but* have been used.

7.3 Talk about it: Animal matters

LEARNING PLAN		
Learning objective	**Learning intentions**	**Success criteria**
4Sc.02	• **Speaking:** Describe an animal using a short sequence of sentences.	• Learners can give a presentation about a special animal.
4Ug.08	• **Use of English:** Use present perfect forms of common verbs to express what has happened (indefinite time). • **Vocabulary:** *kookaburra, lung fish, dinosaur ant.*	• Learners can complete sentences using the present perfect.
21st-century skills		
Critical thinking: Sort and classify animals according to key features.		
Learning to learn: Summarise information and make notes on key topics for their presentations.		

Materials: Learner's Book pages 116–117; Workbook pages 84–85; A list of endangered species: for example, see the species directory on the WWF website; YouTube clip of a kookaburra's 'laugh'; Information about animals from learners' countries for the presentation activity; **Photocopiable 19**

Present perfect

The focus of the Language detective in this lesson is the present perfect, which is formed using the present tense of the verb *have* + past participle. The present perfect is used to refer to experiences up to the present time. For example: *I have been to Australia. I have visited India.*

In Unit 5, learners met the past simple, which is another tense used to express past actions. The difference between the two tenses is that the present perfect:

- focuses more on, or gives more emphasis to, an action, and/or the duration of a state
- can be used to imply that the action hasn't finished.

Here are a couple of examples:

Past simple	Present perfect
I visited India last year. (specified time)	*I have visited India.* (time not specified, so the focus is on the life experience up to the present time).
They lived on Earth for 100 million years. (They don't live on Earth now.)	*They have lived on Earth for 100 million years.* (They still live on Earth.)

Common misconceptions

Misconception	How to identify	How to overcome
Learners may not use the correct pronoun in present perfect sentences, e.g.: *He ~~have~~ has posted some great photos in his blog.*	Write '*I visit India*' '*He visits India*' and '*They visit India*' on the board. Ask learners to rewrite the three sentences in the present perfect.	Practise: Ask learners to complete the 'Focus' and 'Practice' activities on pages 84–85 of the Workbook.

Starter ideas

Mini animal dialogues (5–10 minutes)

- Have a competition to see which team can write the names of the most animals in 1 minute. Encourage teams to write names of Australian animals by giving a bonus point for each one.
- Allow learners 2 minutes to ask each other questions about the animals. Write example questions and answers on the board, e.g. *Have you ever seen a koala? Yes, I have/No, never. Would you like to see a kangaroo? Yes, I'd love to/No, not really.*

Main teaching ideas

1 Talk about the questions (5–10 minutes)

- Help learners to write lists of animals that live in their country/ies.

- Elicit the meaning of *wild, common* and *rare*, and write the headings *Common animals* and *Rare animals* on the board.

> **Critical thinking opportunity:** Tell learners to sort the animals from their lists into the two categories. Tell them to mark *Common animals* with a C and *Rare animals* with an R. If they find this hard, ask questions to help them, e.g. *Do you often see them? Have you ever seen one?/When did you last see one?* Ask learners to discuss in groups why they think the animals they have marked with an 'R' are rare, before sharing ideas as a class.

- Demonstrate what *endangered* means. Show a list and images of endangered animals (see Materials). Discuss why some animals are endangered.

- Allow learners time to discuss the last question from d in pairs, before giving class feedback.

Answers

a   Learner's own answers.

b   Learner's own answers.

c   Suggested answer: (over) hunting (people kill animals too often for clothes or food); the place where they live has been destroyed, etc.

d   Endangered means at risk. Learner's own answers.

2   Look and talk (5–10 minutes)

* Don't worry too much about the correct answers at this stage. The main aim is to pre-teach necessary vocabulary for the listening activity.

* Check learners know the meaning of *habitat*. Give examples of different habitats.

* Focus on the first picture and elicit what is special about the laughing kookaburra. Confirm by playing a clip (there are plenty on YouTube) of a kookaburra's 'laugh'.

* Elicit the meaning of *lung* and *dinosaur*. Learners guess why the lung fish and dinosaur ant have these names. Make suggestions about their habitats.

Answers
Learner's own answers.

3   Listen to Laura (5 minutes)

* Make clear that learners do not need to understand every word of the presentation at this stage. They just need to say which of the three animals from the pictures Laura is talking about. They will listen again for more details.

* Play the audio once and check learners know which animal Laura is talking about.

Audioscript: Track 43

See Learner's Book page 116.

Hello everyone!

Today I'm going to talk about the dinosaur ant. It lives in Australia. It's a rare type of ant, which first appeared on Earth 92 million years ago! This is why it was given the name 'dinosaur' because it lived on Earth at the same time as the dinosaurs. It has a brown body and big black eyes, and it

likes eating seeds, meat and termites. Curiously, it likes to work at night, unlike other ants who work during the day.

Unfortunately, it is an endangered species as its numbers have reduced. Many colonies have died because of climate change and bushfires, which have destroyed their habitat and homes.

I have been to Australia, but I have never seen a dinosaur ant in real life. I've watched some animal documentaries about them, and I'd really like to see a real dinosaur ant one day!

Answers
Dinosaur ant

4   Listen again (5–10 minutes)

* Before listening for the information, ask learners to copy the chart. Encourage predictions. Play the audio and check learners' predictions.

Answers

Name	Dinosaur ant
Curious fact	They work at night
Country	Australia
Characteristics	Brown bodies, big, black eyes
Diet	Seeds, meat and termites
Endangered species (Yes/No)	Yes
Reasons	Climate change and bushfires have destroyed their habitat

5   Listen, repeat and practise the short form of *have* (5 minutes)

* This is a useful activity as learners commonly mispronounce *have*. Play the audio and check learners pronounce the short forms correctly.

Audioscript: Track 44

See Learner's Book page 117.

I have = I've

You have = you've

He/She has = he's/she's

We have = we've

You have = you've

They have = they've

Language detective (10 minutes)

- This lesson's Language detective concentrates on the present perfect, which learners may have heard in the listening activity.

- First, read the examples in the Language detective together and/or elicit examples from the audio. If necessary, download the audioscript, highlight the uses of the present perfect and write these sentences on the board: *The dinosaur ant has existed since 92 million years ago. Their numbers have reduced. Many colonies have died. Climate change and bushfires have destroyed their habitat and homes.*

- Note: Learners can practise question formation (*you, he* and *she*) on **Photocopiable 19.**

> **Digital Classroom:** Use the grammar presentation to revise the Present perfect. The i button will explain how to use the grammar presentation.

Workbook

For further practice of the present perfect, learners look at the Language detective and complete questions 1–3 on pages 84–85.

---

6 Complete the sentences (10 minutes)

- Focus on part a. Elicit the correct answer. Learners complete the other sentences in pairs.

> **Differentiation ideas:** Learners could complete the activity in mixed-ability pairs. More confident writers could provide language support to their partners.

Answers

a   has lived

b   have died

c   have destroyed

d   heard

e   has done

---

7 Do a presentation (20 minutes)

- Write *lung fish* and *kookaburra* on the board. Revisit the learners' suggestions of interesting animals from the Starter activity. Ask learners to vote for the most interesting ones. Create a shortlist of five animals.

- Before learners choose which animal to write the presentation on, create a mind map about each animal. Ask questions to elicit the information in the chart from Activity 4. For example: *Which country is the animal from?*

> **Learning to learn:** Learners could do their research at home by summarising information and making notes for their presentations. Or, if you have access to animal books or the internet in the classroom, learners could work in pairs or small groups to do the research.

- Learners use the information from the chart to form the basis of their presentations.

- You could give learners a copy of the transcript of Laura's presentation to use as a model.

> **Assessment ideas:** When learners are delivering their presentations, check that they are written in sentences and use present perfect forms of common verbs. Make notes on areas where learners might benefit from further support.

Plenary ideas

Consolidation (5 minutes)

- Ask and answer *How long have you…?* questions with stative verbs like *be, have, know, like* and *want*. For example: *How long have you liked your favourite food?*

Homework ideas

Workbook

Questions 1–3 on pages 84–85.

7.4 Write about it: Taking a trip

LEARNING PLAN

Learning objective	Learning intentions	Success criteria
4Wca.03 4Ug.06	• **Writing:** Plan, write, edit and proofread a short sequence of sentences in a paragraph, with support. • **Use of English:** Use present continuous forms with future meaning. • **Vocabulary:** *snorkelling, turtles, rubbish, conservation, conservationist, poison.*	• Learners can plan, write, edit and proofread a blog post. • Learners can use present continuous forms with future meaning to write a blog post about their weekend.

21st-century skills

Communication: Talk about their day, interests and other suitable topics; Share ideas with a peer before displaying on a school blog.

Materials: Learner's Book pages 118–119; Workbook pages 86–87; Paper (see Starter activity); **Photocopiables 20 and 21; Differentiated worksheet 7**

LANGUAGE BACKGROUND

Present continuous with future meaning

The present continuous can be used with future meaning. This is the subject of the Language detective in this lesson.

You can use the present continuous to talk about personal arrangements or fixed plans in the near future, especially if you have decided a time and a place with another person/other people. For example:

*Tomorrow, **we're having** a party.*

***I'm meeting** Chi at 11am at Central Café.*

Common misconceptions

Misconception	How to identify	How to overcome
A common error is using *will* to talk about future arrangements. For example: *My friends and I will go for a picnic tomorrow.* *Will* is used for predictions, promises, spontaneous decisions or future facts, so this sentence sounds unnatural.	Write sentences with *will* and the present continuous. Elicit their function. For example: • *I'll have a sandwich, please.* (spontaneous decision) • *We're having sandwiches for* lunch. (something that has been arranged) • *I'll bring a cake tomorrow.* (promise) • I think there will be sandwiches at the party. (prediction)	Encourage learners to think about the purpose of what they are saying. They should ask themselves whether they want to express: • something that is pre-arranged, usually with another person: in this case, use the present continuous • a prediction: use *will/ going to* • a promise: use *will* • a spontaneous decision: use *will* • a future fact: use *will*. Practise talking about arrangements (see Photocopiable 21).
Learners often use the *present simple* to talk about arrangements, when the *present continuous* is more appropriate. In these cases, the present simple form can sound very unnatural. For example: *I have a party next Saturday. Do you come?*	Write sentences in the present simple and in the present continuous. Elicit which are habits and which are arrangements. *Jim has a party every year. Do you usually go?* *Jim is having a party on Saturday. Are you going to Jim's party?*	

Starter ideas

Holiday miming game (5 minutes)

• On pieces of paper, draw (or write down) activities people do on holiday or business trips. Ask a volunteer to come to the front. Give the volunteer a piece of paper with an activity, e.g. skiing. Ask him/her to mime it. Learners guess the activity and write: [Learner's name] *is skiing.* Continue with other activities. Encourage learners to use the present continuous, as this is covered in the Language detective.

• Take the opportunity to pre-teach words from the blog, e.g. *snorkelling, wildlife, conservation project, endangered species.* Check that learners can remember what endangered means.

Main teaching ideas

1 Talk about why you would take a trip away from home (5 minutes)

• On the board, build up a list of reasons for taking a trip away from home. Ask learners how they can keep in touch with people when they're away.

Answers
Learner's own answers.

2 Read Jack's blog (5–10 minutes)

• Check learners understand the suggestions in a–c and what is meant by *main purpose*.

• Explain that Jack gives lots of details about his trip, but learners only need to identify the most important purpose.

Answers
b

3 What does Jack say about the words in blue? (5 minutes)

• Focus on the first blue word: *snorkelling*. Elicit the correct answer, then do the same for the other blue words (*turtles, rubbish*).

Answers

Snorkelling: He went snorkelling earlier in the day/ He went for the third time.

Turtles: They are an endangered species in this part of Australia/ He has seen two turtles since Tuesday.

Rubbish: His mum collects rubbish from the beach and sea and tests it to see if it contains poisons that can kill turtles.

4 Look at Day 1 and answer the questions (10 minutes)

- Focus on the three questions about Day 1.
- Learners re-read the Day 1 paragraph and look for the answers.
- Ask learners which tense they would expect the information to be written in.

Answers

a He's feeling scared because there are dangerous snakes and spiders.

b He travelled to the campsite from Darwin and ate dinner under the stars.

c They are travelling to the beach so his mum can do her work and they are having a picnic on the beach.

Language detective (5 minutes)

- This lesson's Language detective concentrates on the present continuous with future meaning. The present continuous, for activities in progress, was covered in Unit 2. So learners should already know how to form the present continuous but may not know it can be used with future meaning. Check learners' understanding and elicit how to form the present continuous if necessary.

- Then look at the example in the Language detective. Check learners know that this sentence refers to a future time. Ask concept check questions, such as: *We can use the present continuous for activities happening now; is this activity happening now? (No.) How do we know it refers to the future and not now? (Tomorrow.)*

> **Digital Classroom:** Use the activity 'Future plans' to revise the present continous for future plans. The i button will explain how to use the activity.

> **Workbook**

For further practice of the present continuous for future plans, learners look at the Language detective and complete activities 1–3 on pages 86–87.

---

5 Find more examples (5 minutes)

- Learners re-read the blog and underline the other examples of the present continuous. Then they re-read the sentences carefully and decide if each action is in the future or the present. Elicit which words helped learners make this decision. Learners should choose the following as examples of present continuous for activities in progress: *I'm sitting in my tent. We're camping tonight in the outback. I'm feeling scared.*

Answers

Tomorrow we're travelling to the beach so my mum can do her work. We're having a picnic there too!

6 Make notes and Writing tip (5–10 minutes)

- Learners write notes about Jack and his family in the correct order. The aim of this activity is to provide a model of the writing process for learners to follow when writing their own blog.

- Before learners start, ask them to read the Writing tip. Make sure they know that they only have to write key words when they're making notes, not full sentences.

Answers

Suggested notes:

Day 1: 7 o'clock – set off from Darwin, ate dinner under the stars, camping in the outback.

Day 2: travelling to the beach so his mum can work, having a picnic

Day 4: Morning - dad and Jack snorkelling in the sea – saw lots of different fish, two turtles

Day 5: Morning, (dad and Jack) boat trip and helping Mum to collect rubbish from the beach.

7 Write a blog post about your weekend (20 minutes)

- Learners follow the three steps to write their blog entry. Make sure they understand they need to imagine that now is Saturday evening. Get them to mime what they would be doing on Saturday evening.

- Elicit suggestions for Step 1 about things learners have done, what they are doing now and their plans for the next day.

- In Step 2, help learners write sentences, using the present perfect and present continuous appropriately. Encourage them to start consulting the checklist on **Photocopiable 20**.

> **Communication:** In Step 3, let learners read the different blogs, compare the differences and similarities about their weekends, and offer suggestions and compliments.

> **Differentiation ideas:** This may be a good opportunity for learners to do **Differentiated worksheet 7**.

- Once the blog has been written, focus again on the writing checklist on **Photocopiable 20**.

> **Assessment ideas:** Print out the sample answer. Ask learners to assess it against **Photocopiable 20** before they finalise their blog posts.

8 Display or publish your work (5 minutes)

- Learners display their blogs in the classroom, in a portfolio or on a school blog/website.

Plenary ideas

One minute presentation! (5–10 minutes)

- Invite learners to present their blogs to the class, in a maximum of 60 seconds.

- Learners could do **Photocopiable 21**.

Homework ideas

> **Workbook**
>
> Questions 1–3 on pages 86–87.

- Learners write a paragraph about a trip they are planning.

> **Assessment ideas:** Give written feedback on the paragraph, focusing on the use of the present perfect/present continuous, and adjectives for designing places and activities.

7.5 Read and respond: *Why the Emu Can't Fly*

LEARNING PLAN		
Learning objective	**Learning intentions**	**Success criteria**
4Rm.02	• **Reading:** Read with support a traditional Aboriginal story with confidence and enjoyment. • **Vocabulary:** *jealous, wings, get about, flew away, fool, huge, swiftly, striding, race, sprinted, flapped, landing, rushed at, striking out, puzzled, foolish.*	• Learners can answer questions on a traditional Aboriginal story.
21st-century skills		
Learning to learn: Use pictures to follow a storyline.		
Critical thinking: Explain why things happen.		

Materials: Learner's Book pages 120–123; Workbook pages 88–89; Books containing traditional stories that are popular in the learners' country(ies); Pictures of Indigenous Australians

Starter ideas

Have you read…? (5–10 minutes)

- Ask learners if they know what a traditional story is. Elicit suggestions and then, to gain learners' interest, show the traditional storybooks. Explain what happens in one or two of them.

- Explain that in this lesson they are going to read a traditional Aboriginal Australian story. Briefly tell/remind learners about the Aboriginal Australians and show some pictures of them, if available

Main teaching ideas

1 What traditional stories do you know from your country? (5–10 minutes)

- Allow pairs of learners a few minutes to write down as many traditional stories as they can from their country.

  > **Differentiation ideas:** Give more confident speakers additional questions about traditional stories from their country, e.g. *What happened? Who is the main character?*

- Share the list, then ask and answer the other questions as a class.

Answers
Learner's own answers.

 2 Read and listen (5–10 minutes)

- The story contains lots of information for learners of this level. It is important that reading is enjoyable, so learners should apply the reading strategies they have been developing.

- Make predictions about who the main characters will be. Ask learners who they can see (a turkey and an emu) and *What's happening?* For example: *The emu is running and the turkey is flying, and the turkey is feeding his chicks.*

Answers
Emu and Brush Turkey

Audioscript: Track 45
See Learner's Book pages 120–122.

3 Read and answer the questions (15 minutes)

- Before reading each part of the story, read out the related questions and invite predictions from learners. Pre-teach useful words, like *jealous, wings, get about, flew away, a fool.*

Answers
a   He was jealous.
b   Because only strong birds can get about by walking.
c   He walked.
d   They took off their wings.
e   Brush Turkey.
f   He was angry and sad. He hit the Brush Turkey with his powerful legs.
g   He flew away laughing.
h   It was difficult to find food for all his children.
i   Keep two strong, healthy chicks.
j   He sent all but two of his chicks away.
k   The Emu laughed and told the Brush Turkey he was a fool. 'A bird's strength lies not in his ability to use his wings, but in the number of his children.'

4 What do you think was the true reason that made Emu lose his wings? (5 minutes)

> **Critical thinking opportunity:** Encourage learners to make suggestions and to justify their opinions. Support learners by building up useful vocabulary on the board.

Answers
b – Brush Turkey was jealous of Emu and wanted to hurt him.

5 The message in the story (5 minutes)

- Discuss what the message of the story could be as a class.

Answers
Learner's own answers, e.g. don't believe everything people tell you, jealousy is a powerful feeling.

6 Match the synonyms (5–10 minutes)

- Point out the first of the blue words: *huge*. Repeat the whole sentence and read the suggested synonyms. Encourage learners to guess the meaning of *huge*. Repeat for the other blue words.

Answers

quickly = swiftly

confused = puzzled

very big = huge

silly = foolish

story = tale

hitting = striking out

7 Match the words in green (5–10 minutes)

- Focus on the first green word, *striding*. Read the sentences before and after and encourage learners to guess the meaning from the context.

- Ask learners to work in pairs to match the other green words.

› **Differentiation ideas:** If learners need support with this task, look at the rest of the words together in a separate group.

Answers

a flapped

b race

c striding

d sprinted

e rushed at

f landing

› **Digital Classroom:** Use the activity 'Why emus can't fly: a review' to reinforce reading comprehension of the story. The i button will explain how to use the activity.

8 Values: What to do if you feel jealous (5 minutes)

- Check learners understand the word *jealous* by asking them what sort of things make them feel jealous and *why*.

- Ask and answer the questions as a class.

Answers

a Learner's own answers.

b Think about the good things in your own life and focus on those things.

Plenary ideas

Consolidation (10 minutes)

- There are lots of engaging and fascinating children's books, of various levels, featuring Australian animals.

- Read learners one example, for instance *Aussie Animals* by Rod Campbell (particularly good for less confident readers).

Homework ideas

> **Workbook**
>
> Questions 1–4 on pages 88–89.

- Learners look for a story they like about an animal/ animals (in the library, second-hand bookshop or on the internet – with adult supervision) and bring it to class.

7.6 Project challenge

LEARNING PLAN

Learning objective	Learning intentions	Success criteria
4Wca.03	• **Writing:** Plan, write, edit and proofread a short sequence of sentences in a paragraph, with support.	• Learners can write, edit and proofread an endangered species 'flip-up' class poster.
4Sc.02	• **Speaking:** Describe people, places and objects, and routine past and present actions and events, using a short sequence of sentences.	• Learners can present an international weather report using a short sequence of sentences.

21st-century skills

Communication: Share ideas with peers before a writing/speaking task.

Collaboration: Participate in a shared project, collaborating with others when making choices and decisions.

Materials: Learner's Book pages 124–125; Workbook page 90; **Unit 7 project checklists**; Examples of similar projects (if you don't have examples from previous learners, look on the internet); Books, magazines, pictures or videos about endangered species that are suitable for young learners, e.g. search for 'National Geographic meet some of the world's most endangered animals video' to see a video about endangered animals; Paper/card for making posters; A flip chart stand to show posters (if this isn't available, display on the wall instead); Information about the day's weather in a variety of different countries, from an online or printed source

Starter ideas

Raise interest in the projects (10–15 minutes)

- Tell learners they are either going to make an endangered species 'flip-up' poster or be an international weather reporter.

- Raise interest in the projects by showing examples of children's work on a similar topic from other classes or the internet.

- Revise vocabulary for the challenges in a fun way. For example, for Project B, draw weather symbols on the board. Learners guess what they represent as you are drawing.

- Show a short video clip about endangered species (e.g. see Materials).

Main teaching ideas

Introduce projects (60 minutes)

- Encourage learners to choose one of the projects to work on in pairs or in a group.

- Learners work in pairs or groups, managing and sharing the tasks in the project.

Project A: Make an endangered species 'flip-up' class poster

- Support groups when they are making their lists of endangered species. Encourage each learner to choose one animal that they would like to find out more about.

- The table contains examples of the type of information learners should look for. Make sure they understand the headings in the table and any new vocabulary. Take learners to the school library. Help them to locate information in books and magazines or on the internet (if school rules allow) about their chosen animals.

> **Differentiation ideas:** If groups of learners need support with this project, suggest three or four animals to choose from and bring accessible material about these for your learners to read and interpret.

- Focus on the sentence starters and elicit suggestions about the learners' animals. While learners write their paragraphs, circulate and offer support.

> **Assessment ideas:** Encourage learners to use the checklist to check their paragraphs for errors. Ask them to be as tactful as possible when using the checklist to evaluate other learners' posters.

- Learners display their work on the flip-up poster or the classroom walls.

Project B: Be international weather reporters!

- Elicit and build up a list of countries for learners to choose for their weather report.

- Each group decides on a country to compare with their own country for the weather report. If learners are not all from the same country, tell them to compare two of their countries.

- Help learners make their weather chart, for example by helping them draw an outline of their chosen country. Check learners know that a caption is short text to describe a picture. Elicit ideas for suitable captions. Support learners with any unfamiliar vocabulary.

- Allow time for learners to check the weather online for their chosen country. Circulate and offer support and check that the learners are all working together as a group. If checking on the internet is not practical, distribute information for learners to read, or take the class to the school library to look for information.

- Ask learners to put together the weather reports for their own country and their chosen country using their weather charts and the prompts in step 4. Make sure learners include the name of each country, its outline and the weather report for the day.

- Learners listen to the other groups' presentations. Make sure they have read the checklist before they do this.

> **Assessment ideas:** Encourage learners to be as tactful as possible when using the checklist to evaluate the weather reports.

Plenary ideas

Consolidation (5 minutes)

> **Assessment ideas:** Ask follow-up questions about the posters and weather reports to check understanding/ find out more. For example, *what did you find interesting about their project? How well did your group work together on your project?*

Homework ideas

> **Workbook**
>
> Questions 1–2 on page 90.

- Photocopy the projects (with language mistakes corrected) of the other learners and learners can read them at home.

7.7 What do you know now?

What can we learn about one country?

> **Learning to learn:** Learners have the opportunity to reflect and evaluate their own learning success.

- Reintroduce the question from the start of the unit: *What can we learn about one country?* Discuss learners' responses to the question now and compare them with their comments at the beginning of the unit. How much has changed?

- Focus on the first question. Allow each group of 3–4 learners 1 minute to write down as many examples of extreme weather as possible. Give four points to each group that has written four examples.

- For questions 2, 4, 6 and 7, give four points to the first group to say each answer.

- For questions 3 and 5, groups take turns to recall facts. Build up a list on the board and award one point to each group for each correct fact.

- The winning group is the one with the most points.

Answers

Suggested answers:

1   tornado, flood, blizzard, drought

2   thundery

3   a   It is a big country. There are many different types of people and religions. The currency is the Australian dollar

   b   The landscape is varied. There are deserts and rainforests.

   c   There is little rain in the deserts. It's hot and humid in the rainforest

4   Illegal poaching and loss of habitat due to agriculture

5   Learner's own answers

6   She collected bits of rubbish from the beach and sea. She tested it to see if it contained poisons that could kill the turtles.

7   Brush Turkey tricked Emu into taking off his wings. Emu tricked Brush Turkey into giving his children away.

Look what I can do!

- There are six 'can do' statements. Learners read through the statements and tick the things they can do. Encourage them to reflect on how well they can do these things. Also invite them to think of ways they can improve further, e.g. what strategies they can use, or learn to use.

- If learners find it challenging to read the statements, look through the unit with them and support them to find the relevant information.

- Finally, ask learners to work through the questions on page 91 of the Workbook. Encourage them to talk about what they enjoyed and also about any further support they might need.

〉8 Nature matters

Unit plan

Lesson	Approximate number of learning hours	Outline of learning content	Learning objectives	Resources
1 Nature alert!	1–1.5	Find out about the (environmental) problems our Earth is facing	4Ld.04 4Us.04	Learner's Book Lesson 8.1 Workbook Lesson 8.1 ⬇ Photocopiable 22 ⬇ Differentiated worksheet 8 **Digital Classroom:** Our Earth Relative clauses revision
2 Protecting our planet	1.5–2	Explore how we can change our habits	4Rd.01 4Ug.10	Learner's Book Lesson 8.2 Workbook Lesson 8.2 ⬇ Photocopiable 23 **Digital Classroom:** Recycling What do we have to do?
3 Rethinking our world	1–1.5	Make promises about our environmental habits using **will**	4Sc.03 4Ug.09	Learner's Book Lesson 8.3 Workbook Lesson 8.3 **Digital Classroom:** Which actions are eco-friendly? Promises
4 A personal recount	1–1.5	Write about a visit to a local park, river or coastline	4Wc.02 4Wc.03	Learner's Book Lesson 8.4 Workbook Lesson 8.4 ⬇ Photocopiable 24 **Digital Classroom:** Past simple practice: Beach clean-up Fact or opinion? ⬇ Sample answer for Unit 8
5 *The Future of the Present*	1–1.5	Read a short story about the future of our environment	4Rm.02	Learner's Book Lesson 8.5 Workbook Lesson 8.5 **Digital Classroom:** *The Future of the Present*

(continued)

6 Project challenge	1–1.5	Project A: Make a poster	4Wca.01	Learner's Book Lesson 8.6
			4Wca.02	Workbook Lesson 8.6
		Project B: Design your own recycled monster	4Wc.02	⬇ Unit 8 project checklists

Cross-unit resources

⬇ Unit 8 Audioscripts

⬇ End of Unit 8 test

⬇ Unit 8 Progress report

⬇ Unit 8 Wordlist

BACKGROUND KNOWLEDGE

In Unit 8, learners find out about global environmental problems including air pollution, rising sea levels, plastic pollution, melting ice caps, rubbish and global warming. They explore ways they can protect the Earth and make Earth promises about how they will do so, using the verb *will*.

Lesson 2 encourages learners to *explore rubbish habits*. As well as the literal meaning of *rubbish* (the objects that we throw away), *rubbish* also implies that our habits are bad.

In Lesson 4, learners read about a class's school trip and then write about a school trip they have been on. School trips are known as *field trips* in some countries, e.g. New Zealand, and *excursions* in others. School trips involve learners going on a journey with their teachers away from

school, usually for educational purposes. They learn through experience and observation. Many school trips are day trips in the local area, but often teenage learners visit places that are further afield and spend several days away. For example, learners in the UK might visit the European mainland, e.g. Paris. Popular places to visit for young learners include museums, farms, the theatre or a sporting event.

Learners often use clipboards on school trips. These are small boards with a clip at the top to hold sheets of paper still, so they can be written on.

In Lesson 5, learners read a story called *The Future of the Present*, which was written by a girl in the sixth grade called Malini Venkataraman.

TEACHING SKILLS FOCUS

Language strategies

Language strategies

As stated in Unit 7, language is a way of learning new knowledge. It is vital that language doesn't become a barrier that could limit learners' learning potential. With this in mind, it is recommended that you make yourself aware of the language challenges that learners might face.

For introductory information about language awareness, see Unit 7, pages 147–148.

Your challenge

Look at one of the reading activities in Unit 8. Try to look at it from the perspective of a reader with the same knowledge and skills as your learners. Try to predict the challenges that learners may face. For example, a common problem at this level is that learners think they need to translate every word to understand the text. This can lead to them becoming distracted by the words they don't know. If they start looking up every word in

CONTINUED

their dictionary, reading can feel like a chore. Also, because the meaning of most words is dependent on their context, translating word for word is not the best strategy for understanding a sentence.

Think of ways you can support your learners, using scaffolding techniques. For example, if you predict that learners feel they need to understand every word of a reading, photocopy the text and cross out some of the difficult words (not key words). Ask learners to read the text with the missing

words and to tell you what the general meaning is. Learners can then read the complete text. Point out that even with words missing, the main message is still clear.

If learners lack knowledge of key vocabulary, select (a maximum of) five or six key words and pre-teach these using a fun exercise. For example, type each word and each definition on separate pieces of paper and get groups of learners to match them, before reading.

8.1 Think about it: Nature alert

LEARNING PLAN

Learning objective	Learning intentions	Success criteria
4Ld.04	• **Listening:** Understand, with little or no support, the descriptions describing environmental problems.	• Learners can talk about and answer questions on the descriptions describing environmental problems.
4Us.04	• **Use of English:** Use defining relative clauses, *with which, who, that, where,* to describe people and environmental problems.	• Learners can use defining relative clauses to give extra information about people and environmental problems.
	• **Vocabulary:** *air pollution, plastic pollution, rising sea levels, melting ice caps, rubbish, environment, global warming, eco-friendly, environmentalist.*	

21st-century skills

Collaboration: Explain reasons for own suggestions in a simple way; explain why the text is about whatever they suggested.

Learning to learn: Memorise and repeat key phrases.

Materials: Learner's Book pages 127–129; Workbook pages: 92–93; **Photocopiable 22; Differentiated worksheet 8**

LANGUAGE BACKGROUND

Defining relative clauses

The focus of the Language detective in this lesson is defining relative clauses. These are also known as *identifying* or *restrictive relative clauses*. Defining relative clauses give information about a person, object, place or thing. This information is necessary to define the person or thing. Relative clauses join two sentences into one with a relative pronoun. This lesson focuses on the relative pronouns *who*, *which* and *that*.

Who can only be used with people and *which* is used for things. *That* is used with both people and things in defining relative clauses. Don't use subject pronouns (*He/She/It*) with the relative pronoun.

For example:

A   An environmentalist is a person. *He/She* looks after our natural world.

   An environmentalist is a person *who/that* looks after our natural world.

B   Plastic is a material. *It* is dangerous for oceans.

   Plastic is a material *which/that* is dangerous for oceans.

In defining relative clauses, we often omit the object pronoun. For example:

What do you think of the environmentalist (that) you met?

(You cannot delete the relative pronoun in the examples A and B above, because they are the subjects of the sentence.)

Common misconceptions

Misconception	How to identify	How to overcome
Learners of this level often use the pronoun *which* to refer to people, whereas the correct relative pronouns are *who* or *that*. For example: *Tuncay is the person who I like best in the class.* (In this case the pronoun could be omitted because Tuncay is the object of the sentence.)	Write simple *Which* and *Who* questions on the board, but leave out *Which* and *Who*. For example: ____ is your best friend? ____ do you prefer – football or cricket? Elicit whether *Which* or *Who* should be used. Elicit that *who* cannot be used for things and *which* cannot be used for people.	Following this principle, write pairs of sentences on the board and elicit how to join them with a relative pronoun. For example: *Annisa is a classmate. I sit next to her.* *Annisa is the classmate who I sit next to.* *The Seekers is a story. I like it best. The Seekers is the story which I like best.* *English is a subject. I find it the easiest.* *English is the subject which I find the easiest.*

Starter ideas

Environmental danger anagrams (5 minutes)

- Pre-teach useful vocabulary for Lesson 1. Make anagrams for these dangers: *pollution, plastic,* *melting ice, rubbish, rising sea levels*. For example: *loplution* (pollution).

- See which group of learners can unscramble the words first.

Getting started (10 minutes)

- Learners answer questions a–c in pairs before you work through them as a class.

- In part a, learners compare the two photos. Elicit vocabulary like pollution, plastic and rubbish.

- Explain that when learners answer part b, they should use the present continuous.

- For part c, remind learners that they are using adjectives to describe their feelings.

- Watch the video about global environmental problems, which is a useful introduction to the unit.

Answers
a   One shows the beach clean and tidy. The other photo shows the beach polluted and covered in rubbish.

b   Pollution

c   Learner's own answers

> **Digital Classroom:** Use the video 'Our Earth' to introduce the subject of environmental problems. The i button will explain how to use the video.

Main teaching ideas

1 Works of art (5 minutes)

- The main aim of this activity is to interest learners in the topic and start to build up a list of useful vocabulary they will hear in Activity 3.

- Focus on each work of art. Learners describe what they see in the pictures.

- As a class, encourage speculation about what the pictures are trying to tell us. Take the opportunity to start building up and consolidating useful vocabulary for Activity 3, e.g. *air pollution, plastic pollution, rising sea levels, melting ice caps, rubbish, environment, global warming, eco-friendly, environmentalist.*

Answers
Learner's own answers.

2 Match the environmental problems to the art (5 minutes)

- This activity checks that learners are familiar with vocabulary they will hear in Activity 3. As a class, match the words in the box to the pictures.

Answers
a   melting ice caps

b   rising sea levels

c   air pollution

d   plastic pollution

3 Listen and match (5 minutes)

- Check learners understand the meaning of *dangerous*, *factories* and *flooding*. Ask for predictions about what they will hear, and encourage learners to repeat and memorise key phrases they will hear, e.g. how *factories, flooding* and *plastics* could be *dangerous*.

- Learners memorise and repeat key phrases.

- Explain that there is a lot of information in the descriptions. Learners just need to listen for specific words and expressions to identify the artwork being described.

- If helpful, pause the audio after the first description and elicit which picture the speaker is referring to, before moving on to the other descriptions.

CROSS-CURRICULAR LINKS

Science and Geography: Ask learners to say whether each photo is linked to climate change/global warming, pollution, or both.

Audioscript: Track 46

See Learner's Book page 128.

1   Did you know that air pollution from cars and factories is dangerous for our environment? The heat from these dangerous gases is absorbed by the sea and as it gets hotter it needs more space.

2   So what happens to the sea if it needs more space? Well, it needs to take more of the land we live on, which means sea levels rise. This means there will be more flooding and cities like Venice will eventually disappear.

3   The Earth's ice caps are also melting faster than usual, which is also causing the sea level to rise.

4   Another problem for the sea is plastic and other types of rubbish which humans don't need anymore. Plastic is a big problem for our seas, as it's very dangerous for marine life, so we need to be more eco-friendly by respecting our environment and recycling plastic products. If you're worried about the future of our planet you could become an environmentalist who is someone who tries to protect nature and animals from the effects of climate change.

Answers
1c   2b   3a   4d

Language detective (10 minutes)

* Start by looking at the sentences in the Language detective. Ask learners to point out the relative pronouns.

* Then focus on the relative clauses. Elicit that a relative clause is a useful way to join two shorter sentences together. For example: *An environmentalist is a person. He/she looks after our natural world. An environmentalist is someone <u>who</u> looks after our natural world.*

* See Common misconceptions for common errors and advice on how to overcome them.

* Play the audio again and ask learners to listen for defining relative clauses. Display these on the board. Elicit whether the relative pronoun could be left out: *The Earth's ice caps are also melting faster than usual, <u>which</u> is also causing the sea level to rise.* (NO) *Another problem for the sea is plastic and other types of rubbish <u>which</u> humans don't need anymore.* (Can be omitted or substituted with *that*.) *...you could become an environmentalist <u>who</u> is someone who tries to protect nature and...* (NO)

> **Digital Classroom:** Use the grammar presentation 'Relative clauses revision' to revise defining relative clauses: *who, that, which*. The i button will explain how to use the grammar presentation.

Workbook

For further practice of 'going to', learners look at the Language detective and complete questions 1–3 on pages 94–95.
---

4 Match the sentence halves (10–15 minutes)

* Read out the first halves of the sentences to the class. Check learners know the meaning and pronunciation of the bold words.

* Focus on the first sentence half. Read out the second halves and elicit the correct answer.

* Allow learners time to match the other sentence halves in pairs before giving feedback.

> **Differentiation ideas:** You could put learners in mixed-ability pairs. More confident readers and writers could provide language support.

Answers
1b   2a   3c   4f   5d   6e

5 Read and complete (10 minutes)

* Learners look at the title and the photo. Ask what they can see and encourage suggestions about what the text will be about.

* Learners explain the reasons for their suggestions. They explain why they think the text is about whatever they suggested.

* Before you start the activity, ensure that learners understand defining relative clauses and when to use *who*, *that* or *which*.

* Look at the first gap and elicit the correct answer before allowing learners time to complete the other gaps.

Answers
1   which/that
2   which/that
3   which
4   which
5   who

6 How can you stop plastic from getting into the sea? (10 minutes)

* Write *We should... /We shouldn't...* on the board and elicit suggestions. Learners complete the activity in pairs.

> **Differentiation ideas:** If learners need support with this task, provide them with a prompt sheet. For example: *buy water in plastic bottles/sort rubbish/recycle/re-use/ban the sale of...*

> **Assessment ideas:** Circulate while learners are talking, checking for pronunciation and the use of vocabulary. Encourage more confident speakers to use defining relative clauses, e.g. *The water (that) we drink at school shouldn't come in plastic bottles. We should have a steel bottle that we fill up and re-use.*

Plenary ideas

Consolidation (15 minutes)

* Learners could complete **Photocopiable 22**.

Homework ideas

Workbook

Questions 1–5 on pages 92–93.

> **Differentiation ideas:** Learners complete **Differentiated worksheet 8**.

* Learners write a paragraph about how to stop plastic getting into the sea.

8.2 Environment: Protecting our planet

LEARNING PLAN

Learning objective	Learning intentions	Success criteria
4Rd.01	• **Reading:** Understand, with little or no support, the main points about a scientific-based text.	• Learners can answer questions on text about plastic in our oceans.
4Ug.10	• **Use of English:** Use *have to* to express obligation.	• Learners can use *have to* to express obligation in sentences about the environment.
	• **Vocabulary:** *non-biodegradable, microparticle, reduce, reuse, recycle, ocean, medical products, single use, replace.*	

21st-century skills

Critical thinking: Compare two sets of information and points of view on a topic.

Learning to learn: Summarise information for a selected topic when doing a project.

Materials: Learner's Book pages 130–131; Workbook pages 94–95; **Photocopiable 23**; Photos or images of plastic waste in the sea or on beaches, if possible a sea or ocean near where your learners live (for the Starter activity) – these can be found easily by entering 'plastic in the sea' into a search engine; For the final activity, information about how plastic is recycled and what it can be made into: for example, on the How it works daily website, click on the Environment tab and then search for How are plastic bottles recycled? On the Recycle and recover plastics website, click on Consumers, Kids recycling and then View What Plastics can become (at the bottom of the page)

LANGUAGE BACKGROUND

Have to

The Language focus in this lesson centres on *have to* to express obligation. In British English, *have to* can be used to express an obligation that isn't imposed by the speaker. This can include obligations imposed by laws, rules and regulations, and other people's orders. To express an obligation that is imposed by the speaker, *must* is the preferred form.

The auxiliary verb *do* is used for questions, negatives and short answers. *Don't have to* implies that there is not any obligation to do something. For example:

- We **have to** reduce our use of plastic straws because they pollute our land and water.

- **Do** you **have to** get to school at 8.00 a.m.? Yes, we **do**.

- We **don't have to** go to school on Sundays.

Use *have got to* in informal situations.

Common misconceptions

Misconception	How to identify	How to overcome
Overuse of *must*, when *have to* is more natural. *Must* implies an obligation imposed by the speaker, whereas *has to* is used if there is a general rule. For example: I ~~must get up~~ at 6 o'clock every day. Instead of: I *have to get up at 6 o'clock every day.*	Check learners understand the two different kinds of obligation. Write two example sentences on the board, for example: • *I must wear something nice for the party.* (a personal obligation) • *I have to wear a uniform at school.* (a rule)	Practise. Encourage learners to get into the habit of asking themselves *where* the obligation comes from – either a personal obligation or a general rule. **Note:** Although *must* implies a slightly different meaning in the present, it has no past tense, so in the past tense use *have to* or *needed*.
Using **should** instead of have to. For example: *I can't come on Monday, because I* ~~should~~ *have to go to the dentist.* This misconception usually comes about because of confusion with learners' first languages.	Write these sentences on the board and elicit the difference in meaning. • *You should go to the dentist.* (advice) • *They should be here at 8.30 pm.* (it is very likely or it is ideal/desired) • *They have to be here at 8.30 pm.* (obligation)	Practise using *have to* sentences. Play the *Excuses* game: learners invent excuses for not coming to school, beginning *I can't come to school tomorrow because I have to…* Encourage learners to be as creative as possible. **Note:** Although *should* can also be used in hypothetical cases, it is best not to introduce this use at this level.

Starter ideas

Plastic habits (5 minutes)

- Tell learners they are going to read a text about plastic in the oceans. Gain interest in the topic and generate learners' own ideas about what they will read. Show pictures of beaches and seas, or oceans, contaminated with plastic waste. Elicit words like *medical products, ocean, non-biodegradable, waste, rubbish, tonnes* and *microparticles*, which learners will read in Activity 2. Build up a list of useful words for the reading on the board.

- If necessary, before building up the list, allow learners a few minutes to pool their ideas in groups, while you circulate and offer support by suggesting words they need in English.

Main teaching ideas

1 Look at these things (5 minutes)

- Look at the four images. Answer the questions as a class.
- Take the opportunity to predict what learners will read in the 'Plastic solutions' section of the reading. Ask learners how they can change their habits. Build up suggestions on the board about which habits learners think they need to change.

Answers
All the items are made of plastic. Learner's own answers.

2 Read and listen (10 minutes)

> **Critical thinking opportunity:** Now that learners have some ideas of their own, focus on the Reading tip. Tell them that they will read and listen to a text and compare the ideas on this topic with their own ideas.

- After reading and listening, ask learners if the text mentioned words and ideas they were expecting, and if it suggested the same changes to their habits that they predicted.

Audioscript: Track 47
See Learner's Book page 130.

Answers
Learners' own answers.

> **Digital Classroom:** Use the activity 'Recycling' to practise the reading strategy 'compare and contrast'. The i button will explain how to use the activity.

Vocabulary (10 minutes)

- Learners cover up the Vocabulary feature. Write the words on the board. See which learner can find the words in the text first.
- Look at the context and elicit an example definition for *biodegradable*. Learners work in teams to try

and write their own definition. Circulate and offer support, encouraging learners to use the context in the text where necessary.

- Read the definitions in the box together. Compare them to the learners' definitions and amend where appropriate.

3 Read and answer (5–10 minutes)

- Demonstrate the activity by answering the first question together as a class.
- Learners re-read the text and answer the questions. Circulate and offer support by checking learners understand the words and expressions they need to answer the questions.
- Give class feedback on the answers.

Answers
a   strong

b   Because it's used to make airbags, bicycle helmets and medical products.

c   Because it blows into rivers, which flow into the oceans, and it's not biodegradable.

d   It breaks it into smaller parts called microparticles.

e   We can replace single-use plastic bottles with ones we can reuse. We can use cloth bags instead of plastic bags. Governments need to build better facilities to recycle plastic.

4 Find facts that match the numbers (5 minutes)

- Focus on the first number. Encourage learners to scan the text to find the number and the fact that matches it.
- Allow learners time to do the same for the other numbers before giving class feedback.

Answers
8.8 million tonnes = the amount of plastic waste that goes into our seas every year.

1 million = the amount of single-use plastic bottles bought every minute around the world.

2050 = scientists think that by 2050 there will be more plastic in the sea than fish if we don't change our habits.

Language focus (5 minutes)

- Before focusing on Activity 5, look at the example sentence with *have to* in the Language focus.

- Read the sentence aloud. Encourage learners to practise saying it, in particular the 'v' sound in *have to,* which is pronounced 'f'.

- Learners could complete **Photocopiable 23**.

⟩ **Digital Classroom:** Use the activity 'What do we have to do? to revise all forms of *have to*. The i button will explain how to use the activity.

5 Write three sentences using 'have to' (5 minutes)

- Check learners understand the difference in meaning between *We have to stop doing…* and *We don't have to do…* Elicit examples.

- Allow pairs of learners time to write three sentences of their own.

- Give class feedback and build up a list of examples on the board.

Answers
Suggested answers:

- We have to change our plastic habits.
- We have to stop using plastic bottles.
- We have to use cloth bags instead of plastic bags.
- Governments have to build better facilities to recycle material.

6 Write (5–10 minutes)

- Spend a few minutes introducing the task and brainstorming possible answers. Learners then complete the activity individually

⟩ **Differentiation ideas:** If learners need support with this task, ask them to write one thing they have learned, one interesting thing and one question. You could extend the activity by asking learners to write three things that are interesting and two questions.

- Come back together as a class and share ideas.

Answers
Learner's own answers.

7 Presentation (30 minutes + extra if you visit the school library)

- **Note:** Although *recycled* refers to waste that has been sorted and treated to produce new usable materials, it can also refer to something that is simply reused for a different purpose. There are lots of interesting sites about both interpretations of *recycling* (see Materials). The best sites for your class will depend on the plastic objects available to be re-used in your country.

- If it is practical and school rules allow, learners can look for information on the internet, or you could visit the school library. Learners can summarise the information to produce a poster to show the recycling process.

- To save time in class, you could print some information for learners to use.

- Ask groups of 3–4 learners to decide on the most interesting ideas.

- Learners present their ideas to the class and the class vote for the best idea.

Plenary ideas

Consolidation (15 minutes)

- Write a paragraph about the recycling process. Encourage learners to use scientific vocabulary and to write sentences including *have to*. This can be set for homework if time is short.

⟩ **Assessment ideas:** When learners have finished writing, they could exchange their paragraphs with a partner and provide feedback on the use of vocabulary and sentences including *have to*.

Homework ideas

Workbook
Questions 1–3 on pages 94–95.

8.3 Talk about it: Rethinking our world

LEARNING PLAN

Learning objective	Learning intentions	Success criteria
4Sc.03 4Ug.09	• **Speaking:** Ask questions to find out general information and respond accordingly. • **Use of English:** Use the future form *will* to talk about intentions and promises for the future. • **Vocabulary:** *quiz, green, survey, eco-challenges.*	• Learners can ask questions to find out about personal environmental habits and respond accordingly. • Learners can use the future form *will* to make Earth promises.

21st-century skills

Social responsibilities: Talk about using consumable materials wisely; Understand there is a need to share and protect resources.

Critical thinking: Evaluate ideas, arguments and options; Say whether someone is green or not and give reasons.

Materials: Learner's Book pages 132–133; Workbook pages 96–97; Optional: Pictures of children turning off lights, travelling to school by bike and car, brushing their teeth and drinking from single-use plastic bottles (for the Starter activity)

Common misconceptions

Misconception	How to identify	How to overcome
Learners often think that when talking about a promise, **will + base form** can be substituted with the **present simple**. For example: *She can come with me, I wait for her* The correct form is: *She can come with me, I will wait for her.* This misconception often comes about because it is possible to use the present simple for promises in learners' own languages.	Write two sentences on the board – one that expresses a promise in the future simple tense and one that expresses a habit in the present simple. Ask learners to identify which is the promise and which is the habit. For example: *OK, she can come with me, I'll wait for her.* (Promise) *She comes with me to school.* (Habit)	The best way to overcome this is to practise. If necessary, compare and contrast this rule with learners' languages.

Starter ideas

Are you a planet protector? (5 minutes)

- Explain that this lesson looks at how learners can change habits to become more eco-friendly. Introduce useful words for the listening text in Activity 1 (see Vocabulary). Write *Are you a planet protector?* on the board and check that learners know this means someone who looks after the environment.

- Check learners know what *green* means in an environmental context. Show images of children turning off lights, travelling to school by bike and car, brushing their teeth and drinking from single-use plastic bottles. Elicit which actions are typical of a planet protector. Write these actions on the board and encourage learners to make more suggestions for protecting the planet, e.g. putting waste in the recycling bin, not dropping litter. These can be used for the basis of writing the questions in Activity 4.

> **Social responsibilities:** Use this as an opportunity to ensure that learners understand there is a need to share and protect resources.

Main teaching ideas

1 Listen and tick the pictures (10 minutes)

- Check learners know what a survey is.

- Using the ideas from the Starter activity and the pictures, encourage learners to make predictions about the questions that will be asked in the survey.

- Learners listen to the audio and tick the pictures that show Dani's answers.

- If helpful, re-play the audio, pausing after each question.

> **Audioscript:** Track 48
>
> See Learner's Book page 132.
>
> **Lucia:** Let's try this quiz. How green are you? I'll ask you the questions first.
>
> **Dani:** OK! I'm ready to start!
>
> **Lucia:** Question 1: Do you turn off the lights when you leave a room?
>
> **Dani:** Yes, I do! If I don't, my mum gets angry with me.
>
> **Lucia:** Question 2: Do you ride a bike to school?

> **Dani:** No, I live 10 minutes away from my school, so my mum takes me in the car.
>
> **Lucia:** Question 3: Do you leave the water running when you brush your teeth?
>
> **Dani:** Hmm, yes, I do.
>
> **Lucia:** Question 4: Do you use single-use plastic bottles?
>
> **Dani:** No, I don't. I always drink water from a tap.
>
> **Lucia:** Question 5: Do you grow vegetables?
>
> **Dani:** My mum grows vegetables in our garden and I sometimes help to water them too!
>
> **Lucia:** Well Dani! You have three As and two Bs, so you're quite green, but you need to set yourself more eco-challenges.

Answers
1a   2b   3b   4a   5a

2 How green is Dani? (5–10 minutes)

- Check learners understand the expressions in the quiz summary. Encourage them to guess from the context and ask them concept-check questions. For example, for *You are a number one planet protector! Keep up the good work!*, ask: *Does this person look after the planet? Should this person change something?* For *Set yourself more eco-challenges!* and *Take some of the ideas from this unit and put them into practice!*, ask: *Do these people need to do something?*

Answers
He got As and Bs, so quite green but there is more he can do.

3 Match the phrases (5 minutes)

- Focus on *save water*. Ask learners to point to the picture that shows how to save water.

- Allow learners time to match the remaining expressions before giving feedback. Circulate and support learners before giving class feedback on the correct answers and pronunciation of the expressions.

Answers:
a 3a b 1a c 5a d 2a e 4b f 3b g 5b
h 1b i 2b j 4a

> **Digital Classroom:** Use the activity 'Which actions are eco-friendly?' to review verbs/actions that are and are not eco-friendly. The i button will explain how to use the activity.

4 Do a survey (10–15 minutes)

- Learners use the ideas from the Starter activity as the basis to write five more questions, e.g. *putting waste in the recycling bin, not dropping litter.* → *Do you put waste in the recycling bin?*

- If you didn't do the Starter activity, brainstorm and make a list of ways we can be green on the board.

- Learners ask their questions to three classmates.

> **Differentiation ideas:** If learners don't feel confident about this task, ask them to write and ask three questions rather than five. Challenge learners by asking them to write and ask an extra question.

Answers
Learner's own answers.

5 How green are your friends? (5 minutes)

> **Critical thinking opportunity:** Learners re-read the quiz summary and evaluate how green their friends are. Encourage them to give reasons for their answers.

Answers
Learner's own answers.

6 What Earth promises does Dani make? (10 minutes)

- Write the title *Dani's promises* on the board and the prompts *He will… / He won't…*

- Encourage learners to make predictions about what Dani might promise.

- Listen to the audio and check learners' ideas.

Audioscript: Track 49

See Learner's Book page 133.

Dani: Well in the quiz, I got a mix of A and B answers, so I've been thinking about how I can be more eco-friendly. I've made some Earth promises, which I will start tomorrow.

1   I promise I will get up earlier, so I can ride my bike to school.

2   I promise I won't leave the water running when I'm brushing my teeth.

3   I promise I'll water the plants in the vegetable garden.

Answers

He will get up earlier, so he can ride his bike to school.

He won't leave the water running when he's brushing his teeth.

He will water the plants in the vegetable garden.

Language detective (5 minutes)

- Learners have heard Dani use *will* for promises in Activity 6.

- Focus on the sentences and elicit why the future simple form is used here and not the present simple. Please see the Common misconceptions box for suggestions.

> **Digital Classroom:** Use the activity 'Promises' to revise using *will* to talk about our promises for the future. The i button will explain how to use the activity.

Workbook

For further practice of *will* for promises, learners look at the Language detective and complete questions 1–3 on pages 96–97.

---

7 Listen and repeat (5 minutes)

- Point out the difference in pronunciation between *I'll* and *ill* before playing the audio. Remind learners that the negative contraction is *won't*.

Audioscript: Track 50

See Learner's Book page 133.

8 Write some Earth promises and present them to your class (10 minutes)

- Write the prompts *I will…* and *I won't…* on the board and elicit suggestions.

- Allow learners time to write at least four promises of their own. If they find it difficult to think of ideas, encourage them to look back at Activity 1.

- Circulate and offer support.

Answers

Learner's own answers.

Plenary ideas

Consolidation (10 minutes)

- At the end of the activity, make an Earth promises poster, with a promise from each learner. Review the poster from time to time to see if learners are keeping their promises.

Homework ideas

> **Workbook**
>
> Questions 1– 3 on pages 96–97.

- Learners write an article for the school blog about things classmates are going to do to help the environment. Encourage them to use environmental vocabulary and *will* and *won't*.

8.4 Write about it: A personal recount

LEARNING PLAN

Learning objective	Learning intentions	Success criteria
4Wc.02 **4Wc.03**	• **Writing:** Write, with support, a short sequence of simple sentences which describe people, places and objects, and routine past and present actions and events. • **Writing:** Express, with support, opinions and feelings. • **Vocabulary:** *school trip/field trip, theatre, clipboard, tiny, ducklings, cute, frog, reeds, purpose.*	• Learners can write a personal recount which describes an exciting or memorable school trip. • Learners can express opinions and feelings about the school trip.

21st-century skills

Learning to learn: Use a picture to help them follow and understand a text; Answer *where, how* and *why* questions after reading a paragraph in order to help write own account.

Creative thinking: Narrate own stories using a model.

Materials: Learner's Book pages 134–135; Workbook pages 98–99; **Photocopiable 24;** Pictures of popular places children might go to on school trips in your country, for example a museum or theatre

Starter ideas

Have you ever been to...? (10 minutes)

- Generate interest by showing pictures of young learners on school trips. Check learners understand what we mean by school trip (or a field trip). Build up a list of places where children could go on a school trip.

- Write question prompts on the board, e.g. *Have you been to…? When did you go there?* Elicit when and why the *present perfect* is used, and when and why the *past simple* is used. Elicit sample answers and then tell learners to ask and answer questions in pairs about the places.

- Have a class vote on where most learners would like to go for a school trip.

Main teaching ideas

1 What can you see in this picture? (10 minutes)

- The main aim of the activity is to make predictions about the text, and revise and practise using vocabulary from the unit that they may read.

- First, revise the use of tenses for talking about photos. Write prompts on the board. Check learners know which tense each prompt is written in and why. For example:
  I can see… (*I can see* sounds more natural than *I see*)
  I think the children are going to … (*going to* is used because we are making predictions about intentions that have already been decided)
  They are wearing/looking at/writing… (*present continuous* for actions in progress)

- While learners make suggestions about the picture with a partner, circulate and offer support, for example with vocabulary. Take the opportunity to pre-teach/revise words that will be useful for the reading, e.g. *clipboard, tiny ducklings, cute, frog, the reeds.*

Answers
Suggested answers: a stream/river, grass, a bank, children, boys, girls, trees, a duck, some ducklings.

2 Were your predictions correct? (5 minutes)

- Tell learners not to try to understand every word when they read the text. They just need to say whether their predictions were correct.

- Write prompts for model sentences on the board, e.g. *I thought the children were going to… and I was right/but I was wrong.*

- Encourage learners to tell the class what they got wrong and what they got right using the model.

Answers
Learner's own answers.

3 Find the answers (10 minutes)

- Focus on the first question. Check learners understand what *purpose* means. Ask learners to point out where the information to answer the question is.

- Allow learners about 5 minutes to look for the remaining answers in the text before giving class feedback.

Answers
a   to see if the local river is 'clean' and 'green'
b   excited
c   ducklings, frogs and small fish
d   worksheet on a clipboard
e   shocked

4 Why do we use the past simple in a personal description? (5 minutes)

- Focus on the second sentence of the text. Ask learners which tense the verbs *wanted* and *arranged* are in.

- Allow learners time to find other past simple verbs in the text.

Answers
We use past simple in a personal description when the trip took place in the past (and the writer is describing a series of actions and past states). Regular and irregular verbs: wanted, arranged, was, arrived, waited, took, gave, saw, were, could.

> **Digital Classroom:** Use the activity 'Past simple practice: Beach clean-up' to revise past simple regular and irregular forms. The i button will explain how to use the activity.

5 Label (F) for fact or (O) for opinion and Writing tip (10 minutes)

- The aim of this activity is to demonstrate ways to express fact and opinion, which will be useful when learners write their own accounts in Activity 6.

- Read the Writing tip together before focusing on the four sentences.

- Discuss which sentences express facts and which ones express opinions.

Answers

a fact   b opinion   c fact   d opinion

> **Digital Classroom:** Use the activity 'Fact or opinion?' to practise identifying facts and opinions. The i button will explain how to use the activity.

6 Write a personal recount about an exciting or memorable school trip (20–25 minutes)

> **Critical thinking opportunity:** (Step 1) Learners answer the *where, how* and *what* questions to help them to organise their notes and write their own account.

- Circulate and offer support while learners follow Steps 1 and 2.

> **Differentiation ideas:** If learners need more support with this task, ask them to work in small groups to talk through possible responses to Step 1 before they make notes. Circulate and invite learners to ask you the seven *wh-* questions. Write sample notes for each question, which can be used as a model. Learners also have the model account in the Learner's Book, but the nature of school trips in different schools and countries can vary, so try to provide a model they can easily relate to. For Step 2, you could provide a worksheet showing how to convert the notes into the past simple and continuous, in particular for irregular verbs. For example: *Why did you go? We **were learning** about… so the teacher **arranged**… Where did you go? We **went** to… How did you feel? We/I **felt**…* Answer any questions learners have about including facts and opinions.

- Before learners swap their accounts with a partner, encourage them to focus on the checklist on **Photocopiable 24** (see Activity 7).

> **Assessment ideas:** Print out the sample answer. Ask learners to assess it against **Photocopiable 24** before they finalise their personal recount. Once learners have made any changes, ask them to swap their recounts. They should give each other feedback on how well they wrote about their experiences and feelings, whether there is a clear sequence of events and the use of the past tense.

- Learners could display their recount in the classroom or put it in a portfolio.

Plenary ideas

Consolidation (5 minutes per learner)

- Learners present their recounts to the class.

> **Assessment ideas:** While learners are delivering their presentations, make notes on where they might benefit from further support, particularly on vocabulary and pronunciation. Share some examples of good practice with the class.

Homework ideas

Workbook

Questions 1–5 on pages 98–99.

- Learners write five sentences about their school: two expressing opinions and three expressing facts. Encourage them to use the verbs/expressions from Activity 5.

8.5 Read and respond: The Future of the Present

LEARNING PLAN

Learning objective	Learning intentions	Success criteria
4Rm.02	• **Reading:** Read, with support, a story about the future of our environment with confidence and enjoyment. • **Vocabulary:** *steel, massive, vast, empty, deserted, greenery, remote control, shadow, junk, electronic, dizzy, swirling, emotion.*	• Learners can talk and answer questions on a short story about the future of our environment.

21st-century skills
Learning to learn: Look at pictures in sequence to follow a storyline.
Creative and critical thinking: Engage in activities with fantasy or mystery elements; Describe the consequences of different potential actions of characters in the story.

Materials: Learner's Book pages 136–139; Workbook pages 100–101

Starter ideas

Anagram games (5 minutes)

- Choose five or six words from the text that you expect your learners won't know (see Vocabulary).

- Mix the letters into anagrams, e.g. *samvise* (massive) and have a competition to see who can guess the most words. Learners can work in groups and use a dictionary.

Main teaching ideas

1 What do you think the story is going to be about? (10 minutes)

- Tell learners they are going to read a story called 'The Future of the Present'. Elicit and pre-teach useful words and expressions from the story while learners look at the pictures and describe what's happening: *remote control, storage room, they are pressing the button/ feeling dizzy, their heads are swirling, junk and electronic waste.* (Activities 4 and 5 look at the words *steel, massive, vast, empty, deserted* and *greenery* in more detail.)

Answers
Learner's own answers.

2 Read and listen to the story (10 minutes)

- In order to help learners read the story easily and fluently with good understanding, make it clear, before reading (and listening), that it is not necessary to understand every word. Learners only need to check whether their ideas about the story were correct.

Answers
Learner's own answers.

Audioscript: Track 51
See Learner's Book pages 136–139.

3 Answer the questions (5–10 minutes)

- Allow learners a few minutes to re-read the first part of the story and answer the questions.

Answers
a Play with the remote control car.
b dusty, rusty, old
c Learner's own answers.

4 What adjectives does the writer use? (5 minutes)

- Focus on the next part of the story, on page 137.

- Read the first sentence and write the word *dizzy* on the board. Mime *dizzy* and elicit that it is an adjective.

- Tell learners they have 30 seconds to scan the text on page 137, from *They saw,* and underline all the adjectives they can find. Tell them not to worry about the meaning at this stage. (The adjectives are: *big, steel, strange, massive, red, blue, green, vast, deserted, empty, tall, thorny* and *terrible*.)

- Ask learners which adjectives describe the place (castle) they are in and elicit the first two – *big* and *steel*. Learners look for the other three adjectives. Give class feedback.

Answers
vast, deserted, empty

5 Find words in the story (10 minutes)

- Focus on the first word. Read the relevant part of the story and encourage learners to use the context to find the meaning.

Answers
a massive, vast b strange c deserted d thorny
e empty f greenery

6 Compare the Earth promises Chotu and Pinky made to the ones you made (5 minutes)

- Focus on Chotu and Pinky's Earth promises. Write the beginning of a model sentence on the board: *Chotu and Pinky promised they will not use plastic bags… I promised I will…*

- Ask learners: *Did Chotu and Pinky promise they will not use plastic bags? Did you promise you will not use plastic bags, too?* Elicit model ends to the sentences: *…and so did I. /…but I didn't /…but Chotu and Pinky didn't. / …and so did Chotu and Pinky.*

Answers
Learner's own answers.

7 What emotions did the children experience? (5 minutes)

- Check learners know what *emotion* means. Elicit a list of emotions to demonstrate the meaning to learners. Read the last part of the story again. Tell learners to stop you when you read words that describe the children's emotions.

Answers:

Scared, ashamed, sorry. They realised the effect of their actions and irresponsibility.

8 Would you like to visit the place in the story? (5 minutes)

- Work together. Ask learners the question and encourage them to give reasons why or why not.

Answers
Learner's own answers.

> **Digital Classroom:** Use the activity 'The Future of the Present' to reinforce reading comprehension of 'The Future of the Present'. The i button will explain how to use the activity.

9 Values: being responsible for our environment (5 minutes)

- Work together and build up a list of values about the environment.

Answers
Learner's own answers.

10 Imagine you opened one of the other doors in the story (10 minutes)

> **Creative thinking:** Encourage learners to be as imaginative as possible and to think about possible fantasy or mystery scenarios.

- Circulate during this activity and support learners with any vocabulary they may need in order to describe their pictures.

> **Differentiation ideas:** Extend the activity by challenging learners to think about the consequences of characters taking different actions in the story.

Answers

Learner's own answers.

Plenary ideas

Consolidation (5 minutes per learner)

- Learners present their picture and ideas to the class.

Homework ideas

> **Workbook**
>
> Questions 1–5 on pages 100–101.

- Learners write up their story about what they saw behind the other door.

> **Assessment ideas:** Choose one of the learners' stories that you think is effective and read it to the class. Highlight what you think the learner has done well, focusing on use of vocabulary, e.g. adjectives; and appropriate use of verb tenses, e.g. for past actions and interrupted actions, and promises for the future.

8.6 Project challenge

LEARNING PLAN

Learning objective	Learning intentions	Success criteria
4Wca.01 4Wca.02 4Wc.02	• **Writing:** Use legible handwriting and spell most high-frequency words correctly in written work. • **Writing:** Write a sequence of short sentences to describe a monster made from recycled materials.	• Learners can use legible handwriting in a poster about looking after our environment, with some speed and fluency. • Learners can spell most high-frequency words accurately when writing a poster about looking after our environment. • Learners can write a description about a monster made from recycled materials.

21st-century skills

Collaboration: Manage and share project tasks.

Creative thinking: Use different media to make and design own designs.

Materials: Learner's Book pages 140–141; Workbook page 102; **Unit 8 project checklists**; Examples of *Reduce, Reuse or Recycle* posters from the internet and pictures of *recycled monsters* — these can be easily located by entering *recycled monsters* **or** *Reduce, Reuse or Recycle posters* into a search engine; Glue, scissors, tape, coloured pens; For **Project A:** card for making posters, old magazines that learners can cut out pictures from; real objects and materials that they can stick on the posters; For **Project B:** objects that would otherwise be thrown away to create the monsters

Starter ideas

Raise interest in the projects (10–15 minutes)

- Tell learners that they are either going to make a poster or design their own recycled monster.

- Raise interest in the projects by showing pictures or examples of *Reduce, Reuse or Recycle* posters and recycled monsters. Also show children's work on a similar topic from other classes or the internet.

Main teaching ideas

Introduce projects (60 minutes)

- Encourage learners to choose one of the projects and then follow the steps for their chosen project.

- Learners work in groups, managing and sharing the tasks in the project.

Project A: Make a poster

- Support learners during Steps 1–2. After deciding whether to create a *reduce, reuse* or *recycle poster*, look back together at the Learner's Book. Elicit and build up a list of useful notes for each of the 'R' words on the board.

- In Step 3, encourage learners to use *have to* by writing prompts and examples on the board. Circulate and offer support while learners write their paragraphs. Make sure they write the paragraphs on a piece of paper that they can stick on their poster.

- Allow about 30 minutes for Step 4. If you don't have magazines, learners can find pictures on the internet and draw their own pictures. Encourage learners to stick real objects and materials on the poster. Circulate and offer each group support.

> **Assessment ideas:** Before displaying learners' work, ask learners to complete the checklist with a partner and make any necessary changes.

Project B: Design your own recycled monster

- **Note about Project B:** Although *recycled* usually refers to waste which has been sorted and treated to produce new usable materials, it can also be used to refer to something that is reused for a different purpose, as it is here.

- Use Steps 1–3 to elicit a list of objects that can be re-used to make an interesting recycled monster. Build up a bank of ideas on the board for learners to use. If necessary, show interesting pictures of recycled monsters from the internet. Give priority to images that are made from common and safe waste materials that learners can get hold of easily.

- To build the recycled monster, learners need waste materials. Learners could bring in materials from home, or if your school has recycling you could arrange to get hold of materials that have been discarded for recycling. Remember to advise learners in advance to bring materials from home, or set the task of building the monster for homework.

- Support learners with Step 5 by eliciting suggestions; invite learners to draw sketches of recycled monsters on the board.

- Support learners with Step 7. Elicit the words to express the reasons why learners chose the materials and any special missions the monsters could be on.

> **Assessment ideas:** Before learners present their work to the class, allow them time to consult the checklist and make any necessary changes.

Plenary ideas

Consolidation (10–15 minutes)

> **Assessment ideas:** After learners have presented their posters or monsters to the class, ask follow-up questions to check understanding/find out more. For example, *How well did you communicate with your group on the project? What might you do differently next time?*

Homework ideas

Workbook

Questions 1–10 on page 102.

8.7 What do you know now?

What's happening to our Earth and what can we do to make a difference?

> **Learning to learn:** Learners have the opportunity to reflect and evaluate their own learning success.

- Reintroduce the question from the start of the unit: *What's happening to our Earth and what can we do to make a difference?* Discuss learners' responses to the question now and compare them with their comments at the beginning of the unit. How much has changed?

- Learners work together in pairs or individually to answer questions 1–7.

- Focus on question 1. Look back at Lesson 8.1. Ask: *Which work of art did you like best? Why?* Elicit suggestions and reasons for which work of art learners prefer. Encourage differences of opinion. Circulate and offer support while each group of learners explain and compare their choice and reasons with another group.

- For questions 2–7, encourage learners to discuss their answers with a partner.

Answers

Suggested answers:

1 Learner's own answers.

2 Air pollution, plastic (and other rubbish and chemicals polluting rivers, seas and oceans); any other appropriate answers.

3 Wildlife, marine life (e.g. turtle in Lesson 8.1), ducks in the local river (Lesson 8.4); any other appropriate answers.

4 Learner's own answers.

5 Learner's own answers.

6 Not to use single-use plastic bags, not to waste water, to recycle rubbish, not to waste food, plant more trees; any other appropriate answers.

7 They made a list of Earth promises and shared their Earth promises with their friends and family.

Look what I can do!

- There are five 'can do' statements. Learners read through the statements and tick the things they can do. Encourage them to reflect on how well they can do these things. Also invite them to think of ways they can improve further, e.g. what strategies they can use, or learn to use.

- If learners find it challenging to read the statements, look through the unit with them and support them to find the relevant information.

- Finally, ask learners to work through the questions on page 103 of the Workbook. Encourage them to talk about what they enjoyed and also about any further support they might need.

>9 School's out!

Unit plan

Lesson	Approximate number of learning hours	Outline of learning content	Learning objectives	Resources
1 Do you like a challenge?	1–1.5	Talk about holiday challenges	4Lm.01/4Ld.04/ 4Lo.01 4Sc.03/4So.01 4Ug.02	Learner's Book Lesson 9.1 Workbook Lesson 9.1 ⬇ Photocopiable 25 **Digital Classroom:** Holiday challenges Holiday activities Would you like…?
2 The features of a web page	1–1.5	Research and plan summer camp activities	4TC.07 4SW.03 4SW.05 4Ug.09	Learner's Book Lesson 9.2 Workbook Lesson 9.2 **Digital Classroom:** Digital vocabulary *Going to* for future plans
3 Trip essentials	1–1.5	Plan for an adventure trip	4Lm.01/4Ld.04/ 4Lo.01 4Sc.03/4So.01/ 4Sor.02 4Sc.05	Learner's Book Lesson 9.3 Workbook Lesson 9.3 ⬇ Differentiated worksheet 9 **Digital Classroom:** Why don't we? Holiday fun
4 End-of-year celebration	1–1.5	Write an invitation for an end-of-year celebration	4Wor.03 4Wc.02	Learner's Book Lesson 9.4 Workbook Lesson 9.4 ⬇ Photocopiable 26 **Digital Classroom:** Write an invitation ⬇ Sample answer for Unit 9
5 *Back to school!*	1.5–2	Read a play about going back to school after holidays	4Rm.02/4Rm.01/ 4Rd.01 4Ro.01 4Rd.03	Learner's Book Lesson 9.5 Workbook Lesson 9.5 ⬇ Photocopiable 27 **Digital Classroom:** Ways of responding
6 Project challenge	1–1.5	Project A: A Nature trail map Project B: Create a short play	4Wca.03 4Sc.06	Learner's Book Lesson 9.6 Workbook Lesson 9.6 ⬇ Unit 8 project checklists

(continued)

Cross-unit resources

⬇ Unit 9 Audioscripts

⬇ End of Unit 9 test

⬇ Progress test 3

⬇ Unit 9 Progress report

⬇ Unit 9 Wordlist

BACKGROUND KNOWLEDGE

Unit 9 focuses on celebrating the end of the school year and activities for the school holidays. School holidays vary in duration throughout the world. Children in the UK generally break up from school in late July for 5–6 weeks, and in the USA children get a 10–11 week break, whereas Greek and Italian holidays last 12–13 weeks. In some countries, such as Italy, schools or religious organisations run holiday clubs.

The big question is: *How can we learn from activities?* Many schools suggest challenges for learners to do during the school holidays. Although a challenge is something that requires effort or thought, holiday challenges are usually interesting tasks that aim to get learners to try a new activity. Usually the emphasis is on having fun and avoiding boredom during the school holidays. Learners might try a new activity or learn a new skill, for example learn a few words in a new language, explore a new place, find out about a country they know nothing about, make a new friend, write a thank you letter, make an object from recycled materials, arrange a picnic, make a collage of things they've done over the summer, write a book review, do a simple science experiment, etc. Holiday challenges are often published on school websites. Some schools have a fun competition to see who can complete the most challenges by awarding points for the challenges completed.

Some of the unit vocabulary may need to be put into context for learners. Nature trails are fascinating paths through the countryside where the walker can see interesting plants and animals. A *backpack* is a bag carried on the back; in the UK it is commonly known as a rucksack. Party invitations are slips of paper or invitation cards used to invite guests to a celebration. These are often sent online or by group mobile phone messages, for environmental reasons or convenience. They give details of the party and include a start and finish time in the UK and USA. However, in some countries, such as Brazil, stating a finishing time may be considered rude.

Lesson 9.2 shows an internet blog. This could be an opportunity to revise strategies for keeping safe on the internet.

TEACHING SKILLS FOCUS

Active learning

What can you remember about active learning?

Active learning is an approach where you aim to involve learners in the learning process. When you choose holiday challenges for your learners, remember that the aim is to facilitate them to play an active role in their own learning. Encourage them to ask and answer questions, make discoveries, analyse evidence, connect evidence to knowledge of other subjects and draw conclusions. Page 81 has more general information about active learning.

CONTINUED

Your challenge

The school holidays are an opportunity for you to suggest challenges for your learners to practise their language skills. It is important that these challenges are fun and involve them in the learning process. Here are some ideas.

- Watch at least one programme/film in English, if possible with English subtitles.

- Under parents' supervision, use a website in English to find out about something you are interested in.

- Read a graded reader for your level of English.

- Find a recipe in English and, with the help of an adult, make it.

- Find out about school holidays around the world. Which countries have the most holidays?

- Find out about an English-speaking country or city that you know nothing about, e.g. New Zealand or Sydney.

Choose holiday challenges, from these, or others, that will engage and stimulate your learners. You could award points for each challenge and have a competition to see which learner completes the most challenges.

9.1 Do you like a challenge?

LEARNING PLAN

Learning objective	Learning intentions	Success criteria
4Lm.01/4Ld.04/ 4Lo.01	• **Listening:** Understand and recognise the main points, details and opinions given in listening extracts about holiday challenges.	• Learners can discuss and answer questions on the listening extracts about holiday challenges.
4Ug.02	• **Use of English:** Ask questions using *would like to*.	• Learners can ask and answer questions using *would like to*, to find out about holiday challenges.
4Sc.03/4So.01	• **Speaking:** Give reasons for doing holiday challenges.	• Learners can express, with support, their reasons for doing holiday challenges.
	• **Vocabulary:** *make a den/ make friends/make a cake, bake a cake, go rock climbing/ on a zip wire, explore a new place, design a t-shirt.*	• Learners can use *'would you like + noun'* and *'would you like + verb'* to ask questions about holiday challenges.

21st-century skills

Critical thinking: Compare two sets of information and points of view on the same topic.

Collaboration: Encourage other children by practising inviting them to participate in activities.

Materials: Learner's Book pages 143–145; Workbook pages 104–105; **Photocopiable 25**; Pictures of children doing interesting activities (for Starter activity and Activity 1)

Common misconceptions

Misconception	How to identify	How to overcome
Learners often use *Do you like to...?* instead of *Would you like to?* For example: *Do you like to get together this weekend?*	Write examples of the two structures on the board and elicit the difference in meaning. For example: *Would you like to meet tomorrow?* *Do you like meeting friends?* Ask: *Which is a general question about always?* *Which is an invitation for a specific time?*	Practise, for example using **Photocopiable 25: Would you like to...?**
A common error is to forget to use the *to*. For instance: *Would you <u>like go</u> rock climbing?*	Write two sentences on the board and elicit which is grammatically correct. For example: *Would you <u>like go</u> rock climbing? (incorrect)* *Would you <u>like to go</u> rock climbing? (correct)*	

Starter ideas

Fun miming challenge (5 minutes)

- Pre-teach vocabulary for Activities 3 and 9. Write the names of six different activities on six pieces of paper, but don't show the activities to the class. Tell learners that six volunteers are going to mime one activity each for the class to guess. Give the first slip of paper to the first volunteer, e.g. *making a cake*. Ask questions about what the learner is doing to encourage the class to guess the name of the activity.

Getting started (10 minutes)

- Tell learners they are going to talk about things they can do in the school holidays. Focus on the pictures in the Learner's Book and show other pictures of activities your class enjoy. Elicit/pre-teach the activities learners will see in Lesson 1 (see Vocabulary).

- Focus on question a. Write prompts on the board and practise answering questions with *Do you like + ing*: *...mak<u>ing</u> dens/friends/cakes? ...bak<u>ing</u> cakes? ...go<u>ing</u> rock climbing/on a zip wire?...explor<u>ing</u> new places? ...design<u>ing</u> t-shirts?*

- Learners answer the other questions in pairs.

> **Digital Classroom:** Use the video 'Holiday challenges' to introduce the subject of holiday activities. The i button will explain how to use the video.

Main teaching ideas

1 Talk about challenges (10 minutes)

- Generate interest in challenges. Ask learners what a challenge is and brainstorm examples.

- Then focus on holiday challenges. Show pictures of learners taking part in fun activities that require effort or thought, e.g. a race, rock climbing, making a cake or doing a science experiment (with an adult), etc. Also think back to the video clips.

- Build up a list of suggestions about *why these could be good for learners* on the board.

Answers
Suggested answers:

- A *challenge* is something that takes a big effort to be done successfully and so tests your ability. Examples: Learner's own answers.

- A 'holiday challenge' is a task that you do in the school holidays that makes you learn a new skill or have a new experience.

- A challenge can be good for you because it tests your skills, helps you to improve them and/or learn new skills.

---

2 Put the verbs and nouns together to make holiday activities (5 minutes)

- Make sure learners know the difference between a verb and noun.
- Demonstrate the activity by attempting to match *make* with the nouns. Elicit which combinations are possible.
- Elicit suggestions about the other verbs and give feedback.

Answers

make a den/friends/a cake

bake a cake

go rock climbing/on a zipwire

explore a new place

design a t-shirt

Activities shown in photos: (a) go on a zipwire; (b) go rock climbing; (c) make a den; (d) design a t-shirt.

> **Digital Classroom:** Use the activity 'Holiday activities' to revise putting verbs/nouns together. The i button will explain how to use the activity.

3 Talk about activities (5 minutes)

- Revise the form of useful structures for this activity, e.g. present perfect questions and answers (*Have you ever tried…? Yes I have. No I haven't*, etc.). Build up a model dialogue; revise questions in the present perfect and past simple, and pre-teach *Would you like…*, which will be covered in Activity 8.

Answers

Learner's own answers.

 ## 4 Listen and answer (5 minutes)

- Tell learners they are going to listen for general understanding and five activities. Learners listen to the text and then confer with a partner.
- Elicit and write the answers on the board.

Audioscript: Track 52

See Learner's Book page 145.

Ms Sharma (teacher): Ok, everyone, holidays start next week! So here's your challenge for the holidays!

Your big challenge is to try something new during your holidays–one thing that is new to you, that you haven't done before. This can be trying a new activity or learning a new skill – maybe… let's think…having a go on a zip wire…baking a cake…making a den! It can be exploring a new place or making a new friend. It doesn't have to be something expensive or very difficult. The idea is that the challenge should be fun and make you learn and experience something new. And if you can do two challenges–or even more–then that's even better! Now, get into groups and brainstorm some ideas for challenges. Remember that…

Answers

The teacher's challenge is for all students to try something new during their school holidays, something they haven't done before (trying a new activity or learning a new skill).

Activities mentioned: having a go on a zip wire, baking a cake, making a den, exploring a new place or making a new friend.

5 Listen and answer (5 minutes)

- Encourage learners to make predictions about what the girls will talk about.
- Listen to the audio. Ask learners to answer the questions in groups and then share responses as a class.

Audioscript: Track 53

See Learner's Book page 145.

Lia: What challenge are you going to do? I know what I'm going to do! I want to try rock climbing.

Mina: Why do you want to try rock climbing?

Lia: Because I've never done it before, I want to see how high I can go and it makes your arms and legs stronger. That's decided! I'm going to ask my mum if I can go indoor rock climbing. If she says yes, would you like to go, too?

Mina: Yes please, I'd love to! When can we go?

Lia: I don't know, I need to ask my mum but I'm sure it will be okay. How about you, Ava? Would you like to come too?

Ava: Umm, no thanks, it's not really my thing. I'd like to try…

Answers

a later

b more carefully

c highest

Answers
The girls talk about going rock climbing. Two girls (Lia and Mina) want to try it, one girl (Ava) doesn't.

6 Listen and complete the girls' conversation (5 minutes)

- Learners listen to the audio again and then complete the missing words. Ask learners to answer the question in pairs and then discuss their responses as a class.

Answers

1 would you like to go?

2 Yes please

3 Would you like to come?

4 no thanks

Lia wants to try rock climbing because she's never done it before, she wants to see how high she can go, and it makes your arms and legs stronger.

7 Look at phrases 1–4 in Activity 6 (5 minutes)

- Elicit which form we use and practise by asking learners to invite other learners to do activities.

Answers
We use *would like* + *to* + verb to invite someone to do something:

Replies: *Yes please… / No thanks / No thank you…*

8 Look at the examples in the language focus (5 minutes)

- Read the Language focus together and read the example sentences. Work through 8a as a class, completing the sentence with the correct form of the adverb.

9 Make a list of three new challenges to try in the next school holiday (5 minutes)

- Demonstrate the activity by asking learners for suggestions. Then allow learners time to write their lists and give reasons before giving feedback.

Answers
Learner's own answers.

10 Invite each other to try the challenges (5 minutes)

- Write prompts on the board to elicit the invitation *Would you like to…?* and the answer, *No, thanks. / Yes, I'd love to.*

› **Collaboration:** Encourage learners to work in pairs and practise inviting each other to participate in activities.

› **Differentiation ideas:** As you circulate and offer support, encourage confident speakers to use more complex suggestions from the lesson, e.g. *I'm going to ask my mum if I can… If she says yes, would you like to come, too?* Or: *It's not really my thing.*

Answers
Learner's own answers.

Workbook

For further practice of *would like*, learners look at the Language detective and complete questions 1–3 on pages 106–107.

› **Digital Classroom:** Use the activity 'Would you like…?' to revise making questions with *Would you like…?* The i button will explain how to use the activity.

Plenary ideas

Consolidation (10 minutes)

* Learners work on **Photocopiable 25**.

Homework ideas

Workbook

Questions 1–5 on pages 104–105.

9.2 Digital literacy: Features of a web page

LEARNING PLAN		
Learning objective	**Learning intentions**	**Success criteria**
4Ug.09	• **Digital literacy:** Know that web pages have addresses known as URLs and know how to bookmark these. • **Digital literacy:** Treat others respectfully online and know that they should also be treated with respect. • **Digital literacy:** Know the benefits and risks of online anonymity. • **Digital literacy:** Know that digital communication enables online communities to exist. • **Use of English:** Use future form *be going to* to talk about already decided plans. • **Vocabulary:** *web address/URL, refresh, bookmark star, address bar, minimise, search engine, go forward, go back, friendship bracelets, pet rocks, wall painting, survive in the wild, wild flowers/ trees, wildlife, nature trail, campfire.*	• Learners can bookmark URLs. • Learners can talk about how everyone should be treated respectfully online and that they should also be treated with respect. • Learners can discuss the benefits and risks of online anonymity. • Learners can talk about how digital communication allows online communities to exist. • Learners can use *be going to* to talk about their plans for summer camp.

21st-century skills

Learning to learn: Use pictures to help learners follow a text.

Creative thinking: Design web pages.

Collaboration: Participate in shared projects.

Materials: Learner's Book pages 146–147; Workbook pages 106–107; Poster paper for Activity 4

LANGUAGE BACKGROUND

Going to

The Language detective in this lesson focuses on *going to*. You use *going to* to talk about plans in the future, especially in informal English. When you use *going to*, you emphasise that your intentions have already been decided. For example: *I'm going to try harder.*

Going to can also be used to make predictions about the near future, based on current evidence.

For instance: *It's going to rain – look at those black clouds!*

In Unit 7, learners studied the present continuous with future meaning. Generally speaking, the present continuous refers to something that has been arranged with another person. *Going to* refers to a decision that has been made, or an intention which has been decided.

Often, both *going to* and the present continuous could be used to refer to the same future event.

Common misconceptions

Misconception	How to identify	How to overcome
Learners often do not feel comfortable with *be going to*, especially speakers of languages where this form does not exist, e.g. Italian.	Write two sentences on the board and elicit the difference in meaning. • *I'm telling you about a challenge.* (present continuous – now) • *I'm going to tell you about a challenge.* going to – (near) future intention)	The best way to help learners become more familiar with a new structure is to practise using it, for example with Photocopiable 27: How do you feel?
Learners sometimes use the *present simple* to talk about the future. This is usually incorrect and could cause misunderstanding.	Write sentences on the board and elicit the difference in meaning. • *I take the train.* (habit) • *I'm going to take the train.* (future intention) • *The train leaves at 13.34.* (repeated action).	

Starter ideas

Quiz: Are you an arty-crafty type or an energetic, outdoor person? (5 minutes)

- Write the following questions on the board. Pre-teach/elicit the underlined words.

- A: *Can you create <u>friendship bracelets</u>? Would you like to make <u>pet rocks</u>? Would you like to try <u>wall painting</u>? Do you like singing? Do you like dancing?*

- B: *Do you know how to <u>survive in the wild</u>? Do you like seeing <u>wild</u> flowers and trees? Do you like seeing <u>wildlife</u>? Would you like go on a <u>nature trail</u>? Would you like to tell / listen to stories <u>around a campfire</u>!*

- Learners read and answer *Yes* or *No* to the questions. If they have more positive answers in A than B, tell them they are *an arty-crafty type*. If they have more positive answers in B, they are *an energetic, outdoor person.*

Main teaching ideas

1 **Match the words to the icons (5 minutes)**

- Point to the icons and elicit the correct names. Check learners know the correct pronunciation.

Answers

URL (Uniform Resource Locator): the web address for a page on the internet. Refresh: to make the most recent information appear on an internet page by clicking a button. Bookmark star: the address of a web page that is kept on your computer so that you can find it again easily.

Address Bar: where you type in the address for a site or page.

Minimise: to reduce a page on your screen. Go forward: to advance to another page.

Go back: to return to a page.

> **Digital Classroom:** Use the activity 'Digital vocabulary' to revise digital vocabulary. The i button will explain how to use the activity.

Reading tip (5 minutes)

- Learners look at pictures to help them follow a text.

2 Look at the pictures and talk about the activities (5 minutes)

- Write the prompt *You can* on the board. Elicit suggestions about what you can do in each summer camp.

- Ask learners to tell the class which camp they would like to try.

Answers
Learner's own answers.

3 Read and listen. Then answer the questions (10 minutes)

- Read the questions before looking again at the web page. Play the audio and then ask learners to answer the questions in small groups. If you did the Starter activity, and made predictions from the pictures in Activity 2, learners shouldn't have too much trouble following. Re-play the audio to help learners answer the questions, if necessary.

Audioscript Track 54
See Learner's Book pages 146–147.

Answers
a   Learner's own answers.
b   Learner's own answers.
c   Learner's own answers.
d   sch. = school
e   .uk = country (United Kingdom)

4 Read and answer (5 minutes)

- Introduce the idea of making comments on a website, by asking learners if they ever make comments, and for examples of comments they have seen/made. Ask if they have ever used a false name. Ask what sort of information they should and shouldn't share online.

- Discuss the questions together. Make sure learners understand that they should always be respectful, never give out personal information and always report, to their parents or carers, disrespectful comments or requests for them to reveal personal information.

Answers
a   No, although the second commenter might have used their surname.

b   monster24 and berryman; suggested answer: to protect their privacy.

c   This is an example of bad online behaviour. Always be respectful online towards other people.

Language detective (5 minutes)

- A good starting point is to focus on examples of *going to* in the reading. Check learners understand how to form *going to* and when it should be used. Ask concept check questions, e.g.

  - *Is the activity past, present or future?* (Future)

  - *Was the writer's intention decided before writing the article?* (Yes)

  - *What is the difference between 'We're going to learn new skills?' and 'We're learning new skills' (present continuous)?* (The first is a future action and the second is an action in progress now.)

  - *When can the present continuous be used with future reference?* (For future arrangements, usually agreed with another person.)

> **Digital Classroom:** Use the grammar presentation 'Going to for future plans' to revise 'going to' for future plans. The i button will explain how to use the grammar presentation.

Workbook

For further practice of *going to*, learners look at the Language detective and complete questions 1–3 on pages 108–109.

5 What other activities are they going to do? (5 minutes)

- Write *They're going to…* on the board and encourage learners to complete sentences with the activities from the website.

Answers

Learner's own answers.

---

6 In groups, design your own web page (25 minutes)

- Each group of learners decides which summer camp to advertise and draws their web page on a piece of poster paper.

- Write questions on the board to guide learners, e.g. *Where is it? When is it? What are you going to do on the camp?* Build up a list of suggestions on the board and encourage learners to use the websites in the Learner's Book as a model.

- Circulate and offer advice and support while learners complete their web pages.

⟩ **Creative thinking:** Based on a model, learners design their own web pages.

- When the web pages are finished, display them on the classroom wall.

⟩ **Assessment ideas:** Do a quick quiz to revise digital vocabulary. On mini whiteboards or in their notebooks, ask learners to draw a picture of the bookmark icon, the refresh icon and the 'go back icon'. Ask learners to hold up their pictures. Make a note of learners who are struggling with the vocabulary.

Plenary ideas

Consolidation (10 minutes)

- Build up a list of questions for learners to use, e.g. *Where is the camp? When is it? Are you going to…?*

⟩ **Assessment ideas:** Encourage learners to ask follow-up questions about each other's web pages to check understanding/find out more.

Homework ideas

Workbook

Questions 1–5 on pages 106–107.

- Photocopy the groups' web pages for other learners to read at home.

9.3 Talk about it: Trip essentials

LEARNING PLAN

Learning objective	Learning intentions	Success criteria
4Lm.01/4Ld.04/ 4Lo.01	• **Listening:** Understand and recognise the main points, details and opinions given in a short talk about preparing for a camping trip.	• Learners can talk about and answer questions on a short talk about preparing for a camping trip.
4Sc.03/4So.01/ 4Sor.02	• **Speaking:** Discuss with classmates, making suggestions and giving opinions, what to take on an adventure trip.	• Learners can ask questions to find out general information about what to take on an adventure trip.
4Sc.05	• **Speaking:** Pronounce some familiar words and phrases clearly; others may need to ask for repetition from time to time.	• Learners can express, with support, their opinions about what to take on an adventure trip.
	• **Vocabulary:** *torch, waterproof jacket, sleeping bag, sweatshirt, sun cream, tracksuit bottoms, sunglasses, cap, backpack, tent, insect repellent, rope walking, trekking, nature trail, sightseeing.*	• Learners can initiate, maintain and conclude interaction, with some support, in an exchange about what to take on an adventure trip.
		• Learners can pronounce some phrases for making suggestions clearly.

21st-century skills

Collaboration: Accept others' opinions during a pair or group task.

Collaboration: Help others to complete a task.

Materials: Learner's Book pages 148–149; Workbook pages 108–109; **Differentiated worksheet 9**; A backpack and other objects that you would take on a trip, e.g. a torch, insect repellent, sunglasses, sun cream, etc; alternatively show pictures, or draw the objects on the board (for the Starter activity and Activity 9)

Starter ideas

Let's take a torch (5 minutes)

- Explain that in this lesson, learners are going to look at the kinds of things to pack for an adventure trip.

- Pre-teach the meaning of *Trip essentials* and show/ draw the objects (or pictures) to pre-teach the new vocabulary. Build up a model dialogue on the board, e.g. Speaker A: *Let's take* a torch. Speaker B: *Yes, good idea! / No, we won't need a torch.* Encourage learners to practise the dialogue using the new vocabulary.

Main teaching ideas

1 Talk about what you would need to pack for different kinds of trips (5 minutes)

- Focus on the words in the box and check learners understand the meaning of *pack* in this context. Write different types of trips on the board, e.g. *summer holiday, beach holiday, skiing holiday, school trip.*

- Support learners by writing an example on the board, e.g. *When you go on a school trip, do you pack sun cream? Yes, we need it in the summer.*

- Circulate and offer support while learners ask and answer questions about what they pack for different trips.

> **Differentiation ideas:** If learners need support with this activity, give them a prompt sheet with some sentence starters.

Answers
Learner's own answers.

2 Use the phrases to describe the objects in Activity 1 (5 minutes)

- Read the phrases and then the example. Encourage learners to match *keep you dry* to *waterproof jacket.*

- Nominate learners to match more objects to the phrases, using the prompts in the Learner's Book, and to guess the objects.

Answers
Suggested answers (words can be put into more than one category):

- Clothes/things you wear: *jeans, waterproof jacket, sweatshirt, shorts, tracksuit bottoms, sunglasses, cap, socks, t-shirt, helmet.*

- Something to protect you: *sun cream, sunglasses, helmet, insect repellent.*

- Something to sleep in: *tent, sleeping bag.*

- Something that keeps you dry: *waterproof jacket, tent.*

- Something that gives light: *torch.*

- Something that carries things: *backpack.*

- Things you can fold up: *all clothes listed in 'Clothes' category, tent, sleeping bag.*

3 What kind of adventure trip is Kyra doing? (5 minutes)

- Encourage learners to make predictions about what they will hear in Activity 4, by guessing what might be in Kyra's backpack. Build up a list on the board, including as many words from the listening activity as possible (see Vocabulary).

Answers
Suggested answer: Kyra is doing a camping, trekking or hiking trip.

Learner's own answers for guesses about what is in her backpack.

4 Listen and answer (5–10 minutes)

- Play the audio. Learners write a list of the objects Kyra and her friend packed.

- If helpful, replay the beginning of the recording and check learners understand the girls pack the jacket, but NOT the jeans.

- Check learners have written the six objects correctly. If necessary, replay the recording and pause for learners to write the objects as they hear them. Ask which ones they predicted.

> **Collaboration:** If learners find this task difficult, after listening, but before giving feedback, tell them to compare their lists with a partner.

Audioscript: Track 55

See Learner's Book page 148.

Kyra: Ok, we're camping for two days and one night. The camp leaders are bringing tents and cooking things – I think we have to take everything else ourselves.

Friend: What do you think we'll need? Let's think about clothes first.

Kyra: Ok, how about a waterproof jacket and jeans?

Friend: Waterproof jacket yes – in case it rains – but not jeans! They're too hot to do activities in and take ages to dry if they get wet. Why don't we take tracksuit bottoms? They're light and made of cotton. And let's take shorts too – it might be hot during the day...

Kyra: Yes, you're right. And how about spare socks too – in case our feet get wet? OK, what about at night?

Friend: We'll definitely need sleeping bags to keep us warm in the tent – it gets colder at night. What about packing a torch? I don't think there is any electric light at night...

Kyra:	Ok… Do you think we'll need things for eating? Knives, forks, spoons, bowls, plates…?
Friend:	I don't think so. Cooking equipment are provided, so I think there will be things for eating too…
Kyra:	We're only allowed to take one backpack, so we can't take many things. What else are you going to take? We can take one small personal thing – something special to us.
Friend:	I'm reading a really good book at the moment, so I'll take that. What about you?
Kyra:	I'm going to put some photos in my backpack – so if I miss home, I can look at pictures of my dog!

Answers

Six of the following: *waterproof jacket, tracksuit bottoms, shorts, spare or extra socks, sleeping bags, torch;* personal things: *a book, photos.*

Speaking tip (5 minutes)

• Before learners do Activity 5, read the phrases in blue together. Make sure learners understand that these phrases are used to make suggestions and find solutions.

 5 **Match the sentence halves, listen again and check (5–10 minutes)**

 • Elicit suggestions and then re-listen to the audio and check. In the case of grammatically incorrect suggestions, explain that only a noun or a verb+*ing* can follow *How/What about…?*, and that *Why don't we…? / Let's* require the bare infinitive.

 > **Differentiation ideas:** If learners need more support with this activity, download the audioscript and tell learners to underline the sentences with the expressions.

Answers

1 b 2 d 3 a 4 c

> **Digital Classroom:** Use the activity 'Why don't we? Holiday fun' to revise making suggestions. The i button will explain how to use the activity.

6 **Listen and repeat the girls' suggestions (5 minutes)**

 • Replay the audio as many times as necessary.

 • If learners can't identify where their voices go up and down, demonstrate using your hands.

Audioscript: Track 56

See Learners Book page 149.

1   How about a waterproof jacket and jeans?

2   Why don't we take tracksuit bottoms?

3   Let's take shorts too.

4   What about packing a torch?

Answers

The voice rises in the first part of each suggestion then drops on the last word, which is stressed. Learners should follow the rising and falling intonation with physical actions using hands or fingers to emphasise the point.

7 **Write six things the girls pack and the reasons why (5–10 minutes)**

 • Write the six trip essentials the girls pack on the board.

 • Focus on the words in the box and elicit reasons why the girls take each object.

 • Refer back to the vocabulary in the Starter activity. Ask learners if they would take any objects the girls don't take and why, e.g. *insect repellent – I'd take some insect repellent because there might be lots of insects.*

> **Collaboration:** Learners accept others' opinions during the task by using a tactful answer like *I don't think so* when they give a negative answer.

Answers

Suggested answers:

The girls pack…

- a waterproof jacket – in case it rains
- tracksuit bottoms – because they are light and made of cotton
- shorts – because it might be hot during the day…
- (spare) socks – in case feet get wet
- sleeping bags – to keep them warm in the tent
- a torch – because there might not be any electric light at night.

Learner's own answers.

8 **Which 'special' things do the girls pack? What special thing would you take on a trip like this? Why? (10 minutes)**

- Elicit the girls' 'special' objects and then build up a list of special objects learners would take.
- Invite learners to say why they would take their objects.

Answers

The girls pack a book and photos as their 'special' items.

Learner's own answers.

9 **Choose an adventure trip (10 minutes)**

- Build up a list of interesting places and activities for adventure trips and encourage pairs to choose their trip. Make sure some pairs choose the same trip (for the comparison exercise in Activity 10).
- Show your backpack and objects that you would take on an adventure trip (or pictures of these). Give reasons for your choices.
- Allow pairs time to choose their items and talk about the reasons for packing them. Circulate and support by giving necessary vocabulary where necessary.
- Make a list on the board of which trip each pair is discussing.

Answers

Learner's own answers.

10 **Compare your choices. Which are similar and which are different? (5–10 minutes)**

- Once learners are ready to explain why they are taking objects, tell them to choose a pair who chose the same trip. Circulate and offer support while they explain their choices.
- Don't worry if learners can't find a pair who chose the same trip. The emphasis should be on explaining and listening to each other's choices.

Answers

Learner's own answers.

Plenary ideas

Consolidation (10 minutes)

- Play the 'Guess where I'm going' game. Decide on a place you intend to go for a trip, e.g. the park, but don't tell learners the place.
- Write *I'm going to take…* on the board. Tell the class what you are going to take, e.g. *a picnic, a ball to play with*. Encourage learners to guess where you're going.
- Learners repeat the game in small groups.

Homework ideas

> **Workbook**
>
> Questions 1–3 on pages 108–109.

- Learners write their own dialogue, discussing what to take on a trip. Ask them to perform their dialogues at the start of the next lesson.

〉 **Assessment ideas:** As a class, write a short checklist for learners to use after they have drafted and practised saying their dialogue. For example: *Have I included new vocabulary? Have I used language for making suggestions? Am I confident about performing my dialogue?*

〉 **Differentiation ideas:** Learners could complete **Differentiated worksheet 9.**

9.4 Write about it: End-of-year celebration

LEARNING PLAN

Learning objective	Learning intentions	Success criteria
4Wor.03 **4Wc.02**	• **Writing:** Use, with support, appropriate layout for an invitation and write, with support, a short sequence of simple sentences which describe people, places and objects, and routine past and present actions and events. • **Vocabulary:** *date of birth, guest, passport number, refreshment, smoothies, craft, persuasive, school grounds, compliment.*	• Learners can use an appropriate layout for an invitation to parents to an end-of-year celebration at school. • Learners can write an invitation describing activities and using persuasive language to encourage attendance.

21st-century skills

Creative thinking: Develop new games, dishes, clothes, etc.

Collaboration: Collaborate with others when making choices and decisions; Give simple feedback and suggest ways to improve an idea in a simple way.

Materials: Learner's Book pages 150–151; Workbook pages 110–111; **Photocopiable 26**; Colourful invitations that will appeal to your class (for Activity 1); Blank A4 sheets of paper and drawing pins/re-usable adhesive (for Activity 5)

Starter ideas

Exciting end-of-year celebration! (10 minutes)

- Explain to learners that in this lesson they are going to write an invitation for an end-of-year celebration. Ask learners to tell you about party invitations they have received. *What kinds of parties have they been invited to? What kinds of activities have they done at the parties? What did the invitations look like? Were they plain or decorated? Were they usually sent in the post or via email?*

Main teaching ideas

1 Talk about what information you need to include on an invitation to a party or another event (10 minutes)

- Generate interest by showing colourful party invitations that will appeal to your class. Elicit what learners can see on the invitations.

Answers
The place, the time, the day/date, the reason, the name of the guest(s).

2 Read and check your answers (5 minutes)

- Before reading, make clear that learners are only checking their answers to Activity 1. They do not need to understand all of the information, as they will have the chance to re-read the invitation in more detail later.

Answers
Learner's own answers.

3 Write activities in the circles (10 minutes)

- Before you start the activity, check learners understand *craft* and *refreshments.*

- Elicit which activities go in the circles. Then build up a list of other activities that learners can add to each circle.

Answers

Craft: paint T-shirts, make friendship bracelets.

Sports: running races.

Refreshments: freshly baked cakes, delicious fruit smoothies.

---

4 Read and find (5 minutes)

- Before learners re-read the invitation, check they realise that, here, *making an invitation* is a synonym for *inviting someone*. Ask for predictions about which structure will be used for this (i.e. *would like*) and expressing future plans (*going to*).

Answers

a   We would like to invite…

b   We are going to organise different activities./ There are going to be craft activities.

c   Please come along!

⟩ **Digital Classroom:** Use the activity 'Write an invitation' to help prepare learners for writing, editing and proofreading an invitation. The i button will explain how to use the activity.

5 Write an invitation (15 minutes)

- For Step 1, learners work in groups of 3–4. Distribute three blank sheets of paper to each group and tell learners to write the headings as suggested. While the groups write their ideas, circulate and support learners.

⟩ **Collaboration:** Once learners have written their ideas, stick the pieces of paper around the class to give other learners ideas.

- When learners have chosen the ideas they prefer, encourage them to re-read the invitation in Activity 2 and to use this as a model to help plan and prepare their invitations. During Steps 2 and 3, circulate and support learners.

- Circulate and offer support while learners check other learners' invitations for spelling and grammar mistakes.

⟩ **Collaboration:** Encourage learners to give tactful and sensitive feedback, and to suggest constructive ways to improve the invitation.

Writing tip (5 minutes)

- During Step 3, when learners are looking at the model invitation from Activity 2, draw their attention to the capital letter for Friday. Remind learners to use capital letters for days of the week.

6 Check you have included everything on the checklist (5 minutes)

- Once the invitation has been written, focus on the writing checklist on **Photocopiable 26**.

⟩ **Assessment ideas:** Print out the sample answer. Ask learners to assess it against **Photocopiable 26** and make any changes before they finalise their invitation.

- The invitations could be displayed on the classroom wall and/or photocopied and put into learners' portfolios.

Plenary ideas

Consolidation (10 minutes)

- Practise using persuasive language, like the language in the invitation in Activity 2 (e.g. *Please come along! The cakes will be delicious/ freshly baked. It's going to be fun!*)

- Learners write a dialogue to persuade someone to come to a party or other event.

Homework ideas

Workbook

Questions 1–3 on pages 110–111.

9.5 Read and respond: *Back to school!*

LEARNING PLAN

Learning objective	Learning intentions	Success criteria
4Rm.02/4Rm.01/ 4Rd.01	• **Reading:** Read and understand a play about going back to school, with confidence and enjoyment.	• Talk about and answer questions on a play about going back to school after holidays.
4Ro.01	• **Reading:** Recognise, with little or no support, the opinions and feelings of the characters in the play.	• Discuss the opinions of the children in the play.
4Rd.03	• **Reading:** Deduce meaning from context, with little or no support, in short, simple texts.	• Deduce meaning from context by looking at how exclamation marks are used in the play.
	• **Vocabulary:** *nervous, upset, sick/funny, admit, support, advice, actually, pile, football season.*	

21st-century skills
Social responsibilities: Describe different emotions; Engage in self-talk about emotions; Show concern and compassion for other children when they are hurt or upset.

Materials: Learner's Book pages 152–155; Workbook pages 112–113; Pictures of things that make learners feel different emotions for Starter activity, e.g. nervous (zip wire), upset, happy, sad, excited: newspapers are a good source of people showing emotions, especially the pages about sports like football, rugby or cricket; Use **Photocopiable 27** to support learners by practising using the words for feelings before the main activities, or as a plenary activity for revision

Starter ideas

How do you feel? (5–10 minutes)

- Explain to learners that they are going to read a play about going back to school after a long holiday.

- Elicit/pre-teach *feelings* and useful adjectives, and other ways to talk about feelings/emotions for learners to use in Activity 1. Start by writing basic adjectives like *bad, good, happy, sad* on the board. Show pictures of people showing emotions and elicit which of the adjectives describe their feelings.

› **Social responsibilities:** Write the words *nervous, upset, (feel) sick/funny* (as in strange) on the board, which learners will encounter during the lesson. Elicit situations where learners feel like this and check they understand the meanings. Pre-teach *admit* for later on and ask learners if they always admit their feelings.

Main teaching ideas

1 Talk about how you feel about going back to school after long holidays (5–10 minutes)

- After learners have talked in pairs, build up a list of feelings, and the good and bad things, about going back to school.

- Ask learners if they feel different going back to the same school in the same class compared to starting a new class or a new school.

Answers
Learner's own answers.

2 Look at the picture and the title of the play (5 minutes)

- There is a lot of information in the play. Support learners by gaining interest and encouraging predictions about what they will read.

- Encourage learners to think about why there is an exclamation mark at the end of the title (you will look at this in more detail in Activity 8). Elicit reasons *why* the children might feel *nervous* about going back to school (there might be a new school/class/teacher, or they might have to work a lot), or *happy* (they will see their friends again or they can play sports they like). Ask if they think everyone feels the same and if they think their parents feel the same about going back to work.

Answers
Learner's own answers.

3 Read and listen (5–10 minutes)

- Learners read and listen and check their predictions about how the children are feeling and why. Make it clear that learners do not have to understand every word, just the words that say how the children are feeling and *why*.

Audioscript: Track 57
Learner's Book pages 152–153.

Answers
Learner's own answers.

4 Read and listen to Part 1 again and answer the questions (5–10 minutes)

- Read and check learners understand the three questions. While listening to the play, make sure learners scan the text and look for the answers.

- After re-reading and listening, allow learners a couple of minutes to read Part 1 again and answer the questions.

Audioscript: Track 58
Learner's Book page 153.

Answers

a They feel sad because they don't want to go back to school.

b He always feels the same way the day before going back to school; he doesn't want the holidays to end; he doesn't want to start a new class with the new teacher.

c He's going to tell his mum and dad he's not going back to school.

5 Read and listen to Part 2 again and answer the questions (5–10 minutes)

- Before re-reading Part 2, read the questions and check learners understand *support* in part d and *advice* in part e.

- If it's helpful, pause the audio after Sara says *I'm feeling a bit like that too…* and ask learners for the answer to part a. If learners find the rest of the questions difficult, re-play the relevant part of the audio for each and then ask the question.

Audioscript: Track 59
Learner's Book page 154.

Answers

a Yes.

b Because no one admits it.

c She says even adults feel the same way.

d She says her dad gets nervous when he thinks about the pile of work waiting for him when he gets back from a holiday and hundreds of emails in his inbox.

e She tells them to think about all the good things about going back to school.

6 Find the responses in blue in the play that go with these sentences (5–10 minutes)

- Focus on question a and tell learners to find the phrase *Me neither* in the play. Then allow learners time to re-read Parts 1 and 2 and find the blue responses. Give feedback and practise reading the sentences out loud.

Answers

a	Me neither.	b	Me neither.
c	Me too!	d	Me too!
e	Me too!	f	Really?

> **Digital Classroom:** Use the activity 'Ways of responding' to help revise ways of responding. The i button will explain how to use the activity.

7 Use the words in blue to respond to these statements (5 minutes)

- Check learners know which expressions express agreement (*Me too!* – something both speakers want; *Me neither!* – something they *don't* want) and surprise (*Really?*). Write the expressions on the board.

- Demonstrate the activity by reacting to statement b as a class.

- Allow learners a few minutes to practise in pairs. Make sure they use the correct intonation.

Answers
Learner's own answers.

8 Look at the examples in the language focus (5 minutes).

- Read the Language focus together before focusing on the sentences in Activity 8.

Answers
a   You love going back to school, don't you?
b   He's not happy about it, is he?

9 Listen and repeat (5 minutes)

- Focus on the phrases. Listen to the pronunciation, in particular the stress and intonation.

- Elicit the answer by asking questions like *How do the speakers feel?* Avoid focusing too much on each speaker, as this will be done in Activity 9.

Audioscript: Track 60
Learner's Book page 155.

Answers
Exclamation marks are used to tell us that the speaker wants to emphasise what is being said, often because the speaker feels excited, afraid or upset.

10 Listen again and answer the questions (5 minutes)

- Focus separately on each speaker.

- Listen to the pronunciation, in particular the stress and intonation, and ask questions, e.g. *Is he/she upset, trying to hide something, emphasising that something is correct, surprising or funny?*

Answers

a	Speaker 2	b	Speaker 3
c	Speaker 4	d	Speaker 1

11 Act out the play (10–15 minutes)

- Each learner in the group chooses a role. Circulate and offer support while learners practise acting out the play in groups, helping with pronunciation and expression.

> **Differentiation ideas:** If learners need support with this task, give them a prompt sheet with sentence starters and useful vocabulary.

- Choose groups to act out the play to the class.

12 Values: Being sympathetic (15 minutes + 2 minutes for each pair to present their role play)

> **Social responsibilities:** Encourage learners to think about how people with these problems might feel.

- Look back at the expressions Sara uses to help. Make a note of some useful expressions, e.g. *Hey, how's it going? Oh, dear! What's the matter? No you're not alright! I can tell… I know what it is…you're feeling nervous because….tomorrow, aren't you? Look, it's okay. Everyone feels like… I'm feeling a bit like that too… It's just that no one admits it!*

- Circulate and offer support, while learners write their role play in pairs.

- Learners present their role plays to the class.

⟩ **Assessment ideas:** Give verbal feedback on the role plays, focusing on the use of vocabulary for expressing feelings, expressions used to help and the intonation of these expressions, and the expressions *really/ Me too/ Me neither*.

Plenary ideas

Consolidation (20 minutes)

- Learners complete **Photocopiable 27**.

Homework ideas

Workbook

Questions 1–6 on pages 112–113.

9.6 Project challenge

LEARNING PLAN		
Learning objective	**Learning intentions**	**Success criteria**
4Wca.03 4Sc.06	• **Writing:** Plan, write, edit and proofread a short description with support. • **Speaking:** Produce a short sequence of sentences, maintaining short exchanges, allowing for some hesitation, false starts and reformulation.	• Learners can plan, write, edit and proofread a short sequence of sentences about a nature trail. • Learners can maintain short exchanges about an adventure trip during their performance of the play.
21st-century skills		
Collaboration: Learners work in groups, managing and sharing the tasks in the project.		
Social responsibilities: Empathy and relationship skills – being aware of feelings of others, helping and comforting.		

Materials: Learner's Book pages 156–157; Workbook page 114; **Unit 9 project checklists**; For Project A: ideally you will need to go on a nature trail; alternatively watch a video of children going on a nature trail (if you type 'nature trail' into a search engine, there are lots of ideas); Examples of trail maps: see the Decorah Parks and Recreation website – from the Home page, click on the Trail maps icon

Starter ideas

Raise interest in the projects (10–15 minutes)

- Tell learners that they are either going to make a nature trail map or create a short play.

- Raise interest in the projects by having a class discussion. First, focus on Project A. Talk about the kinds of nature activities that learners do in their countries. What are the landscapes like? Then look at Project B. Talk about what it's like going on an adventure trip. Ask learners what they might feel nervous about, e.g. seeing spiders or other wildlife if they are camping, storms, being afraid of heights if they are going on a zipwire, etc.

- Encourage learners to use vocabulary from the unit during the discussion.

Main teaching ideas

Introduce projects (60 minutes)

- Encourage learners to choose one of the projects and then follow the steps for their chosen project.

- Learners work in groups, managing and sharing the tasks in the project.

Project A: A Nature trail map

- Circulate and offer support to learners while they build up their lists.

- Answer the questions with the class. The last question will depend on the country learners live in. Build up a list of wildlife for learners to refer to when organising their trail.

- If going on a nature trail is not practical, watch a video of children going on a trail.

- Support learners by making sure they know how to use the tenses needed to answer the questions correctly.

- Before learners start Step 2, look at the checklist together to get an overview of what needs to be included.

- For Step 2, show learners examples of trail maps (see Materials). Support learners while they follow the instructions to draw and complete the nature map. If it is practical to do so, learners can look on the internet or in the library and find information about the animals they choose; if not, learners can find out this information for homework.

> **Assessment ideas:** Learners use the **project checklist** to assess how well they carried out the task and make suggestions for improvement.

CROSS-CURRICULAR LINKS

Science: Learners write down the names of plants, animals and insects they see. If necessary, use a book from the library to classify them. Categories could include plants, animals with/ without a backbone, etc.

Geography: Learners practise map drawing skills by producing a map of the trail and key features.

Project B: Create a short play

> **Social responsibilities:** Check learners know the meaning of *afraid*. Focus on the five issues and brainstorm what a sympathetic person could say to make someone with this fear feel better.

- Tell learners to choose one of the issues for their play.

- Focus on each photo and elicit which fear it goes with. Check learners know the correct pronunciaion.

- Circulate and support learners while they are writing their title. Make sure they have chosen two characters, one with a fear, and the other who will be sympathetic and say things to make the other person feel better.

- Circulate and offer support for using sympathetic language, exclamation marks and the present continuous in the notes saying what the characters are doing.

- Invite learners to perform their plays in front of the class.

> **Assessment ideas:** Learners use the **project checklist** to assess how well they carried out the task and make suggestions for improvement.

Answers

a	afraid of water	b	afraid of spiders
c	afraid of the dark	d	afraid of heights
e	afraid of thunderstorms		

Plenary ideas

Reflection (10–15 minutes)

- After learners have completed their projects, have a class discussion about what they enjoyed best about them, and what they would do differently next time. Has doing Project A inspired learners to find out more about nature traiils near their home? What did learners find enjoyable and challenging about creating a play in Project B? Was it harder to write dialogue than to write a description or blog?

Homework ideas

Workbook

Questions 1–4 on page 114.

- Look in the library for a short play to read.

9.7 What do you know now?

How can we learn from activities?

> **Learning to learn:** Learners have the opportunity to reflect and evaluate their own learning success.

- Reintroduce the question from the start of the unit: *How can we learn from activities?* Discuss learners' responses to the question now and compare them with their comments at the beginning of the unit. How much has changed?

- Ask learners to work through the questions in pairs. Demonstrate questions 2, 3 and 4 by writing an example sentence. Allow a few minutes for learners to write sentences. Build up a list of interesting sentences on the board.

- Encourage learners to look back at Lesson 9.5 to help them answer question 5.

Answers

1 Five from: *make a den/friends/a cake; bake a cake; go rock climbing/on a zip wire; explore a new place; design a tshirt*, plus learner's own answers.

2 Learner's own answers (use *going to* + verb).

3 Learner's own answers.

4 Learner's own answers (use *would like to* + verb).

5 She pointed out that lots of people (of all ages) feel nervous about going back to school (or work) and to think about the good things.

Look what I can do!

- There are seven 'can do' statements. Learners read through the statements and tick the things they can do. Encourage them to reflect on how well they can do these things. Also invite them to think of ways they can improve further, e.g. what strategies they can use or learn to use.

- If learners find it challenging to read the statements, look through the unit with them and support them to find the relevant information.

- Finally, ask learners to work through the questions on page 115 of the Workbook. Encourage them to talk about what they enjoyed and also about any further support they might need.

Check your progress 3

Learners answer the eight questions.

Answers

1

Extreme weather	Geographical features	Environment	Holiday activities
drought	desert	global warming	zipwire
blizzard	coast		rock climbing
tornado	coral reef	pollution	
		eco-friendly	wall painting

2 a coral reef

  b eco-friendly

  c blizzard

  d global warming/pollution

  e desert

  f wall painting

3 Learner's own answers.

4 Learner's own answers.

5 Learner's own answers.

6 Learner's own answers.

7 a True

  b False

  c True

  d True

  e False

  f False

8 a I'm ~~do~~ doing a nature study this afternoon.

  b I promise I will ~~to~~ recycle more.

  c I (**have**) never been to Australia.

  d Would you like (**to**) go sightseeing?

  e We are ~~have~~ having a picnic tomorrow.

  f I've ~~learn~~ learnt about the lungfish in class.

Index of photocopiables

The following photocopiables can be downloaded from Cambridge GO.

1 Sports snakes and ladders game (Unit 1, lesson 2)

2 People and places crossword (Unit 1, lesson 3)

3 Checklist for 'Big Clean Up' leaflet (Unit 1, lesson 4)

4 Comparative/superlative quiz cards (Unit 2, lesson 2)

5 Checklist for Mars Rover fact file (Unit 2, lesson 4)

6 Planet present simple cards (Unit 2, lesson 4)

7 Tag questions about people's eco-homes (Unit 3, lesson 2)

8 Modal of deduction cards about eco-homes (Unit 3, lesson 3)

9 Checklist for magazine article/blog (Unit 3, lesson 4)

10 Questions using quantifiers (Unit 4, lesson 2)

11 Words with common roots (Unit 4, lesson 3)

12 Checklist for poem (Unit 4, lesson 4)

13 Past simple time expression cards (Unit 5, lesson 3)

14 Checklist for adventure story (Unit 5, lesson 4)

15 *When/before/after* board game (Unit 5, lesson 5)

16 My school journey (Unit 6, lesson 2)

17 Matching sentence halves (Unit 6, lesson 3)

18 Checklist for description (Unit 6, lesson 4)

19 How long … ? (Unit 7, lesson 3)

20 Checklist for blog post about weekend (Unit 7, lesson 4)

21 Your plans (Unit 7, lesson 4)

22 Environment quiz cards (Unit 8, lesson 1)

23 Do you have to? (Unit 8, lesson 2)

24 Checklist for recount (Unit 8, lesson 4)

25 Would you like to … ? (Unit 9, lesson 1)

26 Checklist for invitation (Unit 9, lesson 4)

27 How do you feel? (Unit 9, lesson 5)

Differentiated worksheet 1 A, B and C: My fun family! (Unit 1, lesson 3)

Differentiated worksheet 2 A, B and C: Practising the present continuous (Unit 2, lesson 3)

Differentiated worksheet 3 A, B and C: Summarising (Unit 3, lesson 5)

Differentiated worksheet 4 A, B and C: *is/are + past participle* (Unit 4, lesson 6)

Differentiated worksheet 5 A, B and C: Language for telling stories 1 (Unit 5, lesson 3)

Differentiated worksheet 6 A, B and C: Language for telling stories 2 (Unit 6, lesson 5)

Differentiated worksheet 7 A, B and C: Holiday fun! (Unit 7, lesson 4)

Differentiated worksheet 8 A, B and C: Defining relative clauses (Unit 8, lesson 1)

Differentiated worksheet 9 A, B and C: Making suggestions (Unit 9, lesson 3)

Photocopiable 1: Sports snakes and ladders game

Do you like/enjoy/hope/want/learn/prefer? (-*ing* vs infinitive)

> **Aim:** Learners play a *Snakes and ladders* style game in groups of four. They ask group members questions using the prompts on the square on which they land.
>
> **Preparation time:** 15 minutes
>
> **Use of language:** Asking and answering present simple questions:
>
> *Do you like/love/enjoy/prefer + verb+ing?*
>
> *Do you hope/want/learn +infinitive?*
>
> **Vocabulary:** *play/do/go,* sports from Lesson 2 (long jump, football, skateboarding, rugby, basketball, karate, running, swimming and tennis).
>
> **Materials:** For each group of learners, one *Sports snakes and ladders board,* one coin with a head/tails side and one small object (e.g. a pencil sharpener) to represent each learner on the board.

Procedure:

- Learners can do this game during Lesson 2 (at the end of Activity 5).
- Build up a list of sports words learners will need for the game and write under the heading *play, do, go.*
- Build up a list of questions learners will need for the game and short answers, e.g.

Do you...?

1	*Do you like...?*	2	*Do you hope...?*	3	*Yes, I do.*
4	*Do you enjoy...?*	5	*Do you learn...?*	6	*No, I don't.*
7	*Do you prefer...?*	8	*Do you want...?*	9	*It's OK.*
	...playing football?		*...to play football?*		

- Distribute one *Sports snakes and ladders board,* and one coin with a head/tails side to each group. Make sure each learner has a small object (e.g. a pencil sharpener) to mark their place on the board.
- Make sure learners understand that if they land on the head of a snake, they go down to the bottom and if they land on the foot of the ladder, they go up to the top of it.
- Choose a group and demonstrate the game. Player 1 tosses the coin. If it lands on the 'heads' side, move forward one space. If it lands on tails, move forwards four spaces. The player uses the prompt on the board to make a question, e.g. Square 1: *Do you enjoy swimming?*
- Check learners understand which questions to ask. Point to random squares and ask for the question and short answer.
- Allow time to play the game while you circulate, giving assistance and noting common errors with form and pronunciation. The game ends when one player reaches the finish.
- Give class feedback on common errors.

Name _____ Date _____

Photocopiable 1: Sports snakes and ladders game

17 *Do you like/enjoy/hope/ want/learn/prefer?* (-ing vs infinitive)	**18** love?	**19**	**20**	**FINISH**
16	**15** hope?	**14**	**13** learn?	
8 learn?	**9** want?	**10** hope?	**11**	**12** like?
7 prefer?		**6** want?	**5** love?	**4** like?
START	**1** enjoy?	**2**	**3** prefer?	

Photocopiable 2: People and places crossword

Aim: Learners practise vocabulary for people and places from Unit 1 by completing a crossword.
Preparation time: 5 minutes
Vocabulary: People and places from Unit 1.
Materials: One photocopy of the crossword for each learner.

Procedure:

- Learners can complete this crossword at the end of Lesson 3.
- Distribute one photocopy of the crossword for each learner.
- Demonstrate the idea by nominating learners to complete 1 Down and 5 Across.
- Allow learners time to complete the crossword in pairs before giving class feedback.

Answers:

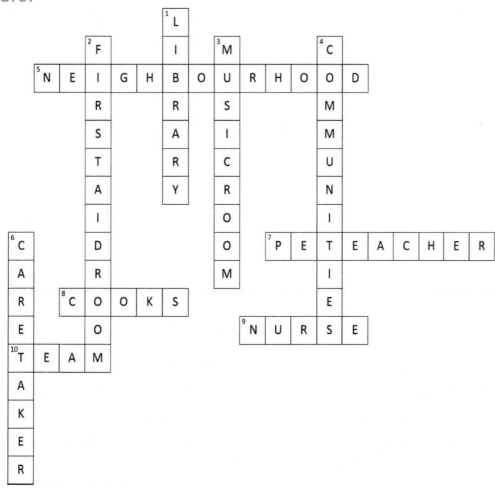

Name _____ **Date** _____

Photocopiable 2: People and places crossword

Down

1 It's got lots of books.

2 (5,3,4) I go there if I'm ill or hurt.

3 (5,4) We learn to play the guitar there.

4 I belong to several of these groups.

6 The name of the person who cleans and fixes things in my school.

Across

5 It's where you live.

7 (1,1,7) He keeps me fit!

8 They prepare our lunch.

9 The person who looks after me if I'm ill or hurt.

10 People who play and train together.

Photocopiable 3: Checklist for 'Big Clean Up' leaflet

Checklist	Have I included it?	Example(s)
The name of the event		
A local charity		
The date, the time		
A slogan		
Imperatives		

Name _____ Date _____

End of Unit 1 test

Vocabulary 1

Complete the words.

Example:

0 f <u>o</u> <u>o</u> t <u>b</u> <u>a</u> <u>l</u> <u>l</u>

1 r _ _ _ _ _ _ _ [1]

2 l _ _ _ j _ _ _ _ [1]

3 k _ _ _ _ _ _ [1]

4 b _ _ _ _ _ _ _ _ _ [1]

5  s _ _ _ _ _ _ _ _ _ _ _ _ [1]

Vocabulary 2

Complete the sentences with the words in the box.

| grandma | caretaker | ~~aunt~~ | nurse | uncle | cook |

Example:

0   Daniel's mum's sister is Daniel's _____aunt_____.

---

6   Daniel's dad's mum is Daniel's _____.   [1]

7   Daniel's mum's brother is Daniel's _____.   [1]

8   The school _____ cleans and fixes things at Daniel's school.   [1]

9   The school _____ prepares Daniel's lunch at school.   [1]

10   Daniel's school _____ looks after him if he hurts his knee at school.   [1]

Grammar 1

Write the correct form of the verb (*-ing* or *to + infinitive*) in each space.

Example:

0   Alan loves _____*fishing*_____ in the lake. (fish)

---

11   Do you enjoy _____ in the sea? (swim)   [1]

12   Do you want _____ my painting? (see)   [1]

13   I'd like to learn _____ a plane! (fly)   [1]

14   My parents enjoy _____ in the park. (walk)   [1]

15   My cousin hopes _____ lots of mountains. (climb)   [1]

Grammar 2

Complete the sentences with *both, too, into* or *on*.

Example:

0   Gary and Richard _____*both*_____ play football.

---

16   Emma is good at maths, and Yan is good at maths _____.   [1]

17   Ollie is _____ surfing.   [1]

18   Hakim writes poems. Assia writes poems _____.   [1]

19   I'm keen _____ vegetables, but my sister likes fruit.   [1]

20   My mum and dad _____ play the guitar.   [1]

Name _____ **Date** _____

Progress test 1

Vocabulary 1

Complete with the words in the box.

| cousin | mum | grandpa | uncle | sister | ~~grandma~~ |

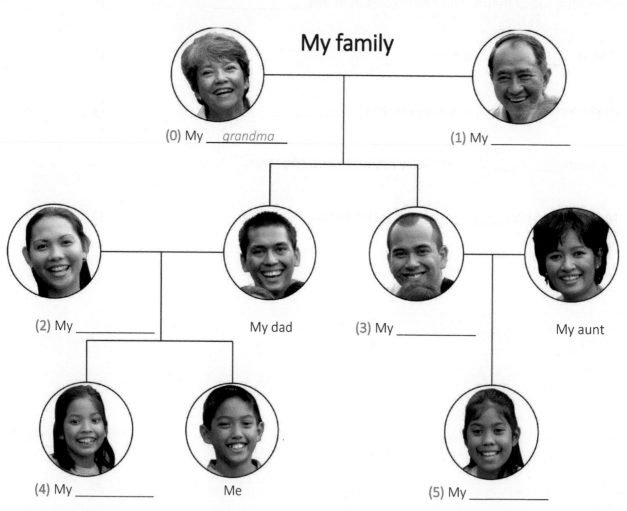

My family

(0) My _____*grandma*_____

(1) My _____

(2) My _____

My dad

(3) My _____

My aunt

(4) My _____

Me

(5) My _____

[Total: 5 marks]

Circle the correct word for each space.

Example:

0   It's _____ in the Arctic.

a high   (b freezing)   c wide

---

6   I like the school nurse. She's very _____.   [1]

a comfortable   b icy   c caring

7   The Amazon River is very _____.   [1]

a long   b helpful   c fun

8   That castle is _____!   [1]

a fair   b enormous   c loving

9   Do you like _____ colours?   [1]

a wooden   b bright   c humid

10   Our school caretaker is always _____.   [1]

a friendly   b modern   c spacious

Grammar 1

Write the correct form of the verb in each space.

Example:

0   The P.E. teacher _____*keeps*_____ all the children fit. (keep)

11   I really enjoy _____ books about sport. (read)   [1]

12   Please, _____ a pencil to draw your picture! (use)   [1]

13   We _____ to the airport now. (drive)   [1]

14   I hope _____ from you soon! (hear)   [1]

15   Andy, _____ you _____ near your school? (live)   [1]

Grammar 2

Complete the sentences with the words in the box.

both	~~into~~	too	about	keen	two

Example:

0   I'm _____*into*_____ running. I go running twice a week.

___

16   We're _____ on rugby.   [1]

17   I like running. My friend Fran likes running _____.   [1]

18   I have _____ sisters and one brother.   [1]

19   Anna and Ben _____ love playing football.   [1]

20   What's unique _____ that sports player?   [1]

Reading 1

Read the information about the Atacama Desert. Are the sentences true (✔) or false (✘)?

Write ✔ or ✘ on the lines.

The Atacama Desert

The Atacama Desert is in Chile, in South America. It is 130 000 km² and it is older than all the other deserts on Earth. In the Sahara Desert, the temperature is sometimes 50 °C, but in the Atacama Desert it is usually only 18 °C.

It hardly ever rains there and it is drier than the Sahara Desert. Scientists go to the Atacama Desert to look at the stars and planets through telescopes because there are about 330 nights every year without any clouds.

The Atacama Desert does not support much life, but some very, very tiny animals called microbes can live there. Scientists think that the planet Mars could also support the same kind of life!

Example:

0   The Atacama Desert is in South America.   ✓

21   The Atacama Desert is the oldest desert on Earth.   _____   [1]

22   The Atacama Desert is hotter than the Sahara Desert.   _____   [1]

23   It never rains in the Atacama Desert.   _____   [1]

24   There are sometimes clouds in the Atacama Desert at night. _____   [1]

25   Scientists think that microbes must live on Mars.   _____   [1]

Reading 2

Read Laila's blog and complete the sentences.

You can use one or two words. You can write a number, too.

The Eiffel Tower

My name's Laila, and I'm visiting Paris, the capital city of France, with my family. Today we've come to see something very special: I'm at the Eiffel Tower. It's amazing! It's a metal tower and it's 324 metres tall.

The tower was built for a special event in Paris in 1889. It was built by a man called Gustave Eiffel. Now it's one of the most famous landmarks in the world and at least 25,000 people visit it every day!

People can visit three floors of the Eiffel Tower. There are restaurants on the first and second floors and we got tickets to go up to the third floor. There are lots of stairs, but we came up in lifts. The views are spectacular and I feel very lucky!

Now I'm looking at the city and I can see a beautiful rainbow far away. What a fantastic day!

Example:

0   Laila and her _____*family*_____ are at the Eiffel Tower.

---

26   The Eiffel Tower is made of _____.   [1]

27   Gustave Eiffel built the tower in Paris for a _____ in 1889.   [1]

28   More than _____ people go to see the Eiffel Tower every day.   [1]

29   Leila is on the _____ of the Eiffel Tower.   [1]

30   Leila can see the city and a _____.   [1]

Writing 1

31   Write about you and your family. What do you do every day?

Write about sports or activities do you enjoy?

Write about 50 words.

_____

_____

_____

_____

_____

_____

_____

_____

_____

_____

_____

_____

_____

_____

_____

_____

[Total: 10 marks]

Writing 2

32   Imagine you are a famous singer. Write a blog about what you are doing today.

Write 50–70 words.

_____

_____

_____

_____

_____

_____

_____

_____

_____

_____

_____

_____

_____

_____

_____

[Total: 10 marks]

Acknowledgements

The authors and publishers acknowledge the following sources of copyright material and are grateful for the permissions granted. While every effort has been made, it has not always been possible to identify the sources of all the material used, or to trace all copyright holders. If any omissions are brought to our notice, we will be happy to include the appropriate acknowledgements on reprinting.

'The Treasure' is based on 'The Gift' by Jennifer Holladay, adaptation translation reprinted with permission of Teaching Tolerance, a project of the Southern Poverty Law Center www.tolerance.org; 'Not a Planet Anymore' by Joshua Seigal, reproduced with permission of the author; excerpt from *The Hobbit* by J.R.R. Tolkien, first published 1937, reproduced with the permission of HarperCollins; 'The Seekers' is a summary of part of 'The Seekers' by Valerie Bloom created for *i-read Fiction 4*, edited by Pie Corbett, published by Cambridge University Press, 2006; Adapted excerpt from *Charlie and the Chocolate Factory* by Roald Dahl, text copyright © 1964, renewed 1992 by Roald Dahl Nominee Limited. Used by permission of Alfred A. Knopf, an imprint of Random House Children's Books, a division of Penguin Random House LLC. All rights reserved; 'Lost in the Desert' by Margo Fallis, adapted and used with permission; 'Why emus can't fly' is retold from an Aboriginal story; *'The Future of The Present'* by Malini Venkataraman, reproduced with the permission of Jeydevi Venkataraman (Malini is currently studying at Lakshmi School, Madurai, she was in 5th grade when she wrote this story).

Thanks to the following for permission to reproduce images:

Lew Robertson; Test 1.1: Ariel Skelley

The All You Can Eat
Gardening Handbook